food and **drink**

BBC

contents

foreword

Food and Drink is television's longest-running food show. In 1982, when it launched, Margaret Thatcher was at war with Argentina, Mick Mills of Ipswich captained England in a doomed World Cup campaign and Bucks Fizz (inexplicably) had two number one hits. It sounds like ancient history, doesn't it? Anyone born that year can now vote. In the intervening period our eating habits have been transformed: eating out is now the norm rather than a rare treat, olive oil is a dressing rather than a laxative and we're as likely to cook Italian, Indian or Chinese as we are English. *Food and Drink* has been there, all the way, to aid and abet the changes in our national diet.

More than 300 programmes, 1000 recipes and 1500 wines later, *Food and Drink* is delighted to offer this new comprehensive guide to cooking, eating and drinking. In keeping with *Food and Drink*'s 'magazine' approach, the book includes reliable advice on food preparation and healthy eating along with the down-to-earth, practical recipes and popular drinks tips that are the programme's hallmark.

What were *Food and Drink*'s roots? Well, for the trainspotters amongst you, let's get the personnel sorted first. Only Jilly Goolden has been with the series from the start. She was accompanied by disc jockey, Simon Bates, in the first run of six programmes. Then Henry Kelly (now Classic FM's star presenter) took over for a run. But in the autumn of 1984 the best known team came together with Chris Kelly and Michael Barry joining Jilly. Oz Clarke sprang on to the scene in 1986 and that was the line-up until Michael Barry relinquished his studio role in 1997. Antony Worrall-Thompson then stepped in.

The persuasive influence of the series is well illustrated by the celebrated apple cutter – a simple device for segmenting and coring an apple. Michael Barry innocently demonstrated this one evening and within 24 hours all UK stores had sold out of the little gadget. To my knowledge at least one factory was set up in Taiwan to satisfy future demand in Britain! Then there was the oxtail stew recipe that led to queues outside butchers and specially flown imports of frozen tails from Europe to keep our viewers' pots boiling. Perhaps the most memorable incident of all was when Anton Mosimann cooked lunch in the Sheffield home of lorry driver, John Wilcock. An extraordinary one in four of viewers that evening actually sat down to write in for the recipe (this was before the days of BBC Online).

During the eighties and nineties *Food and Drink* has also had the important task of monitoring and explaining such food scares as salmonella, listeria, BSE and genetically modified foods. In an era when five supermarkets supply us with three quarters of our food, raw materials arrive by every boat and plane, and large manufacturers have worldwide food brands, we need to feel confident about what we buy.

But, not to belittle such serious issues, food and drink should still be, above all, about enjoyment. So we hope you get maximum pleasure out of this book. Bon appetit.

Peter Bazalgette, Bazal

food and drink

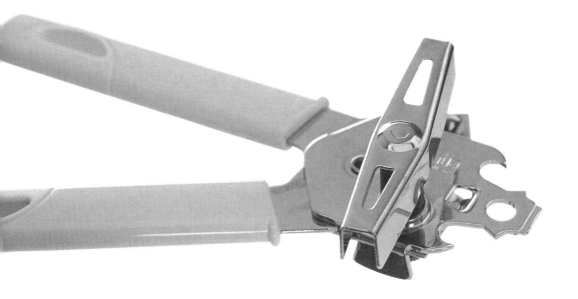

I t could be said that we literally eat to live but we also do far more than that. We appreciate the wide range of food and drink available to us. We see how appetizing fresh produce looks and we breathe in the appealing smells of freshly baked bread, ground coffee, warm chocolate, ripe fruits and the concentrated aromas of a glass of wine. We feel how firm fruit is, to help us decide whether it is ripe and ready to eat or whether we will buy it to use later. We use all our senses before we decide which foods to buy and we feed our senses as well as our hunger when we prepare and cook food.

We also make choices to suit our pockets and preferences, and an increasing number of people want to eat a well balanced diet.

Enjoying food and drink is one of life's greatest pleasures. It is something we do, on average, three times a day; because of this, we sometimes eat out of habit, without appreciating what we are eating. To readers of this book – lovers of good food and drink – all meals should be celebrations of the senses, whether they are for a special occasion or a quick meal to feed hungry children. This book aims to provide the information you need to make the best choice of food and drink in all circumstances.

food for the body

Whatever we are doing, food is needed for energy and to provide materials for growth, repair, reproduction and all the chemical reactions that take place in our bodies at every moment of the day or night. The nutrients in our food are described as macronutrients and micronutrients. Macronutrients are needed in the largest amounts. They are: *carbohydrates*, which provide the body with energy and can be converted into stored energy in the form of body fat; *fats*, which provide energy and can also be turned into body fat; *protein*, which provides amino acids, the building blocks for growth of muscle, lean tissue and repair. Special proteins called enzymes enable and control chemical changes in the body that are essential to life.

Micronutrients include: *minerals*, used in growth and repair and to help regulate body processes, and *vitamins*, needed to regulate body processes (in a similar way to hormones in some instances) and protect against ill health.

Other substances in food that help to keep us healthy include *non-starch polysaccharides* (NSP for short, previously called and better known as dietary fibre). Fibre prevents constipation and helps prevent heart disease and some cancers. NSPs are fermented in the intestines by friendly bacteria, to boost our immune systems and keep us healthy in other ways.

Most foods provide a complex mixture of macro and micronutrients. The key to healthy eating is to eat a wide variety of foods in the right proportion in order to obtain the maximum range of nutrients.

how to eat a balanced diet

There are four main food groups. Eaten in the right proportion, foods from these groups provide everything essential for optimum health and vitality.

Starchy carbohydrate foods Eat six to 14 portions a day, depending on your individual needs. For example, a marathon runner or a teenager during a growth spurt might eat 14 portions of starchy foods a day, whereas a sedentary woman would need only five to six portions per day. Try to eat high fibre varieties where possible.

portion guide
• 3 tablespoons of breakfast cereal
• 2 tablespoons of muesli
• 1 slice of bread or toast
• 1 bread roll, bap or bun
• 1 small pitta bread, naan bread or chapatti
• 3 crackers or crisp breads
• 1 medium potato
• 2 heaped tablespoons boiled rice
• 3 heaped tablespoons boiled pasta
• 1 medium plantain or small sweet potato

Vegetables and fruit Eat five to seven portions a day – and there is more benefit in eating more. Most fruit can be eaten raw, and many vegetables can be eaten raw in salads, or lightly cooked; this retains maximum vitamins and minerals, which, in other foods, are depleted or destroyed by cooking. Include fresh, frozen, chilled and canned vegetables and fruit (except potatoes, which are a starchy food), dried fruits and fruit juice, but not fruit drinks, which contain very little, if any, juice, and also contain added sugars or sweeteners and other non-nutritious ingredients.

portion guide

- 1 medium portion of vegetables, including salad
- 1 piece of fresh fruit
- 6 tablespoons stewed or canned fruit (about 150 g/5 oz)
- 1 small glass of fruit juice (about 100 ml/ 3½ fl oz)

Dairy products Eat two to three portions of lower-fat versions a day. Milk, cheese, yoghurt and fromage frais are all good sources of calcium for strong bones and teeth. And it's not just children who need calcium. Bones and teeth are living, so people of all ages have constant calcium needs. Dairy foods also provide protein for growth and repair and vitamins A and D for eyes and teeth. While everyone over the age of five benefits from eating lower-fat versions, infants and children up to the age of two need full-fat versions.

portion guide

- 1 medium glass of milk (about 200 ml/ 7 fl oz)
- 1 matchbox-sized piece of Cheddar-type cheese (about 40 g/1½ oz)
- 1 small pot of yoghurt, cottage cheese or fromage frais (about 120 g/4½ oz)

Meat, fish and vegetable protein Eat two to four portions a day. If you enjoy meat, eat it lean. Make only occasional use of fatty meat products, such as sausages, pâté, meat pies and burgers.

Government nutrition experts advise people who eat 12 to 14 portions of meat a week to cut down their intake to reduce any possible risk of colon cancer, and possibly of breast, prostate and pancreatic cancer. Eating a lot of vegetables (and fruit) *might* ameliorate any risk among higher meat consumers. Meat-eaters are also advised to replace a couple of meat meals a week with fish, at least one of which should be oily fish.

Two portions of animal protein food per day is adequate for all except the very active; vegetarians might need two to four portions of vegetarian protein foods a day.

portion guide

- 3 medium slices of beef, pork, ham, lamb, liver, kidney, chicken or oily fish (about 50–75 g/2–3 oz)
- 125–150 g/4½–5 oz white fish (not fried in batter)
- 3 fish fingers
- 2 eggs (up to 4 a week)
- 5 tablespoons of baked beans or other cooked pulses, lentils, dhal (about 200 g/7 oz)
- 2 tablespoons of nuts, peanut butter or other nut products (about 65 g /2½ oz)

Foods containing fat Eat one to five portions a day. Too much fat, and saturated fat in particular, increases the risk of heart disease by raising the level of harmful blood cholesterol. Cholesterol can build up in the arteries, slowing down the blood supply to the heart – or even cutting it off completely, causing a heart attack. Diets high in fat also increase the risk of some cancers. But not all fats have the same effect.

Saturated fats come from animal fats, such as meat and dairy produce and hydrogenated vegetable fats in margarine, cakes, savoury snacks and other processed foods, and *trans-fats*, produced when vegetable oils are hydrogenated (hardened) to make margarine and shortening. They raise blood levels of the harmful type of cholesterol, thus increasing the risk of heart disease. They block production of essential fatty acids from vegetable and fish oils in the diet. *Polyunsaturates* (from fish and vegetable oils, except palm and coconut) are called essential fatty acids and must be provided by the diet. There are two families: omega-6, from linoleic acid in vegetable oils such as sunflower; and omega-3, from linolenic acid in other vegetable oils, such as soy and rapeseed, in walnuts and in oily fish such as mackerel, herring, sardines and salmon. We need a minimum of 4 g of omega-6 fatty acids a day and no more than 30 g – up to this level offers protection from heart disease; more risks production of too many free-radicals – particles which can cause changes in blood cholesterol and cells, increasing your risk of heart disease and cancer. We only need 1–2 g of omega-3 fatty acids a day, for membranes in the brain and eyes and production of hormone-like substances.

Risk of heart attack is reduced by these fatty acids, which decrease the tendency of the blood to clot (their anti-inflammatory action also helps arthritis). *Mono-unsaturates* (mainly from olive oil, groundnut and rapeseed oils, avocados, most nuts and some spreads) seem to share the benefits of polyunsaturates.

All fat should be eaten in moderation but some is essential. It also makes food taste good and makes possible the wide variety of methods of cooking that we all love. However, most of us would benefit from eating less fat overall, with a higher proportion of unsaturated and mono-unsaturated fat. We need only a small amount of unsaturated fats each day, around 30 g (1 oz), to enable absorption of fat-soluble vitamins, but we can safely eat more than that. The maximum amount of fat needed depends on age, size and how active you are but, to maintain a healthy weight, most sedentary women should eat no more than 70 g (2¾ oz) of fat a day and men no more than 90 g (3½oz).

portion guide

- 5 g or 1 teaspoon of margarine or butter
- 10 g or 2 teaspoons of low-fat spread
- 5 ml or 1 teaspoon of cooking oil or fat
- 15 g or 1 tablespoon of mayonnaise or vinaigrette dressing
- 15 ml or 1 tablespoon of cream
- 1 packet of crisps

Foods containing sugar Eat up to two portions per day. On average, men eat about 125 g (4½ oz) of sugar a day and women eat about 90g (3½ oz), which accounts for around 20% of total calories. In an ideal diet, this intake would be halved! Dietary sugar comes from honey, treacle, syrup, molasses, and what is added to processed foods, as well as the sugar bowl.

portion guide

- 15 g or 1 tablespoon sugar
- 1 rounded teaspoon of jam/honey
- 2 biscuits
- half a slice of cake or a doughnut or Danish pastry
- 1 small bar of chocolate
- 1 small tube or bag of sweets

Salt (sodium chloride) Sodium is a mineral needed for a variety of body functions. All the sodium that most people need is naturally present in a well balanced diet. Eating too much salt in combination with low potassium intake and being overweight can lead to rising blood pressure. High blood pressure increases the risk of strokes and heart disease. Currently, we eat about 2 to 2½ teaspoons of salt per day. We would benefit from eating less: men less than 7 g per day and women less than 5 g per day. (1 teaspoon = 5 g). You can adjust to a less salty diet by reducing your intake gradually.

alcohol in a balanced diet

The health benefits of red wine might have been exaggerated, but there is research to suggest that moderate drinking, which means two to three units per day for women and three to four units per day for men (but not every day), is associated with reduced risk of heart disease and stroke among men and women aged 45 and over. This equates to no more than 21 units a week for women and 28 for men.

The healthiest pattern of drinking is to enjoy small amounts of alcohol regularly with food – not to drink all the units on one or two days.

Although antioxidants in wine may help reduce the risk of heart disease, ethanol (alcohol) also increases the concentration of beneficial high-density lipoprotein cholesterol (HDL) in the blood and slightly decreases harmful low-density lipoprotein cholesterol (LDL), as well as beneficially affecting other heart-disease risk factors.

Women should, ideally, avoid alcohol while trying to become pregnant but should not worry unduly if they find they are pregnant as long as they have been drinking 'normally'. It would be a good idea to stop drinking if there is a suspicion of pregnancy and once pregnancy is confirmed, until after the fourth month, when one or two units per week are thought to be harmless.

Women are more susceptible to alcohol because of their smaller size and greater proportion of body fat. They also have a greater risk of liver damage and breast cancer than men do.

other drinks

Drink at least six to eight cups, mugs or glasses of liquid (about 1.5–2 litres/2½–3½ pints) each day. Not all should be tea or coffee because these contain stimulants (such as caffeine) and are diuretic, causing you to lose water and nutrients in urine. Sweetened fizzy drinks also contain caffeine and sugar or artificial sweeteners and other non-nutritional additives. Water is best for quenching thirst and hydrating the body.

alcohol units

One unit of alcohol equals:

- half a pint of normal-strength beer or lager

- 1 small glass of wine

- 1 pub measure of spirits

- 1 pub measure of fortified wine, e.g. sherry or Martini.

stocking a fridge and freezer; hygienic food handling

Most people shop only once weekly or even less frequently and, with large amounts and a greater range of fresh and frozen food to keep in good condition for longer periods, the fridge and the freezer have become more important than ever. Fridges and freezers tend to be filled to capacity, especially after shopping trips, and used frequently throughout the day, so it is important to make sure they are loaded correctly and run at the right temperature to keep food in top condition for enjoyment and flavour and to avoid spoilage and contamination.

ten golden rules for fridge safety

- Keep the coldest part of the fridge between 0°C and 5°C (32°F and 41°F). If the fridge is not cold enough, harmful bacteria can grow and may cause food poisoning.
- Keep a fridge thermometer in the coldest part and check the temperature regularly (do not use a mercury thermometer as it could break and contaminate food).
- Keep the most perishable foods, such as cooked meats, in the coldest part of the fridge.
- When shopping, always take chilled and frozen food home quickly.
- Wrap or cover all raw or uncooked foods, so they cannot touch other foods or drip juices (e.g. from raw meat) on to other foods; this could contaminate cooked foods.
- Never overload the fridge; there must be enough space for cold air to circulate between the foods.
- Never put warm or hot food in the fridge; cool it first.
- Do not keep food beyond its 'use-by' date.
- Empty any unused food from cans into a bowl and cover before putting in the fridge to store – do not store food in opened cans; the tin may contaminate the food.
- Open fridge and freezer doors as infrequently as possible.

Fridges keep food fresher for longer. The low temperature slows down or stops growth of most common food-poisoning bacteria (except listeria; see page 18). Clean the fridge itself regularly, preferably before it is reloaded with the weekly shop. Wipe up spills as they occur (before they solidify!).

It is essential to know which part of the fridge is coldest so that the foods can be packed in the best storage conditions. The user handbook gives this information but some generalizations apply. *Larder fridge-freezers*: the bottom shelf above the salad bin is coldest, with the temperature rising towards the top of the fridge. *Frost-free fridges*: in theory, the whole fridge is the same temperature but the door shelves and compartments may be slightly warmer. *Ice-box fridges*: the coldest zone is the top shelf, just below the ice box.

which foods to keep where

Coldest zone (0°C–5°C) Ready meals; soft cheese; pâté; meat; meat pies; cooked meats; fromage frais; home-cooked food; leftovers; cream and cream cakes; custard.

Cool zones Milk; yoghurt; fruit juice; hard cheese; opened jars of mayonnaise and other bottles or jars labelled 'refrigerate after opening' or 'keep refrigerated'; butter; margarine; eggs.

Salad bin This is the warmest part of the fridge, to prevent damage to salad leaves and cucumbers. Put all fresh salad items, tomatoes, lettuces, radishes, cucumbers, avocados and so on in here and keep for 1–2 days.

cans and bottles in the fridge

- Transfer canned foods that are not used immediately to a suitable clean, non-metallic container and store covered in the fridge.
- Wipe milk bottles and other containers that might be dirty or have surface drips (e.g. ketchup bottles, juice containers) before putting them into the fridge.

fridge storage times

These are general guidelines; they do not replace specific storage instructions and use-by dates on packs and labels.

Raw bacon and gammon	1 week	Vegetables	3–4 days
Raw meat and sausages	3 days	Salad	2–3 days
Raw poultry, chops and similar cuts	2 days	Milk	4 days
Raw mince and offal	1 day	Yoghurt	4 days
Raw fish	Use same day	Cream	2 days
Cooked meat	2–3 days	Cheese, hard	1–2 weeks
Cooked meat pies	2 days	Cheese, soft	3 days
Cooked casseroles	2 days	Eggs, pointed end down	2 weeks
Cooked fish	1 day	Egg yolks	2 days
		Egg whites	3 days

fridge maintenance

- Do not overload the fridge.
- Regularly check the temperature and adjust the thermostat as necessary.
- Thaw the fridge as soon as ice begins to build up (if it is not an automatic or frost-free fridge). Ice reduces the fridge's efficiency, so it is less cold and uses more electricity.
- Do not put warm or hot food, which will raise the temperature, inside the fridge. To cool food quickly put it in the coldest part of the kitchen. Alternatively wrap it in a plastic bag or sealable container and put in a basin of cold water or under a running cold tap until cool.
- Return drinks, spreads and other foods to the fridge as soon as possible.

danger zone

Harmful bacteria grow most rapidly in the so called 'danger zone' between 10°C and 63°C (50°F and 145°F) – hence the need to keep refrigerator temperatures below 5°C (41°F). Refrigeration slows down bacteria growth and freezing virtually suspends it.

Cool food quickly before putting in the fridge or freezer – certainly within 1½ hours. Food left out in a warm kitchen provides an ideal breeding ground for food-poisoning bacteria. Cover while cooling – old-fashioned net covers are a good idea; they allow cooling without condensation and keep pests off the food.

using the freezer well

golden rules for freezer safety

- Frozen food should be stored at -22°C – don't let your freezer temperature get higher than -18°C although it can be lower.
- Use a thermometer to check the temperature regularly (not a mercury thermometer). If you do not have a thermometer, keep an eye on your ice-cream: if it is not properly frozen, the freezer temperature is not low enough.
- Keep the freezer as full as possible (unlike the fridge).
- Wrap all food so it does not get freezer burn (a thick white frost that dries the food and also ruins its flavour and texture).
- Label the food with its name and a use-by date – check the storage times in your manufacturer's instruction booklet.
- Open the door as infrequently as possible.
- Check the rubber door seals – if they perish, the freezer will frost up quickly. New seals can be bought.
- Defrost the freezer every six months or when the ice builds up to 1 cm (½ in) thick.

Freezing can preserve the flavour, texture and colour of food and its nutritional value, and keep food safe to eat. Freezing works by converting the water in food to ice, which cannot be used by bacteria to keep them alive or by enzymes that cause food spoilage. The very low temperatures suspend the activity of food-poisoning bacteria, even listeria, which can thrive in a fridge. However, freezing will not kill bacteria so, when food is taken out of the freezer and thawed, it needs to be handled appropriately (see below).

Faster freezing results in better-quality food when it is thawed and cooked, re-heated or eaten. Some freezers have a fast-freeze button, which lowers the temperature – put this on in advance of freezing a lot of food; if you forget, put it on as soon as you put the food in. Slow freezing creates larger ice crystals, which damage the structure of the food, making it soggy.

safe thawing

Some foods can be cooked direct from the freezer without thawing, for example, frozen vegetables and fish fingers, but it is essential that other foods are thawed thoroughly before cooking. Unless they are completely thawed, the temperature at the core of the food may not become high enough during cooking to kill any food-poisoning bacteria that are present. It is always safest to assume that poultry, in particular, will carry salmonella bacteria and treat it accordingly. After thawing, cook and eat food within 24 hours. Never refreeze frozen food as this risks contamination by food-poisoning bacteria and also spoils the texture and flavour of the food.

thawing food in a microwave

Care needs to be taken when thawing food in the microwave oven because it tends to thaw unevenly; food can be partially cooked or dry on the outside while the centre remains frozen.

If the microwave oven does not have an automatic thaw programme, or a thaw setting, use the lowest setting.

If thawing food manually, put the power on for 30 seconds, turn it off for a minute and then repeat until thawed. A standing time of 5 minutes allows the ice crystals to continue to thaw.

If the dish is liquid, such as soup, stock or a casserole, stir during thawing, or break up icy chunks to speed the process.

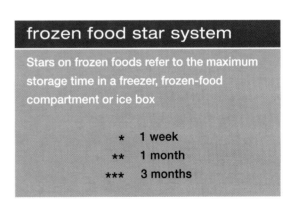

frozen food star system

Stars on frozen foods refer to the maximum storage time in a freezer, frozen-food compartment or ice box

✱	1 week
✱✱	1 month
✱✱✱	3 months

cooking and re-heating

Re-heat food only once. Stir or turn to ensure even re-heating, especially if using the microwave. Make sure food is piping hot (70–75°C/150–160°F) before serving. Serve hot food hot. Serve cooked food as soon as possible. Allowing it to stand around at a warm temperature will let any bacteria that were not destroyed, or that get into the food after cooking, multiply.

pork until the juices run clear when the meat is pierced with a skewer in the thickest part and the flesh is no longer pink. Red meat can, of course, be served less well done if that is to your taste, but the same hygiene rules apply.

Heat does not destroy the toxins produced by another common food-poisoning bacteria called staphylococcus. This bacteria is more common in foods that are handled

freezer storage times

These are general guidelines; they do not replace specific storage instructions and use-by dates on packs and labels.

Raw beef, lamb, chicken, duckling, goose and venison	1 year	Shellfish	2 months
		Butter and margarine	1 year
Raw pork, turkey, game birds and veal	9 months	Soft cheese	6 months
		Hard cheese	3-4 months
Cooked meat dishes and sliced meat in gravy	6 months	Double or whipping cream	6 months
Giblets	3 months	Stock	6 months
Offal and bacon	2 months	Soups and sauces	3 months
Sausages and pâté	1 month	Blanched vegetables	1 year
White fish	4 months	Fruit	1 year
Oily fish	3 months	Baked goods	3 months

Cook to kill! This does not mean overcooking your food, rather, cooking it thoroughly to destroy salmonella and the other common food-poisoning bacteria, such as campylobacter. Most bacteria will not survive in food cooked at 70–80°C/150–175°F for 10 minutes. Use a meat thermometer to check that the centre of the joint or poultry has reached 75°C/160°F. Some meat thermometers give the safe internal cooked temperature for poultry as 90°C/200°F. If you do not have a thermometer, cook poultry and

a lot during preparation, which underlines the need for good personal and kitchen hygiene.

hygienic food handling

It is important to handle food hygienically at all stages during storage, preparation, cooking and serving. Many cases of food poisoning can be prevented if good hygiene (including the techniques in the fridge and freezer sections above) is practised in the home, particularly in the kitchen.

While it is easy to see if food has passed its use-by or sell-by date by looking at the packaging, it is often not possible to tell by looking at a food or smelling it whether it is fit to eat – especially after it has been cooked. That's why it is very important to do as much as possible to prevent food poisoning, especially when preparing food for vulnerable people such as young children, elderly people and pregnant women.

First, wash your hands. Most people know this, but not everyone is aware of the need to keep washing their hands when handling and preparing food. This is very important between handling raw and cooked food. Also wash hands after using the lavatory, coughing, using a handkerchief, touching face or hair and carrying out cleaning or emptying the bin. Keep fingernails short and clean. Do not use the tea towels as a hand towel. Keep a separate hand towel, or dry your hands on kitchen paper.

preparing food

Ideally, use three separate chopping boards for raw poultry or meat; vegetables; cooked meat (e.g. ham) and other foods such as fish, cheese and fruit. This prevents food-poisoning bacteria from being transferred from raw to cooked food. It also prevents your fruit salad being tainted by garlic or onions! If you use the same board, wash well between different types of foods. Wipe work surfaces with a disinfectant cleaner.

Remember that cloths can also spread germs and they provide an ideal breeding ground if they are not kept clean. One bacterium can multiply to 1 million in around 3 hours in a dirty dishcloth, so wash frequently in disinfectant or bleach.

Wash knives and other equipment such as food processors thoroughly during food preparation, as well as after use. Wear rubber gloves and use very hot water and detergent. Always wipe can tops before opening.

cleaning up

Tea towels can spread germs. It is more hygienic to allow utensils to air dry or dry in a dishwasher. Keep the rubbish bin covered and away from food. Empty and clean it frequently.

Keep the sink clean, using a bleach or anti-bacterial product, and do not forget the plug hole and drain. Prevent blockages and nasty smells coming up from around those hidden bends by regular use of a drain-cleaning product.

dealing with food poisoning

Symptoms of food poisoning can appear within an hour or as long as five days after eating contaminated food. Common symptoms are stomach pains and/or vomiting and diarrhoea. Consult a doctor if the sufferer is a baby or child or is pregnant, elderly or ill. In other cases, avoid solid foods, take plenty of fluids to prevent dehydration and try not to prepare food for others while you are ill. If you have to do so, make sure you are very very careful about hygiene.

food-poisoning bacteria

Type of bacteria	Usual food source	Effect of heat	Effect of cold
Salmonella	Raw meat, poultry, eggs	Killed by cooking	Hardly multiplies at 5°C or colder
Campylobacter	Raw meat, poultry, unpasteurized milk	Killed by cooking	No multiplication below 30°C
Listeria	Meat, poultry, soft ripened cheese, pâté, raw vegetables	Killed by cooking	Multiplies a lot at 10°C, a little at 5°C
Staphylococcus	Cold foods that are handled a lot	Toxin not destroyed by normal cooking	Negligible toxin production at 5°C or colder
E Coli 0157	Raw and undercooked meat, raw vegetables, unpasteurised products	Killed by cooking	Slow growth at 5°C

stocking a storecupboard with foods for all occasions

Some people's storecupboard contains enough food for a siege while others run on the Mother Hubbard principle. The ideal lies between these two extremes. You need enough in the cupboard to make a few everyday meals in emergencies, plus items to use on a regular basis with fresh produce from the fridge and items from the freezer. In addition, it's good to have a few luxuries to cheer yourself up when the contents of the fridge and freezer look unpromising.

canned groceries

Coconut milk Avoids the time-consuming task of preparing coconut milk from fresh or desiccated coconut and is vital for Thai and Caribbean dishes.

Fish Anchovies, salmon, tuna, sardines. Canning reduces omega-3 content, so canned oily fish is not quite as beneficial as fresh oily fish, but it is still a valuable protein food, free from saturated fats.

Fruit Better-quality products tend to be canned in natural juice or water, rather than heavy syrup.

Pulses Baked beans, borlotti, cannellini, flageolet, pinto, red and white kidney and butter beans are all huge time-savers and excellent standbys for bulking out casseroles or making last-minute salads. See pages 86–87 for more on pulses.

Vegetables Tomatoes – whole, chopped or baby; sweetcorn kernels; bamboo shoots and water chestnuts.

jars, bottles and cartons

Black treacle For use in baking and desserts and some savoury dishes (great on porridge).

Chutney and pickles Home-made, or commercial lime pickle and mango chutney to accompany Indian dishes.

Golden syrup For use in baking and desserts.

Herbs, dried When fresh or frozen are unavailable: bay leaves, bouquets garnis, oregano, mint, thyme, rosemary, dill or parsley. For more about fresh herbs see pages 41–43.

Honey Clear for glazing and set for use at the table.

Jam Either home-made or bought for use at the table, for cake fillings, for making desserts and baking.

Jellies Redcurrant to serve with meat and as an ingredient in savoury sauces.

Marmite No British kitchen is complete without this nursery food. In addition to making Marmite soldiers for soft-boiled eggs it can also be used as a flavouring in sauces and soups.

Mayonnaise Some brands are better than others so try a small jar first!

Milk, long-life Cows', goats', soya and rice long-life milks are available. None is very nice on cereal or as a drink; keep for emergencies and to make custard and other sauces. Skimmed long-life cows' milk tastes nearest to fresh milk. If you regularly run out of fresh milk, keep a carton of long-life in the fridge; it tastes better well chilled.

Mustard and creamed horseradish sauce Hot English, smooth, milder Dijon or spicier, mild wholegrain mustard. See page 46 for more on mustard. Some people prefer creamed horseradish with their roast beef and it is also mixed with cream cheese as an accompaniment to smoked salmon.

Oil Oil is needed for cooking (olive is tasty; sunflower, corn and groundnut are flavourless). Nut oils (such as walnut or hazelnut) and extra-virgin olive oil, make delicious vinaigrettes. Sesame oil for Chinese dishes. For more about oils see pages 45–46.

Olives and capers Jars are better than cans, for snacks, pizza toppings and pasta sauces.

Oriental sauces Oyster, black bean, fish sauce and many others. Only buy those you use regularly.

Passata Sieved tomatoes in jars, available plain or flavoured and invaluable for use in pasta sauces.

Peanut (and other nut) butter For use at the table and as an ingredient in oriental, African and Caribbean sauces and dips.

Soya sauce Use as a recipe ingredients and to offer seperately at the table with Chinese food.

Spices A basic range of dried spices includes: black peppercorns, cloves, cinnamon (ground or sticks), vanilla pods (or a bottle of vanilla extract, but *not* vanilla flavouring, which is artificial), nutmeg, ground ginger, coriander and cumin (ground or seeds), ground mixed spice (or allspice berries), cayenne (or ground chilli) and turmeric. See also page 21.

Tabasco Or any hot chilli-pepper sauce.

Tahini For hummus and oriental recipes.

Tomato ketchup For when you just have to have some. Also good in barbecue sauces.

Tomato purée Tubes are better than cans.

Vinegar Red and white wine vinegars, cider vinegar and malt vinegar. See page 46 for more on vinegars.

Worcestershire sauce For cooking, Welsh rarebit and the occasional Bloody Mary.

non-perishable stores

Baking powder, cream of tartar and baking soda For baking that needs a raising agent.

Chocolate For the cook to nibble and for cooking. Choose high-quality, plain chocolate with a cocoa-solids content of around 70% for baking and desserts. For more about chocolate, see pages 217–218.

Cocoa For baking and making chocolate drinks; cocoa has a better flavour than drinking chocolate and 'instant' drinks, and is free from additives and sugar.

Coffee With beans and ground coffee, the style is determined by the degree of roasting and the origin of the beans. The darker the roast, the stronger the flavour and aroma whether regular or decaffeinated. Check the strength guide on the pack or shelf label in speciality stores – 1 is the mildest. Choose coffee ground to suit the coffee maker, e.g. finely ground for use in an espresso and filter machine or percolator, more coarsely ground for making coffee in a cafetière. Instant coffee is available as powder, granules or freeze-dried and the brand and style are a matter of personal taste.

Cornflour A quick way to thicken sauces, or to stabilize natural yoghurt (stir in a teaspoonful) to prevent it curdling in sauces.

Custard powder Not a necessity now that cartons of ready-made custard are widely available, but a handy standby nevertheless when in need of comforting custard. For more about making custard, see page 218.

Dried fruit Such as apple, apricots, cranberries, sour cherries, blueberries, mango, papaya, pears, peaches, pineapple, prunes, raisins, sultanas. Buy only what you use frequently.

Dried yeast For baking. For more about yeast and bread-making, see *Bread and Pizza*.

Flour White, brown, wholemeal, whole grain, malted, plain, self-raising, strong flour for bread and pasta, buckwheat and so on. Buy according to frequency of use and need, and store in an airtight (and moisture-proof) container. For a glossary of flours, see pages 175–176.

Grains Such as barley, buckwheat, bulgur and cous cous. Barley usually means *pearl barley*, traditionally used to bulk out soups such as Scotch broth and stews such as Irish stew. Pearl barley benefits from soaking and long cooking, which is probably why it has been superseded by quicker cooking cous cous and bulghur wheat. *Buckwheat* is a small, dark, triangular grain that cooks in about 15 minutes. It can be used in place of rice or other grains and has a sweet, nutty flavour. *Bulghur wheat* is a partially cooked, cracked-wheat grain. This means it is quick to cook – about 15 minutes. Best known as the main ingredient in tabboulleh, in which it is mixed with chopped cucumber, mint and lemons. It can also be eaten like rice as an accompaniment, or added to soup. *Cous cous* is a partially cooked grain made from rolled semolina (the inside of the wheat grain). It does not even need cooking; it can simply be soaked in just-boiled water for about 10 minutes. Use a large enough dish as it swells and increases in volume. Use in place of rice or mix with vegetables.

Lentils and split peas See page 87 for more information.

Mixed peel and glacé cherries If you are a home-baker. Natural-colour glacé cherries are available.

Polenta Even quicker if made in the microwave, polenta is available in 5-minute versions. It is not particularly nutritious but is handy. For more about polenta, see page 85.

Porridge oats Make a hot, filling bowl of cereal for any time of day or night. Make with milk or water, no need to add salt and sweeten to taste.

Rice Keep a long-grain rice in the storecupboard as well as a speciality rice for risotto, plus others to suit your preferences. Freeze spare cooked rice for added convenience. For more about rice, see pages 85–86.

cooking pastes and spice mixtures

Jars of fresh spices, such as ginger, or herbs, such as garlic, coriander and lemon grass, are useful but the flavour is never the same as fresh.

Popular spice mixtures are also very useful: *Cajun seasoning* is a combination of Spanish, French and Caribbean spices: garlic, onion, paprika, black pepper, cumin, mustard powder, cayenne, thyme, oregano and salt. *Chinese five-spice powder* contains star anise, cassia or cinnamon, fennel seeds, cloves and Sichuan pepper. *Garam masala* for Indian cooking (see page 129). *Harissa* is a fiery North-African sauce, a mix of red chillies, garlic, caraway, cumin, coriander, mint and olive oil. *Thai curry pastes* can be red or green; they are a basic mix of garlic, lemon grass, coriander seeds, cumin seeds, black peppercorns, chillies, and galangal. Don't forget your favourite *Indian curry paste* and/or *powder*.

Mushrooms, dried Porcini (English ceps or French ceps), morels or Chinese dried mushrooms, such as shiitake, are flavoursome and excellent in risottos and casseroles. They can be rehydrated with a 15-minute soak and the liquid used in sauces and stocks.

Nuts Almonds, cashews, hazelnuts, pecans, walnuts and pine kernels; they all need to be eaten as soon after purchase as possible and stored in an airtight container. For more about nuts, see pages 161–163.

Pasta, dried All pasta shapes and sizes are indispensable storecupboard standbys. For more about pasta, see *Pasta, Rice and Pulses*.

Salt Sea salt has more flavour and aroma than common table salt. Store salt in an airtight container because it attracts water and will become lumpy in contact with air.

Seeds Sunflower, pumpkin and sesame seeds are useful. For more about seeds, see page 163.

Stock cubes or granules These provide stock in a hurry if there is no fresh or frozen stock available. For more about stock, see *Soups and Starters*.

Sugar White, brown and all shades in between. Buy what you use and store in an airtight (and moisture-proof) container. For more about sugar, see page 202.

fruit and vegetables

ood shopping can be a chore, but it becomes an absolute pleasure when you stand back and admire the colourful array of fruit and vegetables in street markets and on supermarket shelves. Select fruit and vegetables for quality and freshness. Consider how long the produce will last without deteriorating. Store it to retain its freshness and prepare it properly to retain maximum flavour, vitamins and minerals.

a–z of everyday fruit

APPLES, EATING

Buy Autumn is when the new fruit is harvested. Apples are stored in controlled-atmosphere conditions, which delay their ripening so that they are available all year round.

Store In the fridge for a couple of weeks to retain the crispness, but bring to room temperature before eating.

Prepare Wash in soapy water if you want to remove the protective wax used on most apples; rinse it off well. Organic apples will not have been coated with wax, but still give them a wash.

APPLES, COOKING

Bramley Is the only widely grown cooking apple; it is large, green skinned and with a white flesh that is juicy and disintegrates into a purée when cooked. In addition to Bramley you might also see *Lord Derby,* a large, greenish-yellow apple with a purplish-brown flush and coarse and quite dry texture. *Newton Wonder* is a large, flattish apple, with a yellow skin flushed brown red. It is moderately juicy and slightly acidic.

APRICOTS

Buy May–July, when they should be firm but not green, plump with bright, although downy, skin.

Store In the fridge for up to a week or ripen in a brown paper bag at room temperature.

Prepare Wash and eat raw or poach lightly.

AVOCADOS

Buy All year round. Choose even-coloured fruit with unblemished skin. Never trust completely the 'ripe' or 'ready to eat' labels; often this fruit is over-ripe and soft. The fruit should still be quite firm.

Store At room temperature for up to a week, depending on how ripe the fruit is. If it's already ripe, keep it in the fridge and use within a couple of days.

Prepare Run a knife around the circumference through the flesh to the central stone. Twist the halves apart and remove the stone. To remove the skin, slip the end of a teaspoon between flesh and skin to loosen, then lift it off. Dress in lemon juice or vinaigrette to prevent the fruit from browning.

general guidelines on preparing fruit and vegetables

- Always store fresh produce out of direct sunlight, even if storing at room temperature. See page 13 for which fruits and vegetables to store in the fridge.
- Wash and scrub fruit and vegetables to remove surface pesticides and bacteria. Rinse well in cold water and dry carefully.
- Enjoy raw fruit and vegetables as often as possible because even quick cooking reduces vitamin and mineral content.

- Avoid unnecessary peeling; much of the vitamin and mineral content is just below the skin. Peeling also wastes valuable fibre.
- Prepare as close to cooking or serving as possible. Try not to pre-prepare or leave soaking in water, or uncovered in the fridge.

BANANAS

Buy All year round, choosing completely yellow fruit, with a small number of brown specks if you want it for immediate use, or fruit with green skin if it is to have time to ripen.

Store At room temperature for a week, although the fruit will progressively ripen during this time. Don't refrigerate as this turns the skin black.

Prepare Peel and eat! If cooking with the fruit, toss in lemon juice to prevent discolouration.

BLACKBERRIES

Buy (Or pick your own) in late summer and autumn. Blackberries may be cultivated (larger and milder in flavour) or wild (smaller, pippier and more pungent in flavour). Uniform black colour indicates ripeness, as does a 'bloom', especially on hedgerow fruit.

Store In the fridge, unwashed and uncovered, until ready for use. Will go mouldy quickly so use as soon as possible.

CHERRIES

Buy Some varieties are good for cooking and some better for eating. Choose sweet cherries as dessert fruit and acid (sour or bittersweet) cherries such as morello for cooking. Buy evenly coloured bright red to dark purple fruit with fresh-looking stalks.

Store Unwashed in the fridge for 2–3 days.

Prepare Wash and remove the stalks if the fruit is to be cooked, and halve if you have time or an efficient cherry stoner; otherwise leave the stones in – half the fun of eating cherries is removing the stones.

CURRANTS (BLACK, RED, WHITE)

Buy In summer, when fruit is firm, plump and shiny.

Store In the fridge, unwashed and uncovered, for a couple of days.

Prepare Top and tail. Some people find it easier if the fruit is frozen first on its sprigs and the hard berries then pulled off. This causes less damage to the fruit, i.e. less juice is spilled!

FIGS, FRESH

Buy Either fresh green (sometimes called white) or fresh black (sometimes called blue) figs that look plump and have a delicate bloom and are heavy for their size.

Store In a fridge (if not using the same day) for 3–4 days or at room temperature to soften a little.

Prepare Wash well and slice them into halves or quarters to reveal the bright pink-red flesh full of minuscule edible pips.

GOOSEBERRIES

Buy Taut-skinned berries that are bright and glossy. Avoid brown-looking fruit. Green fruit are ready early in the summer before strawberries.

Store In the fridge for a week or in a cool, dry place for a few days.

Prepare Top and tail green fruit using kitchen scissors, although this is not necessary if the fruit is to be sieved. Cook with sugar or with elderflower heads, which sweeten the fruit and add a complementary fragrance. Yellow, white and red gooseberries are riper later in the summer and are dessert fruit that can be eaten raw, although they can be a little too sharp for some tastes.

GRAPES

Buy All year round. Choose well shaped grapes that are plump with tight skins. They may be shiny or have a soft bloom.

Store In the fridge for 4–5 days.

Prepare Wash when ready to eat and pat dry on kitchen paper.

GRAPEFRUIT

Buy All year. Choose firm, well-shaped fruit.

Store In the fridge or at room temperature for a week. Like oranges, the thick skin keeps in the moisture and most citrus fruit is also waxed (sometimes with a fungicide) to retain moisture and prevent mould forming on the fruit.

Prepare Halve and remove seeds, loosen segments with a serrated knife if serving as breakfast halves. Or remove peel and cut into segments.

LEMONS (AND LIMES)

Buy Fruit with hard, gleaming rind and undamaged skin. Choose fruits that feel heavy for their weight and don't have very thick skin. If using the zest, buy unwaxed or organic.

Store At room temperature or in the fridge for a week or longer. The lemon or lime won't ripen further.

Prepare Use flesh or juice as required. Remove pips before putting slices in drinks, or before serving wedges for squeezing over food.

MELONS

Buy Late summer for the best bargains but available all year round. All varieties should have a reasonably unblemished, evenly coloured skin. Some varieties are more scented than others; more scent comes off the stalk end and can be an indication of ripeness. The colour of the flesh is dependent on variety but all should be evenly coloured; a line of darker flesh near the skin indicates that the fruit is unripe. It is important to buy ripe melons, as they do not ripen further once picked from the vine.

Store Either in the fridge or at room temperature for up to 2 weeks, as melons do not continue to ripen after picking. Once cut, wrap and store in the fridge.

Prepare Cut into wedges or, if small, cut in half. Alternatively, cut out balls for use in fruit salads and cocktails.

ORANGES

Buy Different varieties all year round. Whichever variety, a thin skin is best and a fruit that seems heavy for its size. Avoid fruit with soft or bruised areas on the skin.

Store At room temperature for about 10 days or in the fridge if you need to keep them longer.

Prepare If you want to use the skin (zest) choose unwaxed or organic fruit. Use flesh or juice as required. Remove pips before putting slices in drinks or salads.

PEACHES AND NECTARINES

Buy In summer, when skin should be even-coloured and yield slightly to the touch. Be careful to buy ripe fruit as peaches and nectarines do not continue to ripen, they just go soft. Flesh will be a golden yellow, sometimes with a red blush, or white, depending on variety. In 'clingstone' varieties the flesh is not so easily removed from the stone.

Store At room temperature or in the fridge and use as soon as possible.

Prepare The skin of both is edible but many people don't like it. If you blanch fruit in boiling water and then dip it into cold water, the skin should peel off easily. Either eat in the hand or use in fruit salads or recipes.

PEARS

Buy Home-grown varieties such as Conference and Comice, and the relatively new English variety Concorde, ripen in late summer and autumn. Not all of the harvest is released at once; the bulk is stored in controlled-atmosphere conditions that delay ripening so that the fruit can be available 'fresh' all year.

Store At room temperature or in the fridge and use as soon as possible when they have softened slightly.

Prepare No need to peel. Wash and dry then eat in the hand or use in recipes.

Asian Pears are a different species to the pears we are accustomed to. Asian pears are hard and crisp, with a translucent flesh. They are crunchy to eat but they should also be juicy. The flavour is pear-like but different from European and American pears.

PLUMS

Buy Firm, plump, well-coloured plums with unblemished skins. The downy bloom on plums is natural. Avoid fruit with split skins, especially if it has an aroma of fermentation. Victoria plums are firm, juicy and sweet with a mild flavour and an orange-red speckled appearance. Dark red plums – often called culinary plums – are usually best for cooking as they are sharper and more acidic. Yellow and golden plums are often sweeter and best eaten raw.

Store In the fridge and use as soon as possible because plums become over-ripe quickly.

Prepare Eat raw or poached – either whole or halved to remove the stone. There is no need to remove the skin unless you want to use the fruit to make a mousse.

POMEGRANATES

Buy In late autumn, when the shiny, bright-red-skinned fruit appears in the shops.

Store At room temperature; some people suggest until the skin splits which means the fruit is ripe.

Prepare Break open or cut the fruit in half and scoop out the seeds in their sacs of juice, discarding the bitter membrane that acts as pouches for the seeds. Eat fresh by sucking away the seeds.

RASPBERRIES (CLOUDBERRIES, TAYBERRIES, LOGANBERRIES, BOYSENBERRIES)

All these fruits are related, despite their different shapes, flavours and colours.

Buy Plump, brightly coloured berries that are dry, not over-large, and free from mould. If the punnet is see-through, check that the fruit is not squashed and swimming in juice at the bottom. Avoid hard, under-ripe fruit with white patches. Raspberries can vary in colour from quite a deep and dark raspberry pink through lighter shades to golden (or yellow) raspberries, but the latter are not seen often in high-street shops. Cloudberries are popular in Scandinavia and North America; they are golden when ripe and soft and juicy. Loganberries and boysenberries are best cooked. Blackberries (page 24) are also a member of this family.

Store Uncovered and unwashed in the fridge and use within a day if possible. All these berry fruits freeze well.

Prepare Gently pull the stalk to remove the central core and leave whole for eating at once or for cooking.

RHUBARB

Buy Firm, crisp, bright pink, long stems. Avoid any stems with brown markings.

Store In the fridge in a plastic bag for 2–3 days.

Prepare Trim off the leaves and the white base of the stem. Wash well in cold water and pat dry.

STRAWBERRIES

Buy As for raspberries but choose brightly coloured, firm, well shaped and medium-sized fruits with undamaged skin and the stem still attached.

Store Unwashed, in the fridge; but use as soon as possible.

Prepare Wash just before eating and hull the fruit, which means pulling out its central stalk and leaves – unless the fruit are to be eaten with the fingers. For most people, strawberries are best eaten raw with cream, although in France and Italy, they are often served with red wine poured over them. See page 238 for a strawberry jam recipe.

WATERMELONS

Buy In summer for best bargains. As they are very large, wedges or halves are most convenient. The flesh should be bright pink.

Store Cut pieces, wrapped, in the fridge. Whole ones can be stored in a cool, dry, airy place for a week or so.

Prepare Remove skin. Eat in the hand or with a knife and fork. The black seeds are edible (and far too fiddly to remove, except for special recipes). Alternatively use a melon baller or cut into cubes.

a–z of everyday vegetables

BEANS (GREEN, RUNNER, FRENCH, BOBBY)
Buy Firm, fresh-coloured beans that snap when bent.
Store In the salad compartment of the fridge for 5 days.
Prepare Wash and trim the top and bottom. Remove the 'strings' from the sides, if there are any. Leave beans whole or cut into lengths.

BEAN SPROUTS
Buy From the chiller compartment, in plastic bags.
Store In the fridge and comply with the use-by dates (they keep fresh only for a couple of days).
Prepare Rinse well in cold water before use. Pick out any pods or roots and discard any tired-looking sprouts.

BEETROOT
Buy Firm, dry roots that feel hard and are plump.
Store After cutting off the leaves, leaving some stalk, store in the salad compartment of the fridge for 5 days. Avoid bruising, which will cause red juice to leak out in storage and cooking.
Prepare Peel and grate raw for salads or cook whole in skins in boiling water; or steam, bake, microwave or pressure-cook. Remove skins when cool enough to handle.

BROAD BEANS
Buy Small, tender young pods with a fresh green colour. Avoid pods that have any brown blemishes.
Store In the salad compartment of the fridge for up to a week.
Prepare Pod the beans when ready to use. Older beans may need to be removed from their grey skins after podding. Boil or steam.

BROCCOLI (PURPLE SPROUTING, CALABRESE)
Buy With firm, upright stalks and compact, dark green heads. Avoid any yellow-looking florets.
Store In the salad compartment of the fridge for a couple of days.
Prepare Cut large stems into even-sized pieces using as much stem as possible. Wash in cold water.

BRUSSELS SPROUTS

Buy Small, compact, firm, bright green sprouts.

Store In the salad compartment of the fridge, keeping them dry, for 5 days.

Prepare Trim if necessary and score stem with a cross to speed cooking. Do not overcook; they should retain some texture, even crispness.

CABBAGES, GREEN (POINTED CABBAGE, SAVOY OR GREENS, KALE)

Buy Firm, crisp cabbage that is heavy for its size.

Store In the fridge in a perforated bag for a week.

Prepare Break off outer leaves and wash well.

CABBAGES, RED AND WHITE

Buy Smooth, heavy-for-size heads. If the cabbage is cut, buy one that looks recently cut, is wrapped in film to prevent it from drying out and has tight leaves.

Store In a cool, dry place or in the fridge for up to 2 weeks; wrap once cut.

CARROTS

Buy Crisp, firm roots with a good orange colour. If the top is there it should be bright green and fresh.

Store In the salad compartment for a week

CELERY

Buy Compact stalks that are crisp and undamaged. White (blanched) has the best flavour.

Store In the salad compartment for a week.

Prepare Snap stalks off as required.

CHINESE LEAVES (OR CHINESE CABBAGE)

Buy Heavy-for-size heads of this compact pale cabbage that is more barrel-shaped than our more familiar round cabbages.

Store Remove bag if wrapped in plastic and store in a cool, dry place or in the salad bin, where it will keep for weeks although it is much better to use as soon as possible after purchasing.

Prepare By shredding with a sharp knife and washing.

CORN ON THE COB

Buy Corn in the fresh green husk in preference to husked cobs wrapped in cling film. Peek beneath the husks to check that the kernels are plump and moist – the beard or silky threads should feel damp.

Store In the fridge and use as soon as possible.

Prepare Peel off and discard the husk and the threads. Cut off the base and the tip if it is devoid of kernels.

COURGETTES AND MARROWS

Buy Firm, dark green vegetables that feel heavy for their size.

Store In the salad compartment for 5 days.

Prepare Wash both carefully. Peel marrows but use courgettes unpeeled. No need to remove the seeds.

CUCUMBERS

Buy Firm, fleshy, bright green vegetables that are rigid.

Store In the salad compartment of the fridge for up to a week.

GARLIC

Buy Bulbs that are plump and firm. Buy only as many as you are going to use within a week or so.

Store In an airy, dry, cool place – preferably not in the fridge where it could taint other food.

Prepare Peel off the papery skin and chop, mince or crush as required.

Note: Do not store peeled garlic bulbs in oil in the fridge because there is a slight risk of dangerous toxins developing. Some rare cases of botulism have occurred from garlic preserved in oil or being used to flavour oil. *Clostridium botulinum* is frequently found in soil and can infect garlic. If the garlic is stored in acid, such as vinegar, the toxins do not develop but, in a neutral liquid like oil, there is a risk of botulism spores flourishing. Even though the risk is slight, only steep garlic overnight in oil and use within 2 days. Keep the garlic and oil in a fridge. It is still perfectly safe to use fresh garlic in cooking.

LEEKS

Buy Firm white leeks with tight stems and, if possible, the roots and green leafy top still in place, as this is an indication of freshness.

Store In the fridge.

Prepare Trim off roots, base and green tops (which may be used in stocks, soups, etc.). If using whole, prise open the leaves and immerse in cold water to remove any grit and soil; alternatively, slice across and wash the resulting rings, or peel off individual leaves and wash.

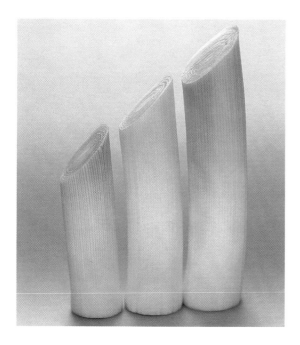

LETTUCES (ALL VARIETIES INCLUDING COS, ICEBERG, LITTLE GEM, LOLLO ROSSO, ROMAINE, ROUND, WEBB'S WONDER)

Buy Firm, fresh-looking lettuce with proud leaves, that feels heavy for its size. Crispness of leaves will depend on variety. Iceberg is usually particularly crisp.

Store Wash as soon as you get it home, dry well and store in a container or bag in the salad compartment for 3–4 days.

Prepare Either remove leaves individually or pull out heart and wash the head under cold running water. Drain and dry using a clean tea towel or salad spinner.

MUSHROOMS (BUTTON, FLAT OR OPEN)

Buy Firm, dry, mushrooms. Avoid any that are damaged or look withered.

Store Keep mushrooms in a paper bag in the fridge for 4–5 days.

Prepare Wipe or brush off any specks of soil or dirt but try to avoid washing unless very dirty. Washing mushrooms can make them slimy and also lessen the flavour. There is no need to peel mushrooms, just trim the ends off the stalks.

ONIONS (INCLUDING SHALLOTS, PICKLING ONIONS, RED ONIONS)

Buy If hard, and crisp, with dry papery skin.

Store In a cool, dark, airy place for several weeks.

Prepare Use a sharp knife to remove the ends then pull away the papery skin before slicing.

PARSNIPS

Buy Small to medium size vegetables that are smooth and firm. Avoid large and old parsnips as the central core may be woody.

Store In a cool, dark, airy dry place for up to 10 days.

PEAS (INCLUDING GARDEN, MANGE TOUT, SUGAR SNAP, SNOW)

Buy Choose bright green, silky pods that look well filled and firm. The same criteria apply to others, except that some will have flat pods and should break crisply.

Store In the salad compartment for 2–3 days.

Prepare Just before use, either shelling or cooking the pods whole after topping and tailing.

PEPPERS, SWEET

Buy Glossy, crisp and unwrinkled peppers.

Store In salad compartment of the fridge, for 7 days.

Prepare To remove the skins, halve, remove seeds, flatten with heel of hand and grill, skin-side uppermost, until the skin is charred. Place in a bowl covered in cling film or inside a loosely knotted plastic bag. When cool enough to handle, peel off and discard the skin.

POTATOES

Buy Tubers that are firm and smooth, whether they are new or main-crop potatoes. Avoid blemished potatoes or any that are sprouting or green. Sweet potatoes should be similarly firm and undamaged. New and salad potatoes should have thin skins.

Store Main-crop potatoes in a cool, dark, airy place for up to 2 weeks or until they start to sprout. Don't store new potatoes for more than a day or two in the fridge because they will go soft.

Prepare Scrub or scrape the potatoes and remove any eyes. No need to peel new or main-crop potatoes but sweet potatoes should be peeled.

frying tonight? do it right

Many people have switched to frying with polyunsaturated vegetable oils for health reasons. However, there has been concern that overheating polyunsaturated oils, which are much less stable when heated than mono-unsaturated oils such as olive oil and rapeseed oil or saturated fats like lard and butter, might create free radicals (substances that can contribute to heart disease and cancer if not kept in check by antioxidant nutrients; refer back to pages 10–11).

Cooking at high temperatures with polyunsaturated fats might also increase production of trans-fats, which are potentially more harmful than saturated fats when it comes to heart disease. (Trans-fats are mainly produced when vegetable oils are hydrogenated – hardened – for use in margarine, shortening and other cooking processes.) So long as you don't use your cooking oil more than eight times and don't heat it to a temperature higher than 170°C/335°F there would seem to be no risk of free-radical damage. Never heat cooking oil to the point where it produces blue smoke. If you do, throw it away.

RADISHES

Buy Preferably in bunches, with the foliage and roots attached. The radish should be clean, red, crisp and heavy for size.

Store In the fridge for up to a week.

Prepare Trim off the roots but leave a little of the stalk and a leaf or two, if small, in place, Scrub well.

SPECIALITY MIXED SALAD LEAVES (INCLUDING ENDIVE, LAMBS LETTUCE, RED CHARD)

Buy Check the use-by date on the bag and buy the freshest available.

Store In the salad compartment of the fridge.

Prepare Rinse well in cold water (even if prewashed) and pat or spin dry.

SPINACH

Buy Those with dark green leaves and a firm crisp stalk; with spinach you want as little stalk as possible and smaller leaves. Avoid yellowing, wilted or bruised leaves or any with rust-coloured blotches.

Store In the salad bin in the fridge.

Prepare Wash the leaves well, in several changes of water, to remove any soil and sandy grit. Cut off any excess stalks.

SWEDES AND TURNIPS

Buy Hard, crisp roots that are heavy for their size.

Store In a cool, dark, airy place, or the fridge for a couple of weeks.

Prepare Scrub and peel before using as required.

TOMATOES

Buy Sun-ripened tomatoes, if possible, as they are best for flavour. A dark red skin indicates ripeness, whatever the variety (unless it is a golden/yellow tomato). Pre-packed varieties may state on the pack that they are special varieties grown for their flavour; the best you can do is try as many varieties as possible and decide for yourself which flavour you prefer. Avoid tomatoes that are light for their size or pale in colour.

are organic fruit and vegetables better?

Not eating enough fruit and vegetables is more harmful to health than hazards from pesticide residues. Government regulations are designed to minimize residues in fruit, which, surveillance shows, do not usually exceed Maximum Residue Levels. However, there are questions over long-term exposure to low doses and also concerns about the so-called 'cocktail effect' (the combined effect of multiple residues). Thorough washing can remove some of the surface pesticides, fungicides, waxes and other treatments but cannot remove systemic pesticides (those taken into the plant during growth). If you plan to use the zest or peel of citrus fruit it is wisest to use organic or unwaxed fruit – the waxes contain fungicide.

Comparisons of nutrient content show some organic produce (grown without chemical pesticides and inorganic fertilizers) contains more vitamins and minerals and has a different physical structure, which is interpreted by some experts as being beneficial.

Organic produce has the potential for better flavour than non-organic, but taste tests are not unanimous and taste is often influenced by familiarity and personal preferences.

Store In the fridge or at room temperature for up to a week to allow the ripening process to continue.

Prepare If removing the skin before use in sauces, plunge into boiling water for 30 seconds, drain and plunge into cold water. Drain and then slit the skin with the point of a sharp knife and peel off. To remove pips and juice (for sauces, some soups and coulis) skin and then roughly chop and drain in a sieve for 30 minutes.

WATERCRESS

Buy Whole bunches rather than ready-trimmed and washed. Choose glossy, dark green leaves and firm stalks.

Store Wash and dry as for lettuce before storing for a couple of days.

Prepare Wash well and remove any roots and flowers; trim off excessive stalks but leave quite a bit of stalk on the leaves as it is flavoursome and nutritious.

exotic
fruit and
vegetables

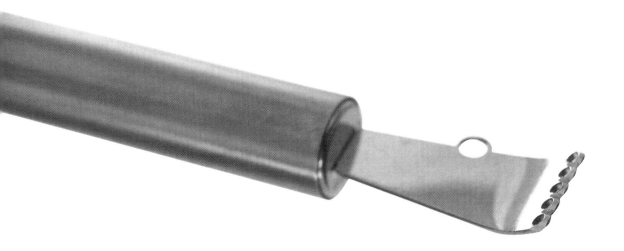

the amazing colours, shapes and sizes of exotic produce brighten the shops and bring a ray of sunshine from faraway tropical places. Along with the sense of excitement induced by seeing such produce, is a sense of bewilderment. How do you tackle a kiwano fruit? What is the best way to peel a prickly pear without being left with fingers full of irritant hairs? And what do these foods taste like? Well, we can't describe everything you see in the shops but here is a guide to those you are most likely to come across.

a-z of exotic fruit

CARAMBOLA (STAR FRUIT OR BILIMBI)

Buy Firm fruit without bruises with an even yellow or orangey colour (although the bilimbi variety remains green). The skin should be bright and waxy and the five prominent sides should be firm.

Store In the fridge for 3 days.

Prepare Wash and slice off the top and bottom, then trim the skin off the corner of each rib of the star. Cut slices across the fruit so that they are star-shaped and add the crisp and juicy flesh to fruit salads.

CHERIMOYA (CUSTARD APPLE OR SOURSOP)

Buy Evenly coloured fruit turning from green to yellow. The bloom on the skin is natural.

Store At room temperature until ripe, then in the fridge.

Prepare Cut the scaly fruit, which, at a quick glance looks like a globe artichoke or a pine cone, in half and scoop out the creamy pulp, discarding the large black seeds. The flavour is reminiscent of pineapple and strawberry.

CRANBERRIES

Buy Fresh fruit around Christmas. The berries should be bright red, plump and firm.

Store In the fridge for a week or so, or freeze.

Prepare Wash and pick over, discarding any damaged or soft berries. Cook with water or orange juice and sweeten this very tart fruit after cooking, to prevent the skins from hardening. Cranberry drinks are used to help treat or prevent urinary tract infections such as cystitis, because they contain compounds that prevent the most common bacteria which cause cystitis from attaching to the bladder wall.

DATES

Buy Large, plump, shiny, fresh dates, with smooth undamaged skin. Dried dates are available in presentation boxes, mainly around Christmas. Dried dates are also available in packs, either stoned or with stones, to be eaten as they are, or chopped and used in baking and desserts. It is worth rinsing these before use as they are often a bit dusty. Slabs of dried dates are the cheapest way of buying dates for cooking. Chop them carefully as they may contain stones or fragments of stones.

Store In the fridge, but bring to room temperature before eating. 'Fresh' dates are frozen after harvesting for export to the UK from many countries, including Israel, Egypt, Morocco, Tunisia and the United States. They have such a high sugar content that the fruit is virtually unaffected and tastes just like fresh once it is thawed.

Prepare Fresh dates can be eaten just as they are – however, some people prefer to remove the outer papery skins and push the stone out.

DATES, MEDJOOL

Buy Dates that look plump. Medjool dates do not have the smooth, shiny skins of natural dates because they are a different variety and their skins are naturally wrinkled, with a matt finish.

Store Like natural dates, medjool dates, which are primarily from Israel, are frozen after harvesting in August and September to provide a year-round supply. Store them in a cool, dry place if they are to be eaten within a week, or in the fridge where they can be stored for around a month.

Prepare Medjool dates need no preparation – they are not sprayed or treated after harvesting and are eaten just as they are.

DURIAN

Buy When the prickly, spine-covered thick skin of this huge, heavy and horned fruit is yellowing.

Store Away from food and human habitation as the smell is disgusting!

Prepare Follow the markings of the segments to cut open and scoop out the flesh, separating the seeds. Eat the flesh uncooked or use in recipes. The seeds are roasted and eaten as nuts.

FEIJOA

Buy Plump fruits with undamaged skin. This duck-egged-sized and -shaped fruit turns from dull green to a yellowish colour on ripening.

Store At room temperature until ripe and then in the fridge.

Prepare Cut in half and eat the grainy flesh, which tastes like a cross between a pineapple and strawberry, from a spoon – discard the jelly-like seeds in the centre.

GRANADILLA (GRENADILLA)

Buy Firm and smooth-skinned examples of this fruit that is an orange version of its purple-brown relative, the passion-fruit.

Store At room temperature – the thick, inedible shell prevents the fleshy interior from dehydrating.

Prepare Halve and scoop out the tangy, fleshy seeds to eat on their own or use to flavour sauces, ice-cream or yoghurt.

GUAVA

Buy This small, round fruit, which is slightly pointed at one end, when the green skin has turned yellowish, indicating it is ripe. The fruit should be firm and heavily perfumed.

Store At room temperature until ripe and then in the fridge for 2–3 days.

Prepare Wash and halve and then eat the flesh, which may be white or strawberry coloured, with a spoon. The flesh is a mixture of grainy, gritty and creamy and the flavour aromatic. Can also be gently cooked.

KIWANO (HORNED MELON OR CUCUMBER)

Buy Firm fruit that feel heavy for their size and have an undamaged skin.

Store In the fridge for a few days.

Prepare The spiky skin is edible but you may prefer only to use the bright-lime-green, seedy flesh inside (which makes a stunning colour contrast to the golden skin); it has the slightly astringent flavour of a sweet and aromatic cucumber.

KIWI FRUIT

Buy All year round but most readily available and cheapest in winter. The brown hairy skin should be covering firm fruit that yields only slightly when pressed.

Store At room temperature or in the fridge. Depending on ripeness when bought, it will keep for up to 2 weeks.

KUMQUATS

Buy Plump and heavy fruit with a firm, shiny skin.

Store This small oval fruit at room temperature.

Prepare Eat whole (the skin is very thin) and spit out the pips. Freeze and use as novelty ice cubes in long drinks.

LOQUAT

Buy Firm, brightly coloured fruit that is still attached to the stem. Avoid any with dull-looking skin.

Store In the fridge.

Prepare Peel and eat fresh or sweeten if the slightly tart flavour is too sour.

LYCHEE

Buy Fruit with a firm, dry skin.

Store Either in the fridge or at room temperature.

Prepare Cut through the leathery, rough, pink-brown skin and peel it off to reveal the pearly translucent flesh, which is sweet and smooth. Do this over a basin to catch the drips from the very juicy flesh. Use whole or take the flesh off the large, black, shiny stone in the centre to put in fruit salads or serve on its own.

MANGO

Buy All year round. Choose fruit with a smooth, firm skin that is not too soft when pressed. Skin colour varies from green to orange and red but does not indicate ripeness; it simply depends on the variety.

Store In the fridge for about 3 days, if ripe. Store at room temperature if the fruit needs to ripen.

Prepare Mango is best eaten uncooked, as cooking destroys the aromatic flavour. It is good on its own or in sorbet and ice-cream, or with chicken. To make a mango 'hedgehog', slice two 'halves' from each side of the large, flat, central stone, cutting as close to the stone as possible. Place the slices skin-side down and cut through the flesh to the skin first lengthways and then across, in evenly spaced, parallel lines. Press the scored flesh up by inverting the mango half to make two 'hedgehogs'. Peel the central band of flesh that was left around the stone and cut the rest of the flesh from the stone.

PAPAYA

Buy A pear-shaped fruit similar in size to a medium to large mango. Available all year. Choose firm fruit that has a bright and even-coloured yellow-green skin; if it is completely green it is not ripe. When it is ripe the fruit gives slightly when held gently in the palm of the hand.

Store At room temperature for a couple of days or, if ripe, in the fridge.

Prepare Halve and remove the black seeds with a spoon. Dress with lime juice to serve. Papaya and pineapple contain a protein-digesting enzyme used in the food industry as a powdered enzyme to tenderize meat. For the same reason, it will prevent setting if included in desserts made with gelatine.

PASSION-FRUIT

Buy Large, heavy fruit with deep purple skins that may be slightly dented in appearance.

Store In the fridge for up to 5 days.

Prepare Cut in half and scoop out the fleshy seeds with a spoon; they can be eaten on their own or used in sauces, fruit salads and other desserts, either as they are or sieved.

PERSIMMON (SHARON FRUIT)

Buy Plump fruit, with shiny, smooth, bright, un-damaged orange skin.

Store In the fridge.

Prepare Only when ripe, as the unripe fruit is hard and astringent. Wash the fruit and halve then eat the sweet jelly-textured flesh with a teaspoon or cut into wedges.

PHYSALIS (CAPE GOOSEBERRY)

Buy Fruit with firm, plump and waxy orange berries.

Store In the fridge or at room temperature.

Prepare Use whole as an exotic topping for a cake or dessert, or the papery 'lantern' can be peeled back so that the berries can be dipped in fondant icing or melted chocolate. The tiny seeds inside are edible.

PINEAPPLE

Buy All year round, choosing fruit that is heavy for its size, which yields slightly when pressed and has a sweet aroma. The green crown should look firm and fresh. The skin does not have to be golden for the fruit to be ripe and it doesn't continue to ripen after picking. 'Super sweet' and 'golden' pineapples are extra sweet.

Store In the fridge but bring to room temperature before eating.

Prepare By cutting off the top and the outer scales of the skin. Use a small knife to remove the eyes, then slice into rings or cut into chunks. If the central core is not tough it can be eaten.

PRICKLY PEAR

Buy Wearing gloves (or use tongs in shops, if provided) as the prickly spines on this cactus fruit stick in the skin and irritate it, and they *are* present even though the skin looks smooth!

Store In the fridge in a paper bag to prevent injuries.

Prepare Using a knife and fork and wear rubber gloves for extra protection. Slice off the top and the base and then cut off the remaining skin. Discard all the skin carefully. No need to cook and the pips are edible.

QUINCE

Buy Firm-skinned fruit that are heavy for their size, if you can find a greengrocer that sells them. The downy covering on this green to yellow fruit that resembles a squat pear is quite natural. Quince sold by greengrocers will be imported; these fruit are larger and more aromatic than the small, hard quince that grows in the UK.

Store In a cool, dry place. Quince is very aromatic so they are best not put in the fridge where they might taint other food. Enjoy the aroma of them in a room.

Prepare Wipe off the down and wash the quince and then peel and put into acidulated water (with added lemon juice) to prevent browning. Most quince – and definitely all UK-grown fruit – needs to be cooked as it is too hard, dry and astringent to eat raw. However, some imports are juicy and soft enough to eat uncooked.

TAMARILLO (TREE TOMATO)

Buy Choose large, firm examples of this egg-shaped fruit with its shiny, deep purple colour.

Store In the fridge.

Prepare Slice off the stalk and the bottom and then peel. When ripe, slice the red (or yellow) flesh, which is bland yet sweet, with its tangy seeds, into salads (sweet or savoury) and use in dessert recipes. Alternatively, bake or poach.

a-z of exotic vegetables

ASPARAGUS

Buy Straight spears with a generous proportion of bud at the tip, which should be compact and pointed. The spear should be firm and look fresh. This applies to both green English asparagus and imported blanched white asparagus.

Store Without washing in the salad compartment for up to 2 days, but it is best used as soon after purchase as possible.

Prepare Scrape the scales off the stalk, working from the bud at the tip towards the base. Towards the end of the season, peel the base of the stems if they are not tender.

AUBERGINE

Buy Glossy, plump, firm vegetables with a smooth skin.

Store In the salad compartment for a week.

Prepare Cut immediately before use as it goes brown quickly. Recipes used to recommend salting to draw out bitter juices, but today's aubergines are not bitter.

CAVOLO NERO

This fashionable, Italian vegetable has slightly bitter-tasting stalks, with thick, dark, curly leaves and looks like curly Savoy cabbage. Treat as for green cabbage, see page 28.

CELERIAC

Buy Small to medium roots with as smooth a surface as possible and, if possible, with the stalk and leaves attached, which is a good indicator of freshness.

Store In a cool dark place or the fridge for up to a week.

Prepare By scrubbing very well if the surface is reasonably smooth; otherwise, peel and cut away the knobbled surface, which harbours grit and soil. Drop into acidulated water as the root does 'rust' quickly on contact with air.

CHARD (SWISS CHARD, RED OR RUBY CHARD OR LEAF BEET)

Buy Swiss chard with a wide, thick and long firm, crisp stalk because the stalk provides the flavour and interest. Red chard and leaf beet should have as little stalk as possible. The leaves of Swiss chard should be large, dark green, and glossy and tender. Red chard and leaf beet leaves are smaller and have red veins.

Store In the salad bin in the fridge.

Prepare Wash the leaves well, particularly red chard, in several changes of water, to remove soil and sandy grit. Cut off excess stalks on the leaf beet and red chard.

CHICORY (BELGIAN ENDIVE, WITLOOF)

Buy Tight heads that are white with a sheen and tipped with fresh-looking, yellow-green leaves.

Store In the fridge for 2–3 days.

Prepare Use whole heads for cooking, or break off individual leaves, or slice lengthways or horizontally for salads.

CHILLIES

Buy Glossy, crisp and unwrinkled chillies.

Store In the salad compartment of the fridge for up to 2 weeks. They will freeze, well packaged, for a year.

Prepare Wear rubber gloves when handling, to prevent the chillies from burning any cuts or sensitive areas such as lips or eyes. Remove stem seeds and, importantly, the ribs – this is where the 'heat' in the chilli resides. Removing it retains the sweet flavour of chillies without too much of the fiery heat.

CURLY AND BATAVIAN ENDIVE (ESCAROLE)

Buy Heavy heads with crisp and fresh-looking, vibrant green leaves.

Store In the salad compartment for 2 days.

Prepare Wash well, by inverting the whole head in a large container of cold water several times, shake dry. Alternatively break off the amount of leaves needed and wash and dry individually.

DAIKON (MOOLI)

Buy Straight, firm, smooth examples of this mild flavoured, long, icicle-like white radish. Avoid over-large daikon as they may be woody and lacking in flavour.

Store Wrapped in the fridge for a couple of weeks.

Prepare Peel and slice to eat raw as an accompaniment to sushi and other oriental dishes, or cook as a vegetable.

FENNEL

Buy Tight, heavy bulbs with fresh green feathery shoots still attached.

Store In the fridge for up to a week.

Prepare Cut off the base and the stalks at the head end and break off the leaves. Alternatively, slice through the entire bulb to get circles of fennel.

heat-seekers' guide to handling chillies

The capsaicin in chillies is responsible for the fiery heat of the chilli. It is a phytochemical (plant chemical) being investigated for its protective health qualities. Capsaicin survives cooking and freezing. The following is a guide in order from mildest to hottest of most common chillies.

Lambok Often labelled mild, the variety originated in Indonesia and has been used on a large scale by the Dutch breeders who export many chillies. Long and thin, it ripens from green to red.

New Mexican A larger chilli, only mildly hot.

Poblano Turns from dark green to red or brown, mildly hot.

Hungarian hot wax Starts yellow and matures to orangey-red. Medium hot.

Cherry Small and round as its name suggests. This chilli is hot stuff.

Jalapeño Shaped like a torpedo with a lot of flavour and heat.

Cayenne Can range from mild to hot – watch out for the yellow ones which are hottest; gets less hot as it turns to orange and red.

Serrano A small and crisp chilli, used in salsas and guacamole.

Thai red and green Small and thin but powerful – the heat goes on and on. Used in Thai curry pastes and mixes.

Thai hot Even smaller than the Thai red and even hotter.

Habanero Also called *Scotch bonnet*, can be green, orange, red or brown. Handle with care.

GLOBE ARTICHOKE

Buy Plump, evenly shaped globes with tight leaves.

Store In the fridge for a few days.

Prepare Cut off the stem and slice off the woody outer leaves. Cut off the top of the globe and then trim the pointed tips off the remaining outer leaves (this makes it neater and easier to eat). The hairy choke in the centre can be removed before or after cooking. To remove before, prise open the top of the head and scrape out the hairy choke with a sharp or serrated vegetable knife. It is probably easier to remove after cooking – plunge into cold water after boiling to halt cooking and make the globe cool enough to handle.

JERUSALEM ARTICHOKE

Buy Large, crisp tubers with as few gnarls and knobbles as possible.

Store Unwashed, in the fridge for up to a week.

Prepare Scrub well if not too knobbly, otherwise peel. Put into acidulated water to prevent them from discolouring.

Boletus A yellow-capped mushroom with a pleasant fruity aroma.

Cep A well flavoured mushroom with a round thin top and long stalk.

Chanterelle or girolle Often described as a furled trumpet, the chanterelle has a characteristic ribbed stalk. The cap is apricot-yellow.

Morel Unmistakable with its pitted cap that looks a bit like a sponge. It can be brown, yellow or cream and sits on top of a thick stalk.

Oyster Pale grey, white or creamy colour with a subtle flavour and chewy texture (recognizable in many Chinese soups and noodle dishes). Bright yellow and pink varieties are available but don't expect the colour to survive the cooking process. Along with shiitake (below) these are the most widely available of the 'wild' mushrooms because they are, in fact, cultivated.

Shiitake Most closely associated with Japanese cuisine, these mushrooms look most like field or cultivated mushrooms in shape, although they are firmer and thinner and the gills are white; don't buy shrivelled ones. The caps are creamy brown – the stalks are usually discarded as they tend to be tough.

KOHLRABI

Buy Firm, good-sized vegetables which may or may not have the leaves attached – the base of the kohlrabi is a stem, although it looks like a root.
Store In a cool, dry place or the fridge for up to a week.
Prepare Cut off the ends of the stalks and the base and scrub well or peel; drop into acidulated water if chopping.

MANGE TOUT

Buy Crisp, green pods, preferably untrimmed.
Store In the fridge for 2–3 days.
Prepare Top and tail with scissors.

MUSHROOMS, WILD

Buy, Store and Prepare Treat wild mushrooms as you would cultivated mushrooms, see page 29, except for the tips given below. In addition, it might be wise to rinse wild mushrooms, particularly varieties such as chanterelle, which has a ribbed stalk in which grit and dust can accumulate.

MUSTARD GREENS

Buy Heavy-for-size heads of this elongated cabbage, with its large, loose leaves, grooved stems and fringed leaves.
Store Remove bag if wrapped in plastic and store in a cool, dry place or in the salad bin of a fridge until leaves appear to wilt, although it is much better to use as soon as possible after purchasing.
Prepare By shredding. The flavour can be too peppery and astringent for some tastes to serve as a vegetable in its own right (although most supermarket versions are quite mild), so use in stir-fries and Chinese dishes.

OKRA (LADIES' FINGERS)

Buy Tender, crisp pods that have well defined ridges on their slightly fuzzy surface. Choose evenly coloured green pods with a fresh-looking sheen, preferably untrimmed and with the stalks intact.

Store Unwashed in the fridge (wet, the okra will go slimy and, while the glutinous texture helps thicken dishes when cooked, it will just make the okra spoil if washed beforehand).

Prepare Wash well and trim off the stalk but not the whole of the end – leave the pod intact. Use whole.

PAK CHOI (BOK CHOY)

Buy Nice compact stems with fresh green, leafy heads. Pak choi is good to eat at all stages, from baby heads to larger ones and even flowering, which is more likely to be found in specialist oriental grocers. The stems may be straight white or greenish and either similar in size to chard or smaller and spoon-shaped.

Store In a cool, dark place for a couple of days or refrigerate for a few days in the salad bin of the fridge.

Prepare Break off the stalks individually and wash the leaves and stalks well in several changes of water. Or immerse the entire head in water and jiggle around to remove soil and sandy grit.

PLANTAINS

Buy This type of banana, which is only eaten cooked, either green (unripe) or ripe. Different varieties ripen to different colours from dark brown (like a standard dessert banana) to a dark red.

Store In a plastic or paper bag. Unlike bananas, plantains can be stored in the fridge without spoiling.

Prepare By boiling in the skin or by peeling and slicing before boiling or frying. Sometimes they are par-boiled before frying. Green (unripe) plantain are almost impossible to peel; you have to cut right through the skin to the fruit, which is difficult without cutting into the fruit itself. It is easiest done in sections along the plantain. Soaking in cold, salted water for half an hour sometimes helps get the skin loose. After boiling, they can also be mashed.

POTATOES, JERSEY ROYAL

Buy In April and May at the beginning of the season that lasts to July, when they get bigger.

Store Don't – eat them as soon as you can.

Prepare Scrape as necessary; use at once.

POTATOES, PINK FIR APPLE, CHARLOTTE, LA RATTE, CORNICHON, BELLE DE FONTENAY

Buy, **Store and Prepare** As for Jersey Royals (above). Available year round from different countries; buy and eat as fresh as possible. *Pink Fir Apple* is a knobbly, pink-skinned small potato. The skin turns brown when cooked. It has firm flesh, good for salads, boiling and sautéing. *Charlotte* is slightly knobbly and creamy coloured with a dense flesh. *La Ratte, Cornichon* and *Belle de Fontenay* are smooth-skinned, small salad potatoes with a waxy yellow firm flesh.

PUMPKINS (AND OTHER SQUASHES)

Buy Hard, heavy-for-size vegetables with a smooth, not-too-thick skin. If buying ready-cut wedges, look for nice bright orange flesh (where appropriate to variety). Avoid any that look dry or shrivelled.

Store Whole squash in cool, dry, airy place, unwrapped, where it will keep for several weeks. Store cut pieces in cling film in the fridge for 5 days.

Prepare Peel varieties with thicker skins, or bake in the skin, and remove seeds before using as required.

ROCKET

Buy Bunches of dark green leaves on fresh stalks.

Store As for lettuce.

Prepare As for lettuce.

SAMPHIRE

Buy Fresh, bright green, juicy and plump sprigs of this salt marsh plant.

Store For 2–3 days in the fridge in a bag or box.

Prepare Rinse well in cold water and pick over, removing any woody stems before cooking. Do not eat samphire raw.

SPROUTED SEEDS (SUCH AS ALFALFA AND BEAN SPROUTS)

Buy Springy-looking sprouts with a fresh smell.

Store In the fridge for 3 days. Puncture any plastic bag or container so the sprouts can breathe.

Prepare By rinsing in cold water, drain well and pat dry on a clean tea towel or kitchen paper.

SWEET POTATOES

Buy Tubers that are evenly sized, firm and smooth and undamaged. Scrape away a little of the skin to check whether the flesh is white or red, if necessary.

Store In a cool dry place for up to a week.

Prepare Brush off any soil, then peel and cut into chunks or slices; alternatively, scrub well and bake them whole.

VINE LEAVES

Buy Fresh ones in summer (at other times of year, pre-packed are available). Choose leaves that are as fresh as possible.

Store Flat in the fridge, between sheets of damp kitchen paper in a plastic bag to keep fresh for a day.

Prepare Blanch, drain, dry and use leaves as directed in recipes.

YAM

Buy Firm and full yams that are light for their size – beneath the bark-like, tough, brown, inedible skin the flesh may be white, yellow or purple. Avoid any that look shrivelled.

Store In a cool, dry, airy place for up to 2 weeks.

Prepare Peel thickly, as the skin is tough, and slice or chop into acidulated water to stop discolouration. Alternatively, wrap in foil and bake whole.

fresh herbs

Combinations of herbs (and spices, see page 21) are at the heart of every food culture. The *bouquet garni* is the best known of French herb combinations, the basic mixture consisting of two or three sprigs of parsley, a sprig of thyme and one or two dried bay leaves. This differs from *herbes de Provence*, the basis of which is a combination of thyme, rosemary, bay, basil and savory. Contrast these classics with the combination of herbs most commonly used in Thai cooking: flatleaf parsley, coriander leaves, kaffir lime leaves and lemon grass. Herbs (and spices) offer a seemingly infinite combination of different rich, memorable and unique flavours.

planting a herb window box

Choose a warm windowsill that has sunlight for at least part of the day. A site sheltered from the wind is best. Do not sow until all danger of frost is past (although parsley, which is slow growing, can benefit from frost before germination).

Sow the seed sparsely so that the herbs are not overcrowded in the pot – you can always thin them out as they start to grow.

Plant individual varieties in separate pots so that they can be watered as required.

Direct sunlight on the soil will encourage germination, but avoid too much as this may dry out the leaves. A mixture of sun and shade is best.

Water sparingly and do not leave the pots standing in deep containers of water as this dilutes the flavour of the leaves and makes the plants limp and droopy.

Harvest by snipping with scissors and leave to continue growing for a week or so before cutting again.

growing herbs
(culinary herbs sold in pots)

Buy Herbs showing luxuriant, vibrant green growth. The plants should be turgid and strong looking and have new growth coming through from the centre of the plant. The idea of pot herbs is to cut from them and then leave them to grow for a few days before snipping again.

Store Following the instructions on the pot or, in the absence of instructions, stand the pot inside near a sunny window but out of cold draughts. Only put the pot outside if the weather is warm and there is no danger of frost or cold temperatures and winds. Water sparsely; herbs that are over-watered do not have the intensity of flavour of herbs given just enough water.

Prepare If all the plant is not to be used, snip or pick off the largest outer leaves first, leaving the younger inner shoots and leaves to continue growing from the centre of the plant.

Pots of growing herbs from the supermarket cannot usually be successfully transferred to the garden because they are hothouse plants that have not been hardened off in preparation for going outside in the British climate, with its variable temperature. Most herbs sold in pots are also annuals so they live only for one season. Common perennial herbs, which grow back each year from the same root, include sage, thyme and rosemary and are not sold in pots (for obvious reasons; you would plant them in the garden and not buy another pot on your next trip to the supermarket!).

packets and bunches of cut herbs

Buy Fresh-looking herbs that are an even colour.

Store Packets in the fridge, unopened, until needed. Small sprays or sprigs of herbs that are to be used for decoration or garnish can be immersed in cold water in the fridge for a couple of days, although this is not suitable for larger quantities. Bunches, e.g. coriander, if rooted, wrap the roots in wet kitchen paper inside a plastic bag to retain the moisture (and keep the fridge clean). If the bunch is of cut stalks, trim 2.5 cm (1 in) off the bottom of the stalks and stand in water in the fridge.

Pop a plastic bag over the top of the bunch to retain moisture and protect the leaves from frost.

Prepare Wash in cold water and dry well on kitchen paper before tearing or chopping.

a-z of fresh herbs

Basil Green or purple leaf with a powerful aromatic, slightly aniseedy flavour and tender leaves, which are often better torn than cut, and added only at the last minute, so the edges don't discolour and the flavour isn't lost. Use with courgettes, feta and mozzarella cheese, fish, Parma ham and peppers, and in pasta dishes, herb butters, salads (especially tomato salads) and salad dressings.

Chervil Small, ferny green leaves with a mild aniseed flavour; good with chicken, mushrooms, eggs (scrambled and omelettes), potatoes and in green salads.

Chives Look like grass with pointed tips, taste of mild onion and are good with soft cheese (French *fines herbes* for flavouring soft cheese includes chives, chervil, tarragon and parsley), eggs, salads, sandwiches, tomatoes.

Coriander (cilantro) Vibrant, dark green leaves on a strong stalk with a strong flavour; used widely in Indian, Thai and Indonesian cooking; also good with avocado, fish, lamb, potatoes, stir-fries and rice.

Dill Dark green, spiky leaves (not as pale and feathery as fennel) with an aniseed flavour, for use with cucumber, fish, ham, salads and salad dressings, smoked fish, potatoes and white sauces.

Fennel Coarser appearance than dill, and another aniseed-flavour herb, with much the same uses.

Kaffir lime leaves Vibrant green leaves that impart a citrus-like flavour to dishes in which they are cooked. Vital in south-east Asian dishes.

Lemon grass Is a thick blade of grass with a distinctive, citrus-lemon flavour and aroma. It has a green stem and creamy white to purple stem base. The base of the stem is crushed and used in recipes and the tougher stems used to infuse flavour into oriental soups and other dishes, being removed at the end.

Marjoram Leaves grow on a compact bush with a stem that can become woody, so use only the leaves. The flavour is similar to oregano but milder. It can be used in omelettes and is good with fish, pasta and pizza, poultry and salads.

Mint The flavour hardly needs describing and it is a classic in combination with potatoes and in mint sauce with lamb. Mint is also vital for popular Moroccan cooking and in Indian and Middle-Eastern dishes: it flavours cous cous and taboulleh. Fresh mint tea has a colour and flavour all of its own.

Oregano Marjoram's slightly stronger-flavoured cousin.

Parsley Needs little introduction, as it is the most widely used herb in Britain. Its bright green colour and curled leaves garnish savoury foods and adorn fishmongers' displays. It goes famously well with fish and in fish cakes, potatoes and other vegetables and shellfish, and in rice salads, white sauces and garlic butter.

Rosemary Fresh spikes of rosemary leaves, with their pungent flavour, are traditionally cooked with lamb and in many Greek dishes using minced lamb and feta cheese and olives. It also goes well with aubergine and in pasta sauces, pâtés and terrines.

Sage With its pointed, greyish-green, rough-textured leaves, has a very strong flavour that is used to balance rich foods, such as goose, liver and pork. Musty dried sage flavour in unattractive stuffings has put many people off but in small amounts sage works well with meat, cheese, onions, apples and in egg dishes.

Tarragon Leaves are long and thin and grow on a straggly tangle of long stems. It is the essential herb in *béarnaise* and tartar sauces and is particularly versatile (especially in French cooking) where it is used to good effect with chicken, game, veal and egg dishes. It makes, arguably, the best-flavoured herb vinegar and is also a good partner to tomatoes and fish.

Thyme The leaves are so tiny they hardly need cutting or chopping. For cooking, the green varieties are most often used, although as an ornamental plant there are also purple, pink, yellow and white varieties. Thyme goes well with chicken, mushrooms, onions, red meat, risotto and vegetables. Use lemon thyme with fish and poultry.

salad and delicatessen meals

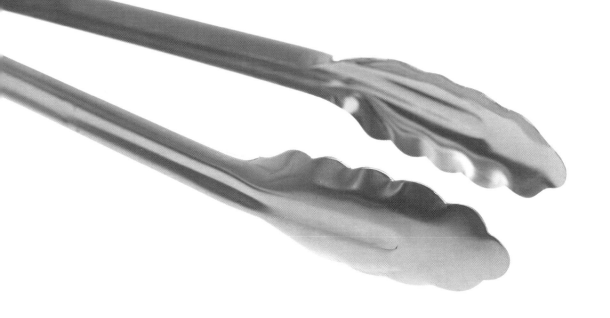

a vast range of salad leaves and other salad vegetables can be used to make tempting and appetizing salads to suit each season of the year. Think of adding olives, eggs, cooked and cured meat or fish, vegetarian dips and pulses or any number of delicatessen foods: salad meals can be as versatile and varied as your imagination.

Experiment with different lettuce bases, from traditional soft green round-head lettuce to crisp, Cos-type lettuce, loose-leaf lollo rosso or oak leaf to make up the bulk of the salad. Then toss in smaller quantities of more exotic leaves, such as rocket or lambs lettuce, purslane or chicory, and watercress. Dress lightly to enhance the flavours.

You can even try adding edible flowers, such as nasturtiums, violas and borage (larger branches of some supermarkets sell bags of edible flowers in summer). Herbs make good additions to salads, as an alternative to being chopped finely in dressings: basil, chervil, chives, coriander, dill, fennel, marjoram or oregano, mint and parsley are all tasty.

For toppings, try croûtons (see page 57) or try adding toasted pine nuts, walnuts, pecans, cashews or pistachio nuts, or toasted sunflower, pumpkin, melon or sesame seeds.

oils for salad dressings

Olive oil With its variety of flavours, olive is the most universally popular oil for salad dressings. It's worth buying extra-virgin olive oil for salad dressings and experimenting with different brands and countries of origin. A Greek extra-virgin olive oil tastes and looks quite different from one from Italy or Spain, just as French Sauvignon Blanc wines differ from New Zealand wines.

Sesame oil This is used mainly for Chinese cooking but blended, with one of the blander oils, makes a distinctive salad dressing – add a dash of soy sauce along with the lemon juice or vinegar for a truly oriental flavour.

Sunflower, groundnut, soy and rapeseed oil These are neutral in flavour.

olive oil

Oil is pressed from olives mechanically (unlike most other oils, which are extracted using chemical solvents and heat processes). The main varieties of olive oil that we see in the shops in the UK are extra-virgin olive oil, virgin olive oil and olive oil. They all taste good and have appetizing aromas and flavours. The exact colours and flavours will differ depending on the country and/or region of origin, with most variety in the extra-virgin olive oil category. Technically, they differ as follows:

Extra-virgin olive oil Perfect flavour, aroma and colour (light yellow to green) and only 1% acidity.
Fine virgin olive oil Perfect flavour, aroma and colour (light yellow to green) and 1.5% acidity.
Olive oil Good flavour, aroma, colour (light yellow).

Labelling Some extra-virgin olive oil labels also state 'first pressing' or 'first cold pressing'; the first pressing producing the best oil. Sometimes the label says 'cold pressing' which shows that the oil was extracted using minimum pressure, to keep the temperature low (higher temperatures impair the quality).

Walnut and hazelnut oils These have fabulous, distinctive flavours of toasted nuts and make delicious dressings – you can blend with a little sunflower oil, to make them go further and temper the flavour.

Both extra-virgin olive oil and nut oils make superb home-made mayonnaise.

vinegars for salad dressings

Wine and cider vinegar make the most successful vinaigrette (oil and vinegar dressing). The different colour and flavour of white and red wine, and cider vinegars will influence the flavour of the salad dressing. More strongly flavoured, dark aromatic vinegars include Italian balsamic vinegar and Spanish sherry vinegar. These mature vinegars make pungent dressings full of character and flavour – use sparingly and mix with a blander white wine or cider vinegar, if necessary.

Steep herbs, shallots, garlic, spices or olives – or raspberries for raspberry vinegar – in vinegar to make flavoured vinegars. They can also be used to add unusual flavours to salad dressings; mix them with light bland oils and vinegars so any subtle flavours are not overwhelmed.

Malt vinegar has a strong, sharp flavour and is more acidic than wine and cider vinegars; it is not suitable for salad dressings. Both malt and distilled malt vinegar are made from malted grains. Distilled is colourless whereas malt vinegar may be light or dark brown, the colour in the darker version coming from added caramel.

Rice vinegar is used mainly in Japanese cooking and is milder than malt vinegar. It may be used in dressings, but is very subtle in flavour.

mustards for salad dressings

Mustard is a great addition to vinaigrette, adding flavour and giving the dressing more body. Hot up the dressing by adding some fiery traditional English mustard, either powdered or ready-made; or give it a more aromatic quality with a milder, creamy-smooth Dijon mustard or wholegrain mustard.

English mustard is the hottest, made mainly from yellow or white mustard seed. Ready-made English mustards may also contain wheat flour, sugar, salt, spices, citric acid and colourings. British versions of French or wholegrain mustards may also contain these, plus vinegar and modified starch, or they may follow more traditional French recipes without the food additives – check the ingredients' list on the label. French mustards are made from brown and black mustard seeds. Dijon is blended with vinegar or wine, salt and spices. The husks of the seeds are removed to make smooth yellow mustard that varies from mild to hot. Meaux mustard (*moutarde – la méthode ancienne*) is made from partially crushed mustard seed blended with vinegar and spices. The speckled appearance comes from the husks of the seed which give it a little crunch; it is medium to hot.

Other mustards, such as German, Swedish and American, tend to be sweeter than English mustard.

balsamic vinegar

Balsamic vinegar originates from the Modena region of Italy. Reduced grape must (the pulpy mixture from pressed grapes) is added to the vinegar which can either be produced in a complicated, slow and traditional way in wooden barrels followed by ageing in oak casks for five to 20 years, or factory-produced, following the old methods but using stainless steel vats and speeding the ageing process.

Good-quality balsamic vinegar has a thicker consistency than most vinegar. It is dark brown to black in colour and should be fruity and sweet with a mellow mature flavour.

American is usually milder, but German and Swedish may be hot or mild. Speciality mustards are flavoured with herbs (basil, garlic, mint, tarragon) and spices (paprika, red and green peppercorns, curry spices) and lemon or horseradish.

delicatessen items

Artichoke hearts Cooked and either canned in brine or bottled in oil for use as an *antipasto*, and in vegetarian pies, salads and pizza toppings.

Black or green olive paste Made from brined olives that are stoned and crushed to a paste with olive oil, then flavoured with salt and possibly herbs and spices. Use as a topping for toast and canapés, spread in the base of quiches, mix with breadcrumbs for a 'crust' for grilled fish and vegetables or add to pasta sauces.

Black or green olives Green olives are harvested before they ripen (turn black) and treated to remove the bitter taste; then they are either pickled in brine or stored in oil. Black olives are left to ripen before harvesting and then pickled in brine; afterwards they may be stored in oil. Olives may also be sun-dried and stoned, or simply cracked, leaving the stone in place, and they can be flavoured with herbs and spices. Green olives may be stoned and stuffed with sweet peppers, anchovies or almonds. Use as an accompaniment to apéritifs, in pizza toppings, sauces and cooked dishes.

Capers The unopened buds of a Mediterranean bush, capers are usually bottled in vinegar or brine with or without flavourings such as herbs and spices. Use in pizza toppings, pasta sauces, with white fish (e.g. skate) or to garnish canapés.

Hummus Greek, Turkish and Middle-Eastern cuisines all use hummus, made from cooked chick-peas crushed with garlic, olive oil and tahini (sesame seed paste). Use as an hors d'oeuvre or part of a *mezze* (selection of hors d'oeuvre), as a dip for crudités (raw vegetables) or a filling for savoury pastry.

Pesto Originates from Genoa on the Ligurian coast of Italy. Basil is chopped and mixed with garlic, pine nuts, olive oil, salt and Parmesan and Sardo cheeses. Use to dress pasta, add to sauces, and stir into minestrone soup, or spread on toast.

Tapenade Crushed black olives mixed with olive oil, capers, salt and crushed anchovies. Use in canapés, in sandwiches such as the French *pan bagna*, on toast, or in sauces.

Taramasalata Made from fish roe (in Greece mullet roe, in the UK cod's roe – either smoked or unsmoked) mixed with breadcrumbs, oil, lemon juice, seasoning, and a variety of other permutations including garlic, vinegar, pepper, herbs and spices. Use as for hummus.

cooked and cured meats

Bacon Cured pork that is either smoked or unsmoked (green) and sliced into rashers that can have a rind or be rindless. Rashers have a layer of smooth, white fat of varying thickness beneath the rind (skin). Cures such as Wiltshire, Canadian (with maple syrup) or dry cure produce variations of flavour and colour. Unsmoked bacon is mildest. Use as traditional accompaniment to eggs for breakfast, in sandwiches (classic BLT), in salads, to protect lean meat (and fish) during cooking, in quiche fillings, in stuffing, pâtés and as a sauce ingredient.

Biltong This originated in South Africa. It is a dried strip of beef that looks like leather. Use as a snack when travelling across the Veldt or as survival food for mountaineering!

Corned beef Cured brisket which has alternating layers of fat and lean when rolled and tied; the deep red colour is the result of preservatives. Cooked corned beef is sold in cans or slices on the delicatessen counter. 'Corned' means cured with salt; grains of salt used to rub the meat in traditional curing methods looked like grains of corn. Use in salads, sandwiches or hot in corned beef hash (fried with potatoes).

Gammon Is usually cured leg of pork that is eaten cooked; however it can be a type of ham when the meat is sliced and eaten cold after being cooked. Gammon 'ham' is saltier than roast and cooked hams that are not brined, particularly unsmoked hams. Gammon steaks are raw for home cooking.

Ham Prepared from pork leg, ham may be cooked (e.g. honey roast, York) or raw (Parma, Serrano) and (like bacon) smoked or unsmoked. First the joint is salted in brine or saltpetre. Smoking is the next process (if applicable); if the ham is to be eaten raw the ham will be hot-smoked to 'cook' it, if it is to be cooked it will be cold-smoked. Cooked ham is then sliced off the bone. However, the majority of ham is made from smaller pieces of meat steeped in brine with other food additives such as polyphosphates, which retain water.

The additives help moisten the meat and allow the ham to hold its shape when the pieces are pressed, or tumbled and massaged together to make boneless 'joints' or blocks of ham. After cooking, this is sliced and packed or sold from delicatessen counters.

Raw hams are 'dry' hams – they are not steeped in brine, whether smoked or not, but are rubbed or injected with salt and then dried in a process which cures and preserves the meat. Best known examples are Parma ham (*prosciutto di Parma*) from Italy, Serrano ham from Spain, Bayonne ham from France and Westphalian and Black Forest hams from Germany. Serve wafer-thin slices with apéritifs (good with sherry) or as a first course with melon, figs and other fruit, or salad.

Pancetta Cured belly pork, originating in Italy, is sliced very thinly as an Italian 'bacon' or cut into strips or diced for use in Italian dishes.

Pastrami Cured and spiced lean silverside beef, dry cooked and rubbed with chilli and peppercorns before being sliced. Use pastrami as a sandwich filling or for a

Scandinavian style topping on rye bread along with gherkins and coleslaw.

Pâté May contain combinations of meat, poultry and game, with aromatic flavourings. Smoked fish and vegetable pâtés (or terrines) are also available. More usually made from meat such as pork and veal, flavoured with wine, garlic and herbs. Maybe smooth or more coarsely cut and packed into a bacon-lined terrine. After cooking it is pressed to remove excess liquid and shape it ready for slicing when cold. Serve with bread and salad as a starter or lunch, spread on toast or crackers, or use to line the pastry that encloses the joint in Beef Wellington.

Salami Strictly speaking a sausage, made from minced meat, often pork, and fat encased in a skin, it is used more like a cold meat. Different countries have their own speciality salamis (and related cooked meats) for use in regional dishes, with apéritifs, as snacks, in salads and sandwiches, as pizza toppings and *antipasti*, or in cooked dishes. Some examples include: *bierwurst*, a German cooked, lightly smoked salami made from pork and beef; *cacciatore*, an Italian pork and beef mixture with spices, garlic and varying degrees of heat; *cervelat,* a mixture of pork and beef, seasoned and smoked, also from Germany. *Chorizo* is a spicy Spanish salami made from pork and/or beef, red pepper, cayenne, chilli and paprika; it may be smoked or unsmoked and is used in Spanish stews and soups or served with sherry as an apéritif. *Csabai* is a mild Hungarian small salami that looks a bit like pepperoni and is seasoned with cracked peppercorns and paprika. *Danish salami* is bright red with chunky pieces of fat and is seasoned with black pepper. *German salami* is usually finely ground, smooth and made with beef and pork and smoked. *Kabanos* is a long, thin, sausage based on pork, seasoned and smoked for use as a snack or *antipasto*. *Milano salami* is a regional Italian speciality, flavoured with garlic and white wine and a mixture of pork and beef. *Pepperoni* is long and thin and made from pork and beef; it is hot and spicy and its small size makes it suitable as a pizza topping. French *saucisson* is a smoked salami (and, confusingly, also a raw sausage) that comes in different regional recipes and sizes flavoured with herbs and pepper.

Speck An oblong strip of cured and smoked pork originating in Austria. Use as an accompaniment to apéritifs or in recipes, like bacon, diced or thinly sliced.

Tongue Ox or beef tongue which has been corned (i.e. salted or pickled) like corned beef and pressed and sold by the slice for use as a cold meat cut.

preserved and smoked fish

Anchovies May be canned or bottled in olive oil or brine with added herbs or olives. Use in canapés, sauces such as pesto, pastes, salads such as Niçoise, pizza toppings.

Rollmop herrings Pickled raw herring flavoured with peppercorns and onions, in sweetened spiced vinegar. Used a lot in Scandinavia and served with crispbread and salad or boiled potatoes.

Salt cod Popular in Portuguese recipes and in Spanish and Greek dishes – usually sold in large fillets that need to be soaked for 24–36 hours in several changes of water, to remove excess salt, before cooking. Use in fish pies and a variety of Portuguese, Mediterranean and Caribbean dishes.

For other preserved fish, see *Fish and Shellfish*.

salad niçoise with seared tuna

serves 4 | preparation time: 20 minutes | cooking time: 8–10 minutes

A deliciously informal dish that can be made as generous as you wish, depending on the amount of vegetables. The tuna is cooked medium rare so that it remains moist, but cook for a minute or two longer if you prefer, or use canned tuna.

2 tuna steaks, about 150 g (5 oz) each
olive oil, for brushing
250 g (8 oz) French beans, trimmed
a bunch of spring onions, trimmed and sliced
450 g (1 lb) plum tomatoes, thickly sliced
½ cucumber, peeled and thickly sliced
4 hard-boiled eggs, shelled and quartered
50 g (2 oz) black olives
50 g (2 oz) anchovies

FOR THE DRESSING:
4 tablespoons olive oil
1 garlic clove, crushed
2 tablespoons red or white wine vinegar
2–3 teaspoons balsamic vinegar
a bunch of fresh basil, shredded
2 tablespoons chopped fresh parsley

Brush both sides of the tuna steak with oil and fry in a very hot frying pan or griddle pan for about 3 minutes on each side. Leave to cool. Cook the beans in boiling water for 3–4 minutes until just tender. Drain and run cold water over the beans until they are cold. Drain well.

Arrange the beans and all other ingredients together on a large platter, or mix together in a large bowl then divide between serving plates. Break the tuna into chunks and arrange on top.

Whisk the remaining olive oil, garlic, red or white wine vinegar and balsamic vinegar together and drizzle over before serving. Sprinkle with basil and parsley.

wine suggestion This favourite Provençal dish needs a well-chilled, high-acidity white wine to do justice to the strong flavours in it. The classic match would be a dry white from Provence (Bellet or Palette), but they are hard to find. Try a dry Chenin or Sauvignon from the Loire or Alsace Riesling instead.

salad niçoise with seared tuna

classic caesar salad

A classic salad that makes a great starter or light supper. Shave off curls of Parmesan using a potato peeler or coarsely grate the cheese.

5 anchovy fillets, finely chopped
1 garlic clove, finely chopped
3 tablespoons olive oil
8 slices of bread
1 Cos lettuce, torn into bite-sized pieces and chilled
50 g (2 oz) Parmesan cheese, shaved or coarsely grated

FOR THE DRESSING:
2 teaspoons Dijon mustard
1 teaspoon sugar
1 tablespoon white wine vinegar
5 tablespoons olive oil
2 tablespoons crème fraîche
a dash of Worcestershire sauce
salt and freshly ground black pepper

In a bowl, mix the anchovies, garlic and oil to a paste. Spread this over each slice of bread and bake for 15–20 minutes until crisp. Cut the toasts into large cubes.

Make the dressing: whisk together the mustard, sugar and vinegar, then gradually whisk in the oil. Whisk in the crème fraîche, season and add a dash of Worcestershire sauce.

Mix together the lettuce and toasts. Drizzle with dressing and sprinkle liberally with shavings of Parmesan cheese.

wine suggestions The pungent, garlicky Caesar dressing and fresh Parmesan here suggest an appropriately bold dry white, but one with enough of a cutting edge of acidity to balance the overall richness. A lightly oaked Chardonnay is fine, but choose a cool-climate wine for the acid grip: Rully or Pouilly-Fuissé from Burgundy or a New Zealand wine.

potato salad

preparation time: 10 minutes | cooking time: 10 minute | serves 4

*No barbecue or summer buffet table is complete without a good
potato salad, but there's more to potato salad than just boiled potatoes
and mayonnaise. You can make it much more interesting with just a few
simple twists.*

Boil about 450 g (1 lb) evenly sized new potatoes (you can scrape or peel
them if you want) in salted water for about 20 minutes, or until they are
just cooked when pierced with a knife. Drain them and add the dressing
while still hot, so that they absorb the flavours.

potato salad dressings

Bacon and tarragon dressing Mix 3 tablespoons
of olive oil, 2 tablespoons of tarragon vinegar,
4 finely chopped shallots and 6 rashers of crispy
fried bacon, chopped. Stir in 3 tablespoons of
mayonnaise.

Mint and lemon juice dressing Mix 2 tablespoons of lemon juice, 5 tablespoons of olive oil
and a small handful of chopped fresh mint. Season
with salt, pepper and a good pinch of sugar to taste.

Wholegrain mustard dressing Whisk 2 teaspoons of wholegrain mustard, 3 tablespoons of
lemon juice, 6 tablespoons of olive oil and
3 tablespoons of mayonnaise together.

Pesto dressing Simply spoon in enough green or
red (sun-dried tomato) pesto to coat, add
mayonnaise if you like, and scatter the potato salad
with toasted pine nuts.

warm cous cous, vegetable and feta salad

serves 6–8 | preparation time: 30 minutes | cooking time: 30 minutes

Mouthfuls of crumbly cheese, warm roasted vegetables and cous cous make this a substantial salad for any time of the year.

1 red pepper, seeded and cut into quarters
2 courgettes, thickly sliced
2 garlic cloves
2 tablespoons olive oil
350 g (12 oz) cous cous
250 g (9 oz) cherry tomatoes, halved
175g (6 oz) feta cheese, crumbled
a small bunch of fresh basil leaves, shredded
1 lemon, cut into wedges

Pre-heat the oven to 220°C/425°F/Gas 7; fan oven 200°C from cold. Place the peppers, courgettes and garlic cloves in a bowl with a little oil and stir to coat everything lightly. Tip into a roasting tin and roast for 30 minutes, until tender.

Meanwhile, pour 600 ml (1 pint) of boiling water over the cous cous and leave to soak until all the water has been absorbed.

Remove the vegetables from the oven and discard the garlic cloves. Place the peppers in a plastic bag, knot the end and leave for 10 minutes; then peel off the skin and cut the flesh into strips.

Place the cous cous in a large serving bowl. Stir well to break up any lumps and add the warm vegetables, cherry tomatoes, feta and basil. Toss together. Whisk all the dressing ingredients together and pour over.

FOR THE DRESSING:
1 tablespoon white wine vinegar
1 tablespoon balsamic vinegar
4 tablespoons olive oil
juice of 1 lemon
salt and freshly ground black pepper

wine suggestion This robust salad recipe will obligingly take either white or red. A subtly oaky, well-built white such as Rioja Blanco Crianza would cope with the earthy textures, while a light to midweight red like Côtes du Roussillon-Villages will stand up to the cheese.

warm cous cous, vegetable and feta salad

soups and starters

first impressions are all-important and the first course of a meal can set the tone for the whole evening. The starter should be inspirational, attractive and act like an apéritif, stimulating the appetite and the senses. The dish should be tasty but not too filling and it should also contrast with what is to follow. Avoid the monotony of a meat-based starter followed by a meat main course, or a creamy soup and a cream sauce with the main course or *crème brûlée* for pudding!

Soups make excellent starters provided they are not too hearty (save these for lunches and suppers as meals in their own right). The basis of all types of soup is high-quality stock; the French call stock *fond*, which literally means 'foundation'. Do not add any of the following to home-made stocks: offal makes it bitter; garlic tends to develop off-flavours; potato makes the stock cloudy; cabbage and its relatives impart a nasty smell and bitter taste.

buying stock

Cartons of fresh stock are now readily available in chiller cabinets and are of excellent quality, but slightly weaker than home-made. They freeze well. Stock cubes are less successful than fresh stock but there is an extensive range including fish, chicken, beef, lamb, bacon, vegetarian, and even speciality ones for ethnic cooking. Many contain monosodium glutamate, which adds to the salty flavour; better-quality ones do not. Try a few brands to discover which best suits your taste. No-added-salt and low-salt versions are available.

storing stock

Meat stock can be stored for 5 days. Chicken stock can be stored for 4 days but should be re-boiled and cooled daily as a food-safety measure. Fish stock should be used within 2 days but is best used on the day it is made. Stock freezes well and may be kept for up to 3 months. Concentrated stock 'ice-cubes' are useful flavour boosters. Reduce stock by two-thirds, pour into an ice-cube tray and freeze.

freezing soup

Soup can be frozen in freezer bags or containers with lids – leave space to allow for expansion. Soup is best thawed overnight at room temperature but using the microwave oven can speed up the process. Do not add cream, yoghurt or eggs before freezing, because they will curdle once thawed. Do not add all the stock or other liquid before freezing (label the container with how much needs to be added once thawed); this saves freezer space and allows for better adjustment of flavour and texture when re-heating after cooking.

croûtons for soup

Cut slightly dry bread into cubes, or into fancy shapes, and fry lightly in butter or olive oil, adding crushed garlic for extra flavour. Once cooked, toss in very finely diced fresh herbs.

accompaniments for soups and starters

Choose from mini bread rolls, poppadums, sliced flavoured bread (e.g. sun-dried tomato, olive, walnut, herb), hot toast, herb or garlic butter.

chicken or turkey stock

makes 2 litres (3½ pints) | preparation time: 10 minutes | cooking time: 1½ hours

This deliciously flavoured stock forms a good base for so many soups, sauces and risottos and is easy to make using the remaining carcass from a roast chicken or, better still, a raw carcass.

1 chicken or turkey carcass and any giblets
1 large onion, cut into wedges
2 cloves
2 carrots, chopped
1 leek, sliced
1 celery stick, sliced
1 teaspoon black peppercorns
1 bay leaf
1 fresh thyme sprig
4 fresh parsley stems

Break up the carcass if it is too large to fit in the pan. Cover with about 2 litres (3½ pints) of cold water and add all the remaining ingredients. Bring up to the boil and then lower the heat and simmer gently, uncovered, for 1–1½ hours. Skim the surface occasionally with a slotted spoon to remove any scum. Strain through a fine sieve into a clean bowl and chill.

Cooking with stock: Reduce the stock by boiling hard until reduced by half, to give a more intense flavour, if you like.

Storing stock: Cool stock before chilling. It will keep in the fridge for up to 3 days or can be frozen for up to 3 months.

fish stock

makes 1.2 litres (2 pints) | preparation time: 5 minutes | cooking time: 20 minutes

This is so quick and simple to cook and makes such a difference to fish soups and stews. Ask your fishmonger or at the supermarket fish counter for some fish bones and they will often give them to you willingly. Use white fish rather than oily fish or the end result will be oily.

750 g (1½ lb) white fish bones, such as plaice or haddock
1 small onion, cut into wedges
1 leek, sliced
1 carrot, sliced
1 bay leaf
4 fresh parsley sprigs
1 fresh dill sprig
1 slice of lemon
4 peppercorns
100 ml (3½ fl oz) dry white wine

Break up the bones a little and place in a large pan with 1.2 litres (2 pints) of cold water and the remaining ingredients. Bring to the boil, then lower the heat and simmer for 20 minutes. Skim off the surface and strain through a fine sieve.

Cooking with stock: Reduce the stock by boiling hard until reduced by half, to give a more intense flavour, if you like.

Storing stock: Cool stock before chilling. It will keep in the fridge for up to 3 days or can be frozen for up to 3 months.

curried parsnip soup

preparation time: 10 minutes | cooking time: 15–20 minutes | serves 6

Delicately spiced and deliciously warming, this simple tasty soup is always a winner.

Cook the onion, garlic and parsnips gently in the butter, cover and cook for 10 minutes. Stir in the flour and curry paste or powder. Cook for 2 minutes, stirring. Pour in the stock gradually, and simmer for 10–15 minutes. When the parsnip is really tender, purée in a liquidizer and then return to the pan and dilute to taste with water. Adjust the seasoning. Re-heat, add the cream if you like and serve with croûtons or crusty bread.

wine suggestion You may feel that a blended soup doesn't need a wine to accompany it, in the sense that it might make for too liquid a combination, but the flavours themselves don't present any problems. A good compromise is a small measure of one of the drier fortified wines, such as a dry *amontillado* sherry or sercial madeira.

1 onion, chopped

1 large garlic clove, split

2 large parsnips, peeled and chopped

2 heaped tablespoons butter

1 tablespoon plain flour

1 tablespoon medium curry paste or 1–2 teaspoons medium curry powder

1.2 litres (2 pints) chicken stock

150 ml (5 fl oz) cream (optional)

red pepper, tomato and garlic soup

preparation time: 20 minutes | cooking time: 1 hour 10 minutes | serves 6

A rich and robust soup that makes a great starter at any time of the year, or a satisfying lunch or supper.

Pre-heat the oven to 200°C/400°F/Gas 6; fan oven 180°C from cold. Place the peppers, onions, tomatoes and garlic in a large, shallow roasting tin. Pour over 2 tablespoons of the oil and season. Roast for 40 minutes, until tender and tinged brown at the edges.

Remove from the oven and cool slightly. Peel the skin off the peppers and tomatoes, then roughly chop with the onions; squeeze the garlic flesh out of the skins.

Heat the remaining tablespoon of oil in a large pan, add the roasted vegetables, garlic and herbs. Add the stock, cover and simmer for 25 minutes.

Remove the thyme, bay leaf and oregano from the pan. Allow the soup to cool slightly, then sieve or purée until it is smooth. Return to the pan, adjust the seasoning and re-heat gently.

Pour the soup into bowls and add a few basil shreds to each one.

4 red peppers, halved and seeded

2 onions, cut into quarters

2 tomatoes (preferably plum), halved lengthways

8 unpeeled garlic cloves

3 tablespoons olive oil

2 fresh thyme sprigs

1 bay leaf

1 fresh oregano sprig

8 fresh basil leaves, torn

1.2 litres (2 pints) chicken or vegetable stock

salt and black pepper

shredded fresh basil, to garnish

thai prawn and noodle soup

serves 4 | preparation time: 15 minutes | cooking time: 15 minutes

This fragrant soup, known as tom yum, can be made with pieces of shredded chicken instead of prawns if you prefer. The lemon grass, kaffir lime leaves, chilli and galangal all give the soup its distinctive, aromatic flavours.

350 g (12 oz) prawns, preferably raw with shells on
½ to 1 red chilli, depending on heat
2 lemon grass stalks, bruised with a rolling pin
3 kaffir lime leaves
2.5 cm (1 in) piece of galangal or fresh root ginger, peeled and chopped
2 garlic cloves, peeled and chopped
2–3 tablespoons fish sauce
100 g (4 oz) medium egg noodles
juice of ½ lime

FOR THE GARNISH:
a few sprigs of fresh coriander
2 tablespoons coriander, chopped
1 lemon, cut into wedges

Shell the prawns, discarding the heads and reserving a few with tails on to garnish. Seed and coarsely chop the chilli.

Heat 1.5 litres (2½ pints) of water with the prawn shells, chopped chilli, lemon grass, lime leaves, galangal or ginger, garlic and fish sauce. Bring to the boil, reduce the heat and simmer for 10 minutes. Strain through a sieve into another pan. Reserve a few pieces of chilli, but discard the remaining contents of the sieve. Bring the stock back to the boil, add the shelled prawns, reserved prawns and noodles and cook for 3–4 minutes until the prawns are pink. Take care not to overcook or they will toughen.

Add the lime juice and season to taste with extra fish sauce, if necessary. Pour into four bowls and garnish with the coriander and reserved chilli. Serve with lime wedges and sprigs of coriander.

wine suggestion The intensity of Thai seasonings calls for a correspondingly assertive wine. You could try something pungently aromatic like a French Sauvignon Blanc, but better still would be a well-chilled pale *fino* sherry, the flavour of which is quite close to oriental rice wine.

thai prawn and noodle soup

prosciutto and shallot salad

serves 4 | preparation time: 5 minutes | cooking time: 12 minutes

Very stylish, very simple and very delicious. The perfect starter!

1 red pepper
3 shallots, peeled
4 tablespoons olive oil
1 teaspoon caster sugar
1 tablespoon balsamic vinegar
salt and freshly ground
black pepper
25 g (1 oz) herb salad
200 g (8 oz) sliced prosciutto

Cut the pepper into quarters. Remove the core and seeds. Grill until the skin has blistered and is blackened. Place in a polythene bag, knot and allow to cool for 10 minutes. Peel off the skin and then cut the pepper into strips.

Gently fry the shallots in 2 tablespoons of the oil for 10 minutes until softened and lightly coloured. Stir in the sugar, turn up the heat and cook for 1–2 minutes until caramelized. Remove from the heat and stir in the remaining oil and the vinegar. Season well.

Put the salad leaves and pepper strips in a bowl, pour over the shallots and dressing and toss together. Arrange on plates, with slices of prosciutto.

wine suggestion A light southern European white with a bit of acidic bite will stand up to the red pepper and rocket in this recipe. A Sicilian or Sardinian white would be an appetizing match, and so would a tot of properly chilled bone-dry *manzanilla* sherry.

asparagus and quail's egg salad with lemon and tarragon dressing

serves 4–6 | preparation time: 10 minutes | cooking time: 5 minutes

450 g (1 lb) asparagus spears
6 quail's eggs
225 g (8 oz) cherry tomatoes
1 bag rocket leaves for the
lemon and tarragon dressing
2 tablespoons tarragon vinegar
1 teaspoon finely grated
lemon rind
¼ teaspoon Dijon mustard
1 tablespoon fresh tarragon
5 tablespoons olive oil
a pinch of sugar
salt and freshly ground
black pepper

Trim off any woody stalks from the asparagus. Place in a shallow frying pan with a little water. Cover lightly with foil or a lid, bring to the boil, then simmer for about 3–4 minutes or until just tender. Drain, then run under the cold tap until cold. Drain well. Boil the quail's eggs for 1½ minutes. Plunge into cold water and allow to cool, then shell.

Arrange the rocket on individual plates with the asparagus, quail's eggs and tomatoes.

Whisk all the dressing ingredients together then drizzle over the salad just before serving.

goats' cheese salad with cranberry dressing

preparation time: 15 minutes | cooking time: 5 minutes | serves 6

This makes a very quick and simple starter or even a light supper. Choose goats' cheese covered in an edible soft rind so that it keeps its shape as it melts. If you don't have cranberry sauce, simply dress the salad with a good vinaigrette.

Cut the goats' cheese into six slices. Lay the French bread on a grill rack and brush both sides with olive oil. Lightly grill one side of the bread until golden. Turn over and lay the cheese on the top. Set aside until ready to serve.

Arrange the apple or pear slices, avocado and lettuce leaves on individual plates.

Whisk all the dressing ingredients together and drizzle over the salad. Just before serving, return the cheese and bread to the grill and grill for 3–5 minutes until the cheese just starts to melt. Serve immediately on top of the salad.

wine suggestion Crisp, sappy Sauvignon Blanc makes an excellent match with goats' cheese, its bracing acidity cutting the richness of texture. Watch out, though: that dressing has citrus juice and wine vinegar in it. A simple Sauvignon from Touraine in the Loire or Hungary will do.

350 g (12 oz) firm goats' cheese with a soft rind
6 slices of French bread
6 tablespoons olive oil
1 apple or pear, sliced
1 large ripe avocado, peeled, stoned and sliced
a bag of mixed lettuce leaves

FOR THE DRESSING:
grated zest and juice of 1 lime
4 tablespoons olive oil
1 teaspoon runny honey
4 tablespoons cranberry sauce
1 tablespoon white wine vinegar
salt and black pepper

smoked salmon and avocado pots

serves 6 | preparation time: 20 minutes

These light, refreshing salmon pots take minutes to make but can be made a day ahead. Serve with Melba toast or brown bread and butter.

350 g (12 oz) smoked salmon
4 tablespoons mayonnaise
100 g (4 oz) full-fat cream cheese
grated zest of ½ lemon
a pinch of cayenne pepper
a small bunch of fresh dill
1 shallot, chopped
1 small avocado, peeled, stoned
and finely chopped
salad leaves and sprigs of dill,
to serve

Line six ramekins or individual moulds with cling film. Cut six strips from the smoked salmon about 2.5 × 25 cm (1 × 10 in). Line the sides of each ramekin with a smoked salmon strip.

Chop the remaining smoked salmon, place in a food processor with the mayonnaise, cream cheese, lemon zest, cayenne, dill and shallot, and whizz until well blended. Stir in the chopped avocado.

Divide between the ramekins or moulds and smooth down lightly. Chill for 4 hours or, preferably, overnight.

To serve, invert on to serving plates, peel off the cling film and serve with salad leaves.

wine suggestion Don't imagine smoked salmon to be a delicate food when it comes to wine. Its oiliness, saltiness and the pungent flavour of the smoke all demand that you think big. Mature Alsace Gewürztraminer or Pinot Gris are brilliant with it, as is the smokiness of richly oaky Chardonnay, from Australia, California or Chile.

smoked salmon and avocado pots

milk, cheese and eggs

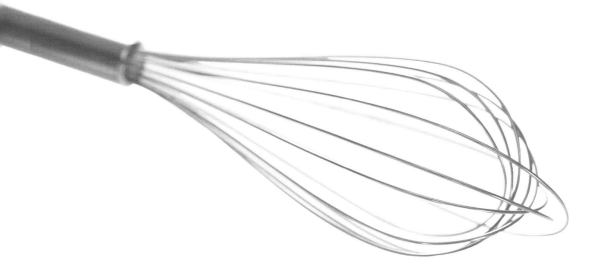

milk, cheese and eggs are frequently used in British cooking and each is a valuable food in its own right. These dairy foods are also important ingredients in breads, cakes, custards, desserts, drinks, flans, ice-cream, mayonnaise, meringues, mousses, soufflés, soups, sweet and savoury sauces, pancakes, puddings, quiches and yoghurt. Milk is the starting point for foods from the dairy. Cream is the fat part of milk and butter is made when milk or cream is churned. Cheese is made from the solids that are produced by curdling milk. Yoghurt is made when friendly bacteria ferment the milk, under controlled conditions, into yoghurt.

milk

All milk, except green-top or raw milk, is pasteurized, to kill bacteria and enzymes, preventing spoilage and eliminating organisms such as those that carry tuberculosis. Most is then homogenized, a process which breaks down the fat molecules to disperse the fat evenly, so that it cannot rise to the top of the milk.

Coconut milk is not the liquid inside the coconut but a liquid produced by pouring boiling water over grated coconut, leaving it to steep and then squeezing the liquid from the pulp and straining it. Double the volume of water to flesh constitutes standard-strength coconut 'milk'. Coconut milk can also be made from coconut cream or creamed coconut, which is solid coconut flesh and fat.

Dried milk This has had all the water evaporated, leaving a powder (or granules). It is usually low-fat milk, which gives a better flavour when reconstituted with water and a longer shelf life.

Evaporated milk (canned) This has had much of the water evaporated at high heat, which gives it a distinct flavour. Evaporated milk contains double the solids of ordinary milk and is 9% fat. It can be whipped like cream. Condensed milk (canned) may be sweetened whole or skimmed milk, reduced by evaporation to a very sweet and thick syrup with fat contents of 9% and 0.3% respectively.

Goats' and sheep's (ewes') milk These can be drunk or used in cooking in the same way as cows' milk; they also make excellent pungent cheese. Goats' milk contains more fat than full-fat cows' milk, around 4%. Sheep's milk is even richer, with a fat content of 4–6%.

non-dairy 'milks' or milk substitutes

A variety of non-dairy 'milks' is sold as an alternative to milk. Soya milk is made from soya beans. The process involves soaking and grinding the beans; then boiling them with more water and filtering the liquid to produce a 'milk'. The basic milk may be treated to remove the soy flavour and other ingredients, such as vegetable oil, concentrated apple juice or other sweetener, additional soya protein, flavourings, vitamins and minerals, may be added to make the 'milk' more palatable and nutritious. Stabilizers and emulsifiers are needed to prevent separation and give the 'milk' an acceptable appearance. There are sugar-free versions and some soya milks contain honey or fruit juice.

If you haven't used soya milk before follow these tips for storing.
- Where applicable, do not dilute until ready to use. Transfer the remainder, undiluted, to a non-metallic container and store in the the fridge.
- Once opened, cartons and the content of cans will keep for up to 5 days in the fridge (unless packaging states otherwise).

Don't overwhip cream Whipping and double cream will curdle if overwhipped. There is no rescue remedy for curdled cream – the only thing you can do is make butter with it! Continue whipping for a couple of minutes until clumps form and then drain the whey and squeeze the curds together into a single lump of butter – mix in salt, if liked, and wrap to store in the fridge.

Chantilly cream (*crème chantilly*) is whipped cream flavoured with sugar and vanilla essence. It can be made lighter by folding in stiffly whisked egg white: allow 1 egg white for every 225 ml (8 fl oz) of double or whipping cream. The egg white will only hold up the cream for about 2 hours, so foods containing this cream need to be used up quickly.

Soured cream Both milk and cream can be soured by the addition of lemon juice (1 teaspoon to 250 ml/8 fl oz) for use in breads, cakes and scones raised with bicarbonate of soda.

Freezing milk, cheese and cream All types of milk (full-fat to skimmed) can be frozen, particularly as virtually all milk sold today is homogenized. Homogenization results in less chance of full-fat milk appearing curdled when it is thawed; it also seems to help prevent flavour changes due to freezing. Thawed milk can be used cold or for cooking. Double cream can also be frozen, but it does not whip well when thawed. Other creams (single and soured, for example) do not freeze well, they separate and have a curdled texture on thawing. Cheese can be frozen for up to 1 month; thaw gradually in the fridge.

Long-life or ultra-heat-treated (UHT) milk This is heated in a sealed container to 138°C/280°F for a few seconds. This sterilizes the milk for a long life but spoils the flavour; the flavour of lowest-fat milk is least affected. Use this milk for cooking.

Non-dairy 'milks' Rice, oats, sunflower oil and pea protein may all be used to produce non-dairy 'milks'.

cream

Cream is made from pasteurized or sterilized milk (unless the pack states that it is unpasteurized). Most cream is also homogenized to keep the fat evenly dispersed and make the cream smoother and more consistent.

Half-cream Literally half cream and half milk, so it is light and thin, more like rich milk. It tastes like top of the milk. Use for adding to drinks and enriching milk puddings or pouring on cereal and porridge for a treat.

Single cream Contains no less than 18% fat but this is still too low for whipping (to whip into smooth whipped cream the fat content must be 35%). It tastes smooth, rich and velvety. Use for quiche fillings, thickening soups and sauces (but do not boil, as it separates) or pour over desserts or stir into coffee.

Extra-thick single cream A thicker, homogenized version of single cream with the same fat content. It cannot be whipped. Use as for single cream.

Whipping cream Has a higher fat content than single cream, at around 35%. It doubles in volume when whipped – the colder it is, the greater the volume. Overwhipping results in separation. It tastes lighter than double cream; use for folding into mousses and cold soufflés, for piping and as a pouring cream.

Double cream With a fat content of no less than 48%, this is heavy enough to float on soups and liqueur coffees. It whips as for whipping cream and it tastes very rich and smooth. Use whipped for folding into mousses and soufflés and other desserts. The main ingredient in crème brûlée, some ice-creams and syllabub and the most luxurious pouring cream.

Extra-thick double cream Has been homogenized to make it thicker. Use this as a spooning cream, without whipping.

Clotted cream So rich (more than 60% fat) that it can be cut with a knife. It is traditionally made in Devon, Somerset and Cornwall, by heating and then cooling creamy milk. The cream rises to the surface and forms a thick crust, which is skimmed off. It tastes very rich and concentrated. Use clotted cream as a filler for scones with jam or serve with hot desserts.

Soured cream Single cream with a friendly bacteria added to make a thicker, creamier texture. It tastes slightly acidic (like yoghurt) but is still creamy and thick. Use as a cooking ingredient and to make dips and salad dressings, or serve with baked potatoes (add herbs). Spoon on to desserts. Serve with Mexican food, beef stroganoff, goulash and borscht and use to top blinis. It will separate at high temperatures.

Crème fraîche The French version of soured cream. The fat content varies between 30 and 50% (or even higher). There are also half-fat and lower-fat versions; it can be heated without separating, but to be on the safe side, stir in a teaspoon of cornflour before you use in cooking. It has a slightly acidic flavour, like soured cream, is richer, thicker and creamier.

Smetana (smatana) A cross between soured cream and yoghurt, it is made with skimmed milk, single cream and a culture to sour it. Smetana tastes more like yoghurt than cream and has a pouring consistency (containing only 10% fat). Use it in soups and drinks, pour it onto cereal or use it as an ingredient in baking.

Cultured buttermilk Very low in fat, traditionally this was made when friendly bacteria 'soured' the buttermilk that was left over once the cream had been removed from the milk during churning to make butter. Today, a culture is added to skimmed milk. It tastes like thin natural low-fat yoghurt. Use to make scones and soda bread or pour on breakfast cereal.

yoghurt

Yoghurt is a traditional food in many countries; from the Balkans, where for centuries it has been associated with health and longevity, to India and Arabic countries, where it provides a safe drink in hot climates where milk is not pasteurized or refrigerated.

Yoghurt is made by fermenting milk with friendly bacteria that feed on lactose (milk sugar) to produce lactic acid, which thickens the milk and gives natural yoghurt its tangy flavour. The bacteria such as *streptococcus thermophilus*, *bifido* bacteria and *lactobacilli are* added to the milk, which is warmed to around 42°C/110°F for 2–3 hours, then it is chilled quickly to halt fermentation.

Many ingredients are added to yoghurt, from fruit to modified starches (to make it thicker and creamier), sugar, colourings and flavourings. Low-fat and low-sugar yoghurts are available. Several brands claim 'probiotic' health benefits, due to the bacteria they contain. It is claimed the bacteria ferment undigested food in the large intestine to produce anti-cancer agents and boost the immune system.

yoghurt for cooking

Yoghurt will separate and give a cooked dish a curdled appearance but this does not affect the flavour. If the appearance is important, yoghurt can be stabilized by stirring 1 teaspoon of cornflour with 150 g (5 oz) of yoghurt (the amount in an individual carton), before you add it.

Use yoghurt as a dessert or for breakfast, as a snack, to thicken soups and sauces, as a marinade, as a dip or accompaniment, e.g. raita with Indian meals. Make into drinks and use in recipes for frozen yoghurt, sorbets and ice-creams.

fresh cheeses

Fresh cheeses are also called unripened cheeses. They are made in a similar way to yoghurt, adding a culture to milk to sour it, followed by an animal or vegetable rennet to separate the milk into curds (solid particles) and whey (liquid). The curds are cut and drained and then either beaten to a smooth paste to make soft cheeses such as cream cheese and fromage frais, or they are washed and drained in moulds to make cottage cheese and curd cheese. Salt and flavourings are then added.

These cheeses can be used in sweet and savoury recipes, such as cheesecakes or pasta fillings (lasagne and ravioli), as ingredients in dips, mousses and desserts, to top jacket potatoes or for spreading on crackers and sandwich fillings.

Cottage cheese Contains distinctive firm, grainy curds, which are a result of the curds being warmed in the whey, drained and washed in water before being mixed with cream. Cottage cheese is fairly bland; there are sweet and savoury varieties that may have added herbs, fruit and vegetables.

Curd cheese With a mild slightly acidic flavour, this is soft and spreadable. The curds are drained and blended with a salt and skimmed milk powder. Natural and flavoured varieties are available.

Cream cheese Made from single or double cream, this tastes very rich and buttery. The French cheese Neufchâtel is a slightly lower-fat cream cheese with a fat content around 25%. It is often shaped into cylinders and heart shapes and served as a dessert.

Fromage frais Of French origin, this is made from skimmed milk but, after the curds are separated from the whey, cream is added; depending on how much, it can be virtually-fat-free up to rich and thick. Fruit and flavourings are often added to make alternatives to yoghurt. Plain versions can be used as an alternative to cream or to make dips and as an ingredient in desserts, although it does not heat well.

Full-fat soft cheese Lower in fat than cream cheese, this has a creamy, savoury flavour and is the classic accompaniment to smoked salmon on bagels.

Mascarpone A rich Italian cream cheese, made from fresh cream that is heated and whipped to give a thick, smooth texture. It tastes slightly sweet and is the basis of the famous Italian dessert *tiramisu*. Also good in cheesecakes and pasta sauces.

Quark Made from skimmed milk curdled by lactic acid and then rennet. The curds are separated from the whey by draining to produce a virtually-fat-free cheese; cream is added to the higher-fat versions. Quark has a chalky texture and slightly acidic taste but this is not apparent when it is used in German pastries and cheesecakes.

Ricotta A rich Italian version of cottage cheese, with a similar bland taste but creamier and thicker. The cheese is made either from whey or a mixture of whey and full-fat milk or cream. After the curds are cut they are traditionally drained in perforated pyramid moulds which gives the cheese on a delicatessen counter its distinctive shape, although much is sold pre-packaged in cartons.

cheese

Cheese is an extremely versatile food. Traditional British cheeses (see page 73) are popular in ploughman's lunches, served with pickle and salad, as toppings for jacket potatoes, for cheese on toast, in cheese sauces, as a topping for gratin recipes, in soufflés and quiche and pasta fillings. They also appear alongside cheese from other countries on a cheese board for a special occasion or to replace dessert at the end of a meal.

choosing cheese

Speciality cheese shops, and some cheese counters in supermarkets, may offer a sliver of cheese to taste before buying, but most cheese today is bought prepacked so it cannot be judged by smell or flavour until after purchase. Cheese should smell appetizing and have a fresh or pungent odour according to variety, but no cheese should be so overripe that it has a hint of ammonia in its aroma.

If the cheese has a rind, it should be firm and crusty but the cheese beneath it should not look dry.

storing cheese

Take cheese out of any cling film or plastic wrap and store it loosely wrapped in waxed paper or a freezer film that will prevent it from drying out but will not make it sweat and become wet and slimy. Ideally, cheese should be stored at around 10°C/50°F but, for practical purposes, it is stored in the fridge so put it in the 'warmest' part of the fridge (see page 13). Hard cheeses can be grated ready for use and stored in a container in the fridge for about a week.

cooking with cheese

Take care when cooking with cheese because, if overheated, it will coagulate and the fat will separate out and form strings. That is why cheese is usually added off the heat to a cheese sauce, once the other ingredients have been amalgamated. This is not such as problem with Parmesan, Gruyère and Swiss cheese for melting into fondue or raclette cheese, the cut surface of which melts in front of a special grill and is served liquefied over boiled potatoes.

Mature well-flavoured cheeses are best for giving dishes and sauces a cheese flavour: less goes further with Parmesan, Gruyère and mature Cheddar.

Cheeses used as toppings need to melt well. Mozzarella has a bland taste but it melts into a wonderful stringy texture to top pizzas. Cheddar and other hard British cheeses melt well. Gruyère is grated to give a melted but crisp surface on French onion soup. Soft goats' cheese is often melted on top of croûtes and for melted goats' cheese salads.

presenting a cheese board

Choose only the best quality cheese when the cheese is to be eaten on its own. A well balanced cheese board could include examples of cheeses made from several different types of milk: cows', goats' and sheep's. Another theme could be all British cheeses, or all goats' cheese. Remember to supply several knives so that the blue cheese knife doesn't turn any unused cheese blue!

Serve cheese with walnut bread, crusty white or brown bread, savoury crackers or sweet digestive-style biscuits, plus grapes, pears, melon or fresh berries, walnuts and celery.

soft cheeses

Bel Paese (Italy) This is a sweet, buttery, pale yellow cheese with a smooth springy texture and a shiny golden rind.

Brie (France) Soft and creamy, with varying fat levels and encased in a velvety white rind; the flavour is quite mild but more mature Brie will have a darker, bulging ripe centre that spills out when cut. Wedges cut from the large disc of the whole cheese need to be used within a few days before they dry out.

Camembert (France) Is made in small rounds so that it is usual to buy a whole or half a cheese. The pungency depends on maturity and whether the milk was pasteurized or unpasteurized, the latter being more flavoursome. Like Brie, the cheese liquefies as it ripens and is made with varying fat levels.

Chaumes (France) A washed-rind cheese with a shiny gold rind and a soft texture. This cheese has a strong aroma and needs to be stored away from other foods it may taint.

Coulommiers (or Petit Brie, France) The name given to smaller versions of Brie, but still too big to buy a whole cheese for normal domestic needs. As it ripens it tastes more like Camembert than Brie.

Epoisses (France) A pungent cheese from Burgundy, with an orange-red rind and a soft, earthy centre.

Fet(t)a (Greece) A soft cheese with a high moisture content; it is uncooked and matured in brine. It is therefore salty, with a hard, crumbly texture and sharp flavour. Originally made from sheeps' milk, it is now also made from cows' milk. Eat with olives and tomatoes and bread.

Gubbeen (Ireland) A rich, creamy texture; it is dense and firm inside its orange rind.

Livarot (France) A Normandy cheese, wrapped with strips of sedge (to prevent the cheese from collapsing). It has a washed, shiny brown rind and a pungent smell from ripening in humid, unventilated rooms. The cheese is supple and golden in colour with a strong flavour.

Pont l'Evèque (France) A strong smell and a rich but milder flavour than the aroma might suggest. It is supple and pale gold inside its ridged, golden-brown rind. Made in small squares and sold boxed.

Port Salut (France) Has a deep orange washed rind, with a subtle, textured yellow centre. It is very smooth with a savoury flavour that is quite mild.

Reblochon (France) Usually sold boxed in a small disc. It has a pinkish-brown washed rind and is pale and creamy inside, with a slightly fruity taste.

Stinking Bishop (England) The British equivalent of Munster, the washed, orange-red rind cheese which is distinctively pungent. This cheese lives up to its olfactory name, with its smooth centre becoming runny when ripe.

Vacherin (France, Switzerland) Ripens to a runny texture, like Brie, and has a sweet and nutty flavour.

blue cheeses

Blue cheeses tend to be either creamy or crumbly, with a piquant, strong flavour; they are a vital addition to a cheese board. Blue cheese can also be cooked. It is good in sauces and in pastry fillings and croquettes. Blue cheeses tend to be salty so do not serve with salty biscuits and be cautious about seasoning dishes that contain cooked blue cheese. When buying, avoid any cheeses with grey patches or that look wet or sticky.

Bleu de Bresse (France) Small and soft with a white rind and delicate blue veining, this cheese is creamy sweet and mild.

Blue Cheshire A golden version of the Cheshire hard cheese with scant green veining. Blue Cheshire has a buttery taste and texture.

Cabrales (Spain) Made mainly with cows' milk, sometimes with the addition of goats' and ewes' milk. A strong-smelling cheese with blue-brown veining and a strong flavour.

Danish Blue (Denmark) Has a very pale colour and a lot of blue-green veining. The cheese is strong and tangy in flavour and quite soft to slice, with a buttery, spreadable texture.

Dolcelatte (Italy) A factory-made Gorgonzola. The name means 'sweet milk' and it is a milder version of Gorgonzola.

Dorset Blue Vinny (England) A hard cheese with a dry texture and sharp tangy flavour.

Gorgonzola (Italy) A soft, moist, smelly, creamy-blue cheese, with a blue-green veining and mellow, creamy flavour. Also available in an aged version, with a firmer texture and stronger flavour. In Italy, it is used to stuff soft fruits or crumbled on to salads and into salad dressings; and it is used in cooking, because it tends not to be as salty as some blue cheeses.

Shropshire Blue (England) A smooth-textured cheese with a yellow-orange colour and blue veining.

Stilton (England) The so-called King of English cheeses. The strong, tangy flavour is mature and creamy, with attractive blue-green veining and a totally individual taste. Hard to better.

hard cheeses

These are the cheeses by which nations are known. They are the everyday cheeses that are eaten with bread or grated for cooking. Despite their familiarity, well made examples are far from contemptible and never mundane. Generally speaking, the more mature a hard cheese the better the quality and flavour – and the higher the price.

Hard cheeses feature in sandwiches, on toast, in sauces, and on salads. In Britain, Cheddar-style cheeses are the most popular; in France, Gruyère is the everyday cheese used in the Croque Monsieur (a toasted ham and cheese sandwich), the Swiss have Emmenthal, with its nutty taste and unique large eyes (holes) and Appenzeller (and the frequently mentioned Gruyère); the Italians have pecorino romano, a close relative of Parmesan (parmigiano-reggiano), but less

british regional (territorial) cheeses

All these hard cheeses are very high in fat. Their fat content is similar, 31–33%.

Caerphilly (Wales) Made from skimmed milk, which gives it a white colour. Caerphilly has a salty, fresh taste with a hint of lemon, and a flaky texture.
Cheddar Varying from mild to mature and originating in the Cheddar Gorge area of Somerset.
Cheshire Light and crumbly and pale in colour, unless it is red Cheshire, which is in reality yellow, the colour derived from the addition of anatto (a natural vegetable dye). There is also blue Cheshire, which has green veining and quite a soft texture.
Double Gloucester A hard block cheese with a bright orange colour (from annatto). It has a close, smooth texture and slices well. Its flavour can resemble Cheddar.

Lancashire A pale, firm, hard cheese with a mild sharp flavour when mature, although most examples are not very sharp.
Red Leicester Another hard cheese coloured with anatto. It is compact and grainy in texture with a flavour similar to mild Cheddar.
Wensleydale A crumbly, slightly salty white cheese with a mild flavour that is pleasantly sour and similar to Caerphilly. Famed in Yorkshire for its partnership with apple pie, Wensleydale has now hit the big time in Hollywood, through its association with Wallace and Gromit.
Cornish Yarg Another British cheese: it is white and hard and wrapped in nettles, which impart its characteristic flavour.

expensive and prestigious. The Norwegians have Jarlsberg; a rich yellow cheese with large eyes and a buttery taste a little like Emmenthal. Norway also produces the strange, brownish, sweet Gjetöst cheese, sold in small bricks. It is sliced thinly and eaten for breakfast on crisp bread. The Dutch have Gouda in many stages of maturity and varieties (some containing cumin seed, caraway seeds and herbs) rarely seen outside the Netherlands. The Cypriots, Lebanese and Syrians share a passion for Haloumi, a sheeps' or cows' milk cheese matured in brine and white in colour (with similarities to Feta). It is often sliced and grilled or shallow-fried but is not particularly flavoursome.

goats'-milk cheeses

Goats' cheeses range from quite mild to pungent. The texture is different from cows' milk cheeses, being soft and more chalky than crumbly, unless it is a Cheddar-style cheese made from goats' milk.

Bûcheron A log of goats' cheese with a familiar white mould rind. Often sold sliced and wrapped – a creamy, slightly tangy, rich flavour.

Cabécou and cailladou The small, flat, round, goats' cheeses from Languedoc and the Aquitaine, ranging from semi-soft to firm.

Chevret, chevreton, chevrotins All three are goats' cheeses from the Savoie area of the Alps, lightly pressed into rounds or small flattened cones; the flavour will depend on the age. Also known as *tomme de chèvre*, the term that covers a lot of different goats' cheese made in the Savoie.

Crottins de chavignol The kind of smelly, salty, sharp cheeses that put a lot of people off goats' cheese; having said that, they are delicious to some and flavours vary widely.

sheep's-milk cheeses

Sheep's cheese is creamier, richer and higher in fat than cows'-milk cheese.

Beenleigh blue (Devon) Has a pungent, spicy flavour.

Lanark blue (Scotland) A hand-made cheese made from unpasteurized milk and vegetarian rennet. Creamy white with a blue-green vein reminiscent of Roquefort.

Manchego (Spain) Rich and creamy, with a sweet nutty flavour, small eyes and wax-coated rind.

Pecorino (Italy) Made from cooked sheep's milk. The texture is granular, like Parmesan; it is used mainly for cooking and grating but young cheeses are sometimes put on a cheese board.

Roquefort (France) A creamy coloured cheese with green veining. It owes its unique tangy flavour to being ripened in limestone caves in the region of the town of Roquefort, where it originates.

butter

Butter is made from pasteurized or unpasteurized cream, which is churned until the butter solids separate from the buttermilk. It is about 82% fat. All butter should be refrigerated. Keep it wrapped in the paper or tub in which it was sold to prevent it from drying out or becoming tainted. Butter can be frozen for 4–5 months.

Unsalted butter is best for cooking, both for flavour and because it burns less easily.

eggs

Eggs from many different birds can be eaten but it is hen's eggs that we use for everyday cooking. The choices are between methods of production and size.

Several terms appear on egg boxes but most are marketing jargon rather than specific legal categories. In general, eggs are either from the battery system or they are free range (hens are reared inside but with access to an outside run) or organic (hens are reared with constant access to pasture during the day).

The colour of the shell derives from the breed of hen; it is not an indication of nutritional status of the egg.

A deep colour in the yolk may be an indication of a well nourished hen and a nutritious egg in truly free-range eggs, but the colour of yolks in commercially produced eggs is determined by natural colourings which are added to the hens' feed.

choosing eggs

Eggs need to be fresh, so check the best-before date on egg boxes when buying. This is set at 21 days after the egg was laid. To test for freshness, break an egg on to a saucer; the yolk should stand up and be well formed – very fresh eggs are best for poaching. There should be two distinct layers in the white, an inner circle and a thinner outer circle. A stale egg is flatter, with indistinguishable layers in the white. Another test is how the egg floats in water. An egg that floats on its side is fresh. An egg that floats vertically with the rounded end up is 2–3 weeks old. An egg that floats on the surface is very old and should be thrown away.

storing eggs

Store eggs pointed-side down in the fridge, either in the box in which they were bought, which will prevent them from picking up odours and stop them from dehydrating, or in the egg tray. Lightly beaten egg yolks can be refrigerated for 1–2 days in a covered container. Put a little cold water on top to prevent a crust forming, before covering with cling film.

Uncooked eggs can be frozen out of their shells for up to 3 months. Single eggs would dry out rapidly but a quantity of about six, lightly beaten together, will freeze. Add half a teaspoon of salt or sugar to prevent the mixture becoming gelatinous. Separated whites may be frozen without the addition of salt or sugar.

egg rescue remedies

If whisked for too long, egg whites separate and turn grainy, making it difficult to fold them into other ingredients. Once mixed, they lose volume quickly and will not 'hold up' a mixture. To rescue the situation, add another unbeaten egg white for every four that are already whisked and continue whisking for 30 seconds until they are smooth.

Eggs are often difficult to shell after boiling. To remedy this, plunge them into cold water. This helps detach the membrane from the shell. Shelling under cold running water also helps.

tips on whisking egg whites

- Greater volume is achieved from eggs that are 3–4 days old.
- Some chefs recommend a pinch of salt to make the whites easier to beat to firm peaks and a pinch of cream of tartar to stabilize the beaten foam.
- An unlined copper bowl and a balloon whisk achieve the maximum volume when whisking eggs. Glass bowls are least successful, because the egg white slides off the sides.
- Make sure that both the bowl and utensils are free from any trace of grease or water when whisking egg whites.
- A chilled bowl and whisk makes the job easier.
- If you are using a copper bowl, follow the cleaning instructions and rub the bowl with a tablespoon of salt and a cut lemon or tablespoon of vinegar up to 2 hours before use, to remove any toxic copper deposits. Rinse and dry the bowl thoroughly.

raw eggs and salmonella

Raw eggs or lightly cooked eggs, or dishes and drinks that contain them, will not have been cooked sufficiently to kill any salmonella present. Because eggs (along with poultry and meat) are the foods most likely to be infected with salmonella, vulnerable groups, such as babies, pregnant women and the elderly are advised to avoid undercooked eggs. Eggs should be hard-boiled for at least 7 minutes; fried eggs should be cooked for 3 minutes each side, scrambled eggs should be cooked until they are firm. Other foods, such as mayonnaise, egg custard, hollandaise sauce, meringues, ice-creams, sorbets, soufflés and mousses and royal icing should all be avoided unless made from pasteurized egg.

how to cook eggs

Eggs are very sensitive to heat and, ideally, should be brought to room temperature before cooking. Egg yolks should never be added directly to a hot mixture as they will cook almost immediately; instead, add a little of the hot mixture to the lightly beaten yolks to warm them slightly first. Eggs overcook very easily and just a few seconds can make a difference between a tender egg and a dry, tough one. Eggs continue to cook if left in a hot dish.

boiled eggs

Bring the water to the boil before adding the eggs. Once boiling, reduce the heat to a simmer and add the eggs. The water should cover the eggs. Simmer for the time stated below.

boiled egg cooking times

Soft-boiled eggs	**4½–5 minutes**
(white is softly set and yolk is runny)	
Medium-cooked eggs	**7 minutes**
(white is set and yolk is firm and creamy)	
Hard-boiled eggs	**10–12 minutes**
(where the white and yolk are firm)	

poached eggs

Eggs poached directly in water produce a very moist, soft egg. They are delicious on buttered toast or served with smoked haddock and are often served in salads too. Poaching pans with specially moulded cups are also available but, since the egg does not touch the water, the egg will have a much firmer texture closer to that of a boiled egg.

You will need at least 7.5 cm (3 in) depth of boiling water in a shallow or wide pan. Add 3 tablespoons vinegar to every 1 litre (1¾ pints) of water (this will help seal the white); do not use salt as this will break it up. Bring the water to a rolling boil and break the

egg sizes

Eggs are sold in four sizes, small, medium, large and very large. These replace the previous size scale of 0–7. Each size falls within a 10 g weight band. Many recipes, especially for baking, refer to size-3 eggs, which is equivalent to large.

New sizes	Old sizes
Very large	0, 1
Large	1, 2, 3
Medium	3, 4, 5
Small	5, 6, 7

egg carefully into a bubbling area so that the bubbles spin the egg and set the white around the yolk. Lower the heat to just below a simmer and poach for about 4 minutes. To test, lift the egg out with a slotted spoon and press. The white should be set and the yolk still soft. Serve immediately if using hot or place in cold water if serving cold.

scrambled eggs

Good scrambled eggs need careful cooking since they can quickly become overcooked and tough. Season the eggs with a little salt and freshly ground black pepper before cooking and, if you like, add a tablespoon of cream or milk. If flavouring with fresh herbs, add them before cooking; if you want to add strips of smoked salmon, or ham, add it as the egg starts to thicken.

Whisk the eggs (allowing 2 eggs per person) with salt and black pepper and add 1 tablespoon of cream or milk if you like. Melt a knob of butter until foaming and then pour in the egg. Stir constantly over a medium heat until the egg starts to cook on the base. Keep stirring until the eggs become creamy, but thinner than the consistency you want. Remove from the heat and continue stirring as the eggs will continue to cook in the pan. Stir until thickened and serve at once.

omelette

The most popular omelette is a simple folded one, often made just with eggs and seasoning or flavoured with herbs. Popular fillings include grated cheese, ham or cooked bacon, mushrooms or prawns, which are added at the end of cooking.

To make a folded omelette Allow 2 eggs per person. Whisk the eggs with a fork until frothy, with a little salt and black pepper. Heat 25 g (1 oz) of butter in an omelette pan or shallow frying pan until foaming. Pour in the eggs and stir with a fork until they start to thicken. Pull the egg that sets at the side of the pan into the

fried eggs

There is arguably no tastier snack than fried egg on toast or a fried egg with bacon.

Use a non-stick pan, if possible. Heat 1–2 table-spoons of butter or oil until hot but not smoking. Crack the eggs into a cup and slide into the pan. Fry over a medium heat, spooning the fat over the white and yolk, until the white is firm but the yolk is still soft. Flip the egg over and briefly brown it on the other side. In America, the term 'over easy' is used, to mean an egg cooked on both sides and 'sunny side up' for an egg that has been fried just on one side.

middle, tipping the pan to pour the uncooked eggs to the side. Keep the mixture moving until all the runny egg has become softly set. Stop stirring and continue cooking until the top of the omelette has just set. Add the filling and serve.

To make a soufflé omelette These are made by whisking the egg whites until they form soft peaks then folding in the yolks. They may be cooked entirely on the hob or finished off in a hot oven. Most often, they are sweetened with 1 tablespoon sugar per egg and served folded with raspberry jam and dusted with icing sugar.

basic pancakes

makes 10–12 | preparation time: 5 minutes | cooking time: 15 minutes

100 g (4 oz) plain flour
1 egg
300 ml (10 fl oz) semi-skimmed milk
sunflower oil, for frying

Place the flour in a bowl. Make a well in the centre and add the egg and half the milk. Using a wooden spoon or balloon whisk, beat the eggs and milk together, incorporating the flour at the same time. When the mixture starts to thicken, gradually add the remaining milk until the consistency is that of thin cream (make sure there are no lumps).

Heat a little oil in a small heavy-based crêpe or frying pan. Pour in enough batter to cover the base of the pan thinly, swirling the batter around the pan to form an even layer. Cook for 1 minute or so until small holes start to appear in the pancake.

Using a palette knife, carefully flip the pancake over and cook for 1 minute. Remove from the pan. Repeat this process until you have used all the batter. As you make the pancakes, stack them on a plate, separating them with greaseproof paper. Keep them warm, wrapped in foil in a low oven.

note You can add a little caster sugar to the batter to sweeten it if you wish, or a good pinch of salt if you want to make pancakes with a savoury filling.

pancake varieties

Butterscotch sauce Melt 75 g (3 oz) of butter and 75 g (3 oz) of golden syrup and pour over the pancakes. Serve with ice-cream.

Sultana pancakes Add 1 tablespoon of caster sugar and 50 g (2 oz) of sultanas to the basic batter.

Apple pancakes Serve with caramelized apple slices: heat 75 g (3 oz) of butter and 75 g (3 oz) of sugar in a pan, add 6 peeled eating apples, cut into wedges, and cook until tender. Add a pinch of ground cinnamon and serve with cream.

cheese soufflé

preparation time: 15 minutes │ cooking time: 30–35 minutes │ serves 4–6

Cheese soufflés are much simpler to make than you imagine. They are based on a white sauce (which you can make in advance) with egg whites folded in, and make a light, tasty supper.

Pre-heat the oven to 200°C/400°F/Gas 6/fan oven 180°C. Generously butter a 1.25-litre (2-pint) soufflé dish or four individual 300 ml (10 fl oz) dishes, then sprinkle with one tablespoon of the Parmesan. Tap around the dish so that the cheese covers the inside evenly.

Melt the butter in a large pan, add the flour and cook for 1 minute, stirring all the time. Gradually blend in the milk, stirring constantly until the sauce is thickened and smooth. Simmer for about 3 minutes, stirring occasionally.

Cool the sauce briefly, then stir in the mustard powder, egg yolks, Gruyère and all but one tablespoon of the remaining Parmesan. Add salt and freshly ground black pepper to taste; mix well.

In a clean, dry bowl, whisk the egg whites until stiff and dry. Fold a quarter of the egg whites into the sauce, then fold in the remainder, cutting through the mixture and turning it over with a large metal spoon until the egg white is evenly mixed throughout the sauce, taking care not to knock out the air.

Turn the soufflé mixture into the prepared dish and place the dish on a baking sheet or cover with cling film and keep for up to 1 hour before cooking. Sprinkle with the reserved Parmesan. Bake for 30–35 minutes for the large soufflé, or 25–30 minutes for the smaller, individual ones, until well risen and golden brown. Serve immediately.

50 g (2 oz) butter, plus extra for greasing
25 g (1 oz) Parmesan cheese, freshly grated
40 g (1½ oz) plain flour
300 ml (10 fl oz) hot milk
½ teaspoon English mustard powder
4 eggs, separated
75 g (3 oz) Gruyère cheese, grated
salt and freshly ground black pepper

tips

Pre-heat the oven for 20 minutes to get it really hot before cooking the soufflé(s).
Use a large pan to make the sauce. It is easier to fold in the egg whites, without knocking out too much air, when you have a larger surface area.
Put the soufflé dish on a baking sheet so that it is easy to remove from the oven.

Fold a little whisked egg white into the sauce before adding the remainder. This softens the sauce, making it easier to add the rest, and ensures that as little air as possible is knocked out of the mixture.

mushroom and parmesan baked eggs

serves 4 | preparation time: 5 minutes | cooking time: 18–20 minutes

These delicate, savoury custards make a great starter or light supper. Serve with fingers of buttered toast.

25 g (1 oz) butter
100 g (4 oz) mushrooms, sliced
142 ml carton of double cream
4 large eggs
15 g (½ oz) Parmesan cheese, finely grated
salt and freshly ground black pepper
buttered fingers of toast, to serve

Pre-heat the oven to 190°C/375°F/Gas 5/fan oven 170°C. Use a little of the butter to grease four ramekin dishes lightly. Cook the mushrooms with the remaining butter for 2–3 minutes in a small pan until just soft, then divide between the dishes.

Pour the cream over the mushrooms and season with a little salt and freshly ground black pepper.

Break an egg gently into each dish and sprinkle with the Parmesan cheese. Place the dishes in a small roasting tin and pour enough hot water into the tin to come half way up the sides of the ramekins.

Bake for 15 minutes for a softly set egg, and 18 minutes for a more firmly set egg. Serve with buttered toast.

wine suggestion This is a rather grand first course that requires a white wine with enough savoury concentration to handle the cream, eggs and cheese in the recipe. Almost any lavishly oaked Chardonnay would fit the bill, or you might ring the changes with a wood-matured Marsanne or Verdelho from Australia.

mushroom and parmesan baked eggs

pasta, rice and pulses

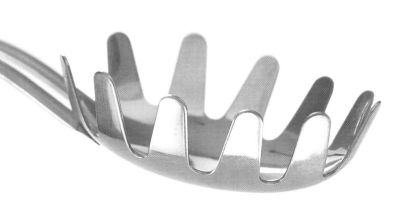

there are hundreds of different pasta shapes and sizes but the basic choice is between fresh and dry. Dry pasta is most widely used, even in Italy, because it is convenient and has a long shelf life. Dry pasta is usually made from just flour and water, but it may also contain egg. Fresh pasta is made from flour, water, egg and, usually, olive oil; both may also contain flavourings and seasonings. While fresh pasta has become popular in the UK, most Italian families eat dried pasta daily and buy or make fresh pasta for special occasions.

Pasta is made from several different types of flour: durum wheat flour (also called semolina flour), plain unbleached flour, wholemeal flour, rye flour and buckwheat flour. The best quality wheat pasta is made from durum wheat, which may also be described on the pack as pure semolina. Which shape you choose is a matter of personal preference, although some shapes hold the sauce better than others do. Spaghetti distributes a sauce well as do shells, snails, quills and twists (which are easier to eat than spaghetti).

Food technology has made special diet pasta for people who cannot tolerate wheat or rye flour possible, by using vegetable, corn and other starch to make pasta. Italian grade 00 flour (also called *type 00* or *farino tipo 00*), available from Italian food shops and some supermarkets, is best for home-made pasta because it absorbs liquid easily. Its fine, soft texture makes it easier to knead and roll out and it has a delicate flavour and texture. Other special flours for making pasta are sold by supermarkets and food stores. Strong plain flour can be substituted for Italian flour.

Noodles are the Asian equivalent of pasta and are made with wheat flour or rice flour, or from vegetable starch such as soya, mung or other beans. Dried noodles can be boiled like pasta, fresh or previously boiled ones can be used in stir-fries. Egg noodles may be dried or fresh and are often packaged wrapped into a ball. Cellophane noodles are made from dried ground mung beans and are eaten more as a vegetable; they need to be soaked before they are boiled.

Although most noodles are cooked by boiling, some oriental noodles are made into sheets such as for spring rolls or wrappers for wontons; these are filled and deep-fried.

know your pasta shapes

Bigoli Thick spaghetti, sometimes made from wholemeal flour.

Cannelloni Oblongs of pasta rolled up into tubes and filled before baking, usually in a sauce.

Capelli d'angeli Means 'angels' hair', a reference to the thinness of the strand.

Conchiglie Pasta shells; *conchigliette* are small shells. These are good for serving with sauce, which becomes trapped in the shells.

Ditali 'Little thimbles' that look like tiny cups full of sauce when cooked.

Elicoidali Straighter, slightly larger and not quite as bent as elbow macaroni.

Farfalle Butterfly-shaped pasta, sometimes described as 'bow ties'. Larger and smaller versions are *farfalloi* and *farfallette* respectively. Good for serving with meat sauces.

Fettuccine Long, flat ribbons or strips. Fettucine is similar to *linguine*.

Fusilli Twists of pasta, may be any colour.

Lasagne Very wide pieces of pasta, which may be strips or nearer to rectangles in shape, with either a straight or crimped edge. For layering with different sauces and baking in the oven.

Linguine Long, flat, ribbon noodles ('noodles' generally refers to flat pasta).

Lumache Snail-shaped pasta.

Orecchiette 'Little ears'; they look like tiny cones that have been bent into an ear shape.

Pappardelle Long, wide strips of pasta with a distinctive crimped edge.

Pastina Includes a variety of miniature pasta, cut into stars and letters of the alphabet, often served for babies and toddlers, or used in soups and broth.

Penne Short tubes with a diagonal quill-like end, either ridged or smooth. Larger and smaller versions are *pennoni* and *pennini*, respectively. Good for serving with sauce, which fills the tubes.

Rigati Ridged, hollow pasta tubes, the most popular version is *rigatoni*; larger ones are *grossi rigati* and smaller ones *rigoletti*. Good for baking in sauce.

Tagliatelle Similar to *fettuccine* but thinner; good for bolognese-style sauces.

Vermicelli Fine strands, thinner than spaghetti and usually dried into coils or little nests.

Fresh pasta is often filled to make familiar pasta shapes such as ravioli, tortellini and cappelleti. The fillings can be based on meat, fish or vegetables. Flat, unfilled egg pasta is the most popular; it is available either plain or flavoured and coloured with herbs and vegetables, in varieties such as spaghetti, tagliarini, fettucine, tagliatelle, pappardelle – and, of course, lasagne.

cooking pasta

Pasta should be added to a large pan of boiling water. Addition of salt is a matter of personal preference, but 1 tablespoon of oil helps keep the shapes or strands of pasta separate. Once boiling, the heat is lowered so that the pasta is kept at a rolling boil until it is *al dente*,

pasta dressings

Once cooked, pasta can simply be tossed in olive oil (good with torn basil leaves) or butter (good with torn sage leaves) or a grating of fresh Parmesan cheese. Vinaigrette of lemon juice and olive oil with black pepper is another simple option. Finely chopped fresh herbs and flavouring such as capers, olives and anchovies can also be thrown in with pasta if you do not want to make a cooked sauce. Pesto sauce (see page 47) is simple and quick if purchased either fresh from the chiller cabinet or in a jar.

tender but still with some bite. Follow the cooking instructions on the pack. In general, fresh pasta takes 1–2 minutes to cook and filled fresh pasta 3–5 minutes. Dried pasta takes 5–12 minutes to cook, depending on its thickness, the size of the pieces or whether it is wholemeal (which takes longer).

polenta

Polenta is a staple of northern Italy because the corn from which it is made grows easily there, whereas rice, the staple of southern Italy, does not. Polenta is a maize (corn) flour that can be coarse or fine; both are simmered with water to make a thick paste that can be served as an alternative to rice or potatoes. The paste can also be transferred to an oiled baking tin, baked in the oven and then cut into slices and eaten hot or cold, or grilled. Grated cheese is a good addition, because polenta has a rather bland flavour. Include sweetcorn, mushrooms or sun-dried tomatoes or put slices of cheese on top of polenta to be grilled.

Polenta is traditionally added to boiling water but this can lead to a lumpy paste. It is easier to add it to cold water and bring it to the boil. Pre-cooked polenta takes only a matter of 5 or 10 minutes to cook, but is frowned on by many Italian cooks, who prefer the flavour of slow-cooked polenta stirred in a big saucepan on the hob for 30–40 minutes. When made over an open fire, polenta develops a smoky flavour.

rice

Rice feeds more than half the world's population, especially in Asia. It can be brown or white, long-grain, medium-grain or short-grain. Both white and brown rice have the inedible husk removed after harvesting.

American long-grain rice Used to be called 'Carolina rice', from the area in which is grown; now it is grown elsewhere. Grains are thicker than basmati.

Arborio An Italian variety of short-grain rice used for making risotto because it absorbs a lot of stock during cooking without becoming unpleasantly soft and sticky.

Basmati rice A prestigious long-grain variety grown in the foothills of the Himalayas and prized for its aromatic flavour. The best accompaniment to Indian food.

Brown rice Retains the bran layer and germ, which are removed when husked rice is polished to produce white rice. White rice lacks the B vitamins, vitamin E and fibre found in brown rice. Takes 30–40 minutes to cook.

Camargue red rice From the eponymous region of southern France. It is medium-grain rice with a red skin and a nutty flavour. It takes 30 minutes or more to cook.

Carnaroli Similar to arborio but less plentiful and therefore more expensive.

Easy-cook rice So called because the grains do not stick together. The rice is partially cooked under pressure before milling; this has the advantage of driving some of the vitamins and minerals from the husk into the grain, but it also slightly hardens the grain, making it slower to cook.

Long-grain rice Grains have pointed ends and stay separate when cooked. Serve with Asian dishes: jambalaya; pillau; biriyani; pilaff.

Medium-grain rice Plumper than long-grain rice and moister and stickier, but it can be used in all savoury recipes where long-grain rice is indicated.

Short-grain rice Also called round or pudding rice and, as these names suggest, it is used for rice puddings and is plump and round in appearance.

Sticky rice Sold in speciality food suppliers, this has a high starch content that make the rice sticky for use in sushi and other dishes.

Thai fragrant or jasmine rice Long-grained, slightly sticky and with an aromatic fragrance of jasmine.

Valencia Short-grain rice grown in the Valencia area of Spain and some parts of Portugal. It is used for authentic paella.

Wild rice The seed of an aquatic grass and not a grain. Longer and thinner than long-grain rice, it has a dark brown colour, earthy flavour and chewy texture. It takes about 40 minutes to steam or boil.

cooking rice

Rice expands to twice its volume when cooked. During cooking, starches are released that make the grains of rice stick together. This is desirable in some recipes, for example, sushi, but, where separate, fluffy grains of rice are required, rinsing after cooking can be necessary.

Rice will absorb a lot of water during cooking: 450 g (1 lb) absorbs about 600 ml (1 pint). As a general rule, add salt to the water before cooking though it can be added later. If you want perfectly cooked, separate grains, it is a good idea to rinse standard long-grain rice. Pour cold water over it and swirl around with your fingertips, then pour off the water. Repeat twice or until the water is clear. Basmati, risotto and paella rice do not usually need to be washed.

All rice is cooked when the centre of the grain is tender on biting.

Absorption method This is the most common method for long-grain or basmati and gives soft, fluffy grains. It is easy for the water to boil off too quickly, though, and for the rice to burn on the base of the pan. The rice and water must be accurately measured so that all the water is absorbed. It is usually one part rice, to two parts water; tip the weighed rice into a measuring jug, check its volume and cook it in twice as much water. Or measure 1 cup of rice to 2 cups of water. Tip the rice, water and salt into a pan and bring to the boil. Stir once, then cover and turn down the heat to a simmer. Simmer until all the water has been absorbed, about 10–12 minutes for white rice.

Boiling method Add the rice to a large pan of boiling, salted water. Return to the boil, lower the heat and simmer until cooked. Then drain in a sieve. This is an easy method but the rice can be quite wet. It is the best method for brown rice.

Microwave method This method is no quicker, but guarantees perfectly cooked, separate grains every time. The rice and water must be accurately measured; one part rice to two parts boiling water. Place in a glass bowl and cover with plastic wrap. Pierce the top to allow steam to escape. Cook on high for 11–12 minutes, depending on the wattage of the oven.

Oven method Put the rice in an ovenproof dish, with a layer of foil lined with greaseproof paper as a lid if the dish does not have a lid. Allow one part rice to two parts water and bake at 180°C/350°F/Gas 4/fan oven 160°C for 15–18 minutes.

Steaming method Put rice in a steamer over boiling water. Stir every so often to ensure even cooking. It will take 5 minutes longer than by other methods.

pulses

This term is used to describe dried beans, peas and lentils. Generally, the older the pulses the harder and drier they become and the longer they take to cook and the tougher they are. Buy pulses from a shop with a good turnover. Store them in an airtight container.

Most dried pulses need to be soaked before cooking, so that they absorb water, which results in more tender cooked pulses and a quicker cooking time. Soak pulses in twice their volume, e.g. 1 litre (1¾ pints) of water to 450 g (1 lb) of dried pulses. Soaking in boiling water speeds the soaking time to a couple of hours; otherwise soak overnight in cold water. Alternatively, wash the pulses, bring to the boil for 2 minutes, remove from the heat and leave to soak for 1 hour.

All pulses (except lentils) need to be boiled for at least 10 minutes during cooking, to deactivate a substance that can otherwise lead to stomach upsets.

Pulses are cooked when the inside is tender.

feast of beans

There are many different types of bean; make regular use of all of them for a varied and healthy diet.

Aduki (or azuki) beans Small, dark red or yellow. Popular in Japanese cuisine, they are usually used to make sweet dessert pastes and confectionery but can be used in the normal savoury way in the West.

Black-eye beans Small, creamy-coloured beans with a black eye. They are called cowpeas in American cookery books and used in recipes for 'Soul Food' from the South. They are also good in curries.

Black kidney beans Lose a lot of their colour during cooking but make stunning black-bean soups, popular in the American South. The black-bean sauces or pastes used in oriental cooking are not made from black kidney beans but from fermented soybeans.

Borlotti (or pinto) beans Have a mild flavour. They are used in soups, Italian salads and are cooked with other vegetables.

Butter beans Large, flat, kidney-shaped beans of beige colour and waxy texture.

Cannellini beans A white variety of haricot or kidney beans used widely in Italy and South America.

Chick-peas Another versatile pulse (called garbanzo beans in America). Chick-peas are beige in colour, with a slightly wrinkled appearance. The dried peas take a long time to soak and cook. Canned chick-peas are by far the most convenient. They are used widely in Mediterranean cuisine (mainly Spanish, Italian and Turkish), soups, stews and falafel, but are probably best known as one of the main ingredients in hummus.

Flageolet beans are a pretty pale green and are used mainly in France and Italy. They have a delicate flavour.

Ful médames Small brown beans. The name has become the name of the national dish of Egypt, in which the beans are combined with hard-boiled eggs and garlic, parsley, lemons and olive oil. The dish is eaten with flat Arab bread and accompanied by tahini.

Haricot beans Medium-size white beans, popular around the world in dishes from the French cassoulet to American Boston baked beans. In the US, they are also called navy beans.

Lentils can be whole, such as green and brown Continental lentils, or split, such as red lentils. Lentils and split peas are the basis of Indian dhals. Different lentils and spices make for a great variety of dhals. The slate-grey Puy lentil, which takes its name from the French town of Le Puy, is the most fashionable and is served as a vegetable or as a purée accompanying fish and meat. Whole green lentils are also served as a vegetable and a salad or a purée.

Mung beans Small, dark green beans more familiar in their sprouted form as Chinese bean sprouts.

Pinto beans See *Borlotti beans*.

Red kidney beans Widely used in vegetarian cooking, these beans are also used in Mexican chilli con carne and other dishes from the south of the United States; in France they are cooked with wine and bacon.

Soya beans More often eaten in products made from the soy bean: soya milk, tofu (bean curd), soy protein meat substitutes, soy and other sauces, as well as the less familiar products of soy such as tempeh, a firm white paste.

Split peas Are either yellow or green. Pea and ham soup is a British classic, as is pease pudding. Split peas make smooth satisfying soups and do not need to be soaked before cooking.

macaroni with rich cheese sauce

serves 4 | preparation time: 5 minutes | cooking time: 12–20 minutes

Rich and comforting, this makes a quick snack or supper for the whole family. Serve plain or pour it on top of lightly sautéd vegetables, or a bolognese sauce and bake until golden. The cheese sauce is also excellent poured over cauliflower maybe sprinkled with crispy bacon or poured over lasagne.

350 g (12 oz) macaroni or fusilli

FOR THE SAUCE:
25 g (1 oz) butter
25 g (1 oz) plain flour
450 ml (15 fl oz) milk
100 g (4 oz) mature Cheddar cheese, grated
1 teaspoon English mustard
3 tablespoons crème fraîche (optional)
salt and freshly ground black pepper
25 g (1 oz) Parmesan cheese, grated

Boil the pasta in plenty of salted water for 8–10 minutes until tender. Drain well.

Melt the butter in a medium-size pan. Stir in the flour and cook for 1 minute. Gradually whisk in the milk a little at a time, stirring constantly until thick and smooth. Simmer for 2 minutes until the flour has cooked. Remove from the heat, stir in the cheese, mustard and salt and pepper. Stir in the crème fraîche for extra richness, if you like. Pour over the macaroni, sprinkle with Parmesan and either serve immediately or, better still, pour into an ovenproof dish and bake, topped with 25 g (1 oz) of breadcrumbs, for 15–20 minutes at 200°C/400°F/Gas 6; fan oven 180°C from cold.

basic white sauce

If you want to make a white sauce to serve with fish or vegetables, simply omit the cheese and mustard. Bring the milk to a simmer, with chopped onion, a bay leaf and a few peppercorns if you like, and then leave off the heat to infuse, to give it more flavour, before stirring it into the flour.

Make a sweet white sauce by adding 1 tablespoon of caster sugar instead of the cheese, mustard and seasoning. This can be served with puddings instead of custard.
Vary the thickness of the sauce by adding more milk for a thinner sauce.

bolognese sauce

preparation time: 15 minutes | cooking time: 30 minutes | serves 4

This classic tomato sauce is simple to make. Add minced beef or lamb or, if you prefer, vegetables, to make a great spaghetti sauce.

Fry the carrot, celery, onion and garlic in oil until the onion is softened but not browned. Add the meat and fry until browned, then pour over the canned tomatoes and their juice, and add the tomato purée. Simmer gently for 30 minutes.

   Add the parsley and check the seasoning. Remove from the heat and serve with 350 g (12 oz) of pasta, cooked until tender and drained.

wine suggestion Spaghetti (or any other pasta) with bolognese sauce would be unthinkable without a good Italian red to go with it. Chianti Classico is an exact match, its keen edge of acidity dealing with the acid in the tomatoes, but other Italian reds such as Montepulciano d'Abruzzo or Barbera from Piedmont work equally well.

1 carrot, peeled and chopped
1 celery stick, chopped
1 onion, chopped
1 garlic clove, crushed
2 tablespoons olive oil
225 g (8 oz) minced beef or lamb
400 g (14 oz) can of tomatoes
2 tablespoons tomato puree
2 tablespoons chopped
**   fresh parsley**
salt and freshly ground
**   black pepper**

pepper and mozzarella pasta sauce

preparation time: 5 minutes | cooking time: 10 minutes | serves 4

Heat 2 tablespoons of olive oil in a frying pan, add 1 orange pepper and 1 red pepper, seeded and cut into strips, and 1 finely chopped onion. Fry for 10–15 minutes, until the onion is tender and the peppers are soft. Add 2 crushed garlic cloves and a 400 g (14 oz) can of chopped tomatoes. Simmer for 10 minutes and then stir in 150 g (5 oz) of cubed mozzarella. Season well. Serve with 350 g (12 oz) of pasta, cooked until tender and drained.

crispy bacon and soft cheese pasta sauce

serves 4 | **preparation time: 5 minutes** | **cooking time: 10 minutes**

Grill 225 g (8 oz) of bacon until crisp, then drain on kitchen paper and snip or chop into pieces. In a small pan, melt 100 g (4 oz) of soft cheese with garlic and herbs and 150 ml (5 fl oz) of single cream over a low heat, stirring until it makes a smooth sauce. Stir in 100 g (4 oz) of frozen peas and cook for 3 minutes or until cooked. Stir in the bacon. Serve with about 350 g (12 oz) of pasta, boiled until tender and drained. Sprinkle with chopped fresh parsley.

tuna and anchovy pasta sauce

serves 4 | **preparation time: 5 minutes** | **cooking time: 10 minutes**

Heat a couple of tablespoons of oil in a pan and add 1 chopped onion. Cook gently until the onion is tender, then add 6 anchovy fillets, 50 g (2 oz) of black or green olives, a can of chopped tomatoes, a pinch of chilli powder and a drained 200 g (7 oz) can of tuna in oil. Season well and simmer for 5 minutes. Serve with 350 g (12 oz) of pasta, boiled until tender and drained.

leek and mascarpone pasta sauce

serves 4 | **preparation time: 5 minutes** | **cooking time: 10 minutes**

Melt 50 g (2 oz) of butter in a frying pan and very gently fry 450 g (1 lb) of thinly sliced leeks until soft but not browned. Pour in 150 ml (5 fl oz) of dry white wine and leave to simmer until the wine has reduced by about half. Add a 250 g (8 oz) tub of mascarpone cheese and 50 g (2 oz) of freshly grated Parmesan. Stir into 350 g (12 oz) of pasta, boiled until tender and drained.

crispy bacon and soft cheese pasta sauce

parmesan risotto

serves 6 | preparation time: 5 minutes | cooking time: 15–20 minutes

This is the most basic and delicious risotto. Add mushrooms, peas, bacon, ham, blue cheese, chopped herbs or any cooked vegetable that takes your fancy, about halfway through cooking.

25 g (1 oz) unsalted butter
5 tablespoons olive oil
1 onion, finely chopped
600 g (1 lb 5 oz) risotto rice
about 1.5 litres (2¾ pints)
good-quality chicken, meat or
vegetable stock, kept at
simmering point
6–7 tablespoons freshly grated
Parmesan cheese
salt and freshly ground
black pepper

In a frying pan, heat the butter and half the olive oil, then fry the onion for about 10 minutes over a low heat until the onion is softened but not browned. Gently stir in the rice and fry for 2–3 minutes.

Add one ladleful of hot stock to the pan and stir frequently; wait until the rice has absorbed all the liquid before adding the next ladleful.

Continue to stir in the stock gradually until the rice is almost completely soft and creamy. This will take up to 20 minutes.

Stir in the cheese and remaining olive oil. Season to taste and serve.

wine suggestion   Red or white will rub along quite happily with classic Parmesan risotto, the red perhaps just shading it. Sangiovese-based Tuscans or Piedmont Barbera are well suited, and would also match the mushroom or tomato variations below. If white is your preference, try characterful Vernaccia di San Gimignano from Tuscany.

risotto variations

Risotto con i funghi **(Mushroom risotto)** Omit the Parmesan and add a clove of crushed garlic to the onion when frying. Soak 25 g (1 oz) of dried porcini mushrooms in a little warm water for 20 minutes. Then, halfway through cooking, add the dried mushrooms and their soaking liquid (discarding any grit at the bottom), plus 350 g (12 oz) of fresh mushrooms, and continue cooking.

Risotto al pomodoro **(Tomato risotto)** Omit the Parmesan. Add 450 g (1 lb) of peeled, seeded and chopped plum tomatoes, 1 tablespoon of tomato purée and 6–8 chopped sun-dried tomatoes halfway through cooking. Stir in 2–3 tablespoons of chopped fresh parsley just before serving.

lentil and vegetable dhal

preparation time: 15 minutes | cooking time: 20 minutes | serves 2

A delicious, satisfying supper using canned lentils for speed.

Place the lentils, bay leaf, coriander and cumin seeds and 300 ml (10 fl oz) of water in a pan and bring to the boil. Cover and simmer for 15 minutes until the lentils are pulpy and most of the water has been absorbed. Discard the bay leaf.

Meanwhile, heat 1 tablespoon of the oil in a small frying pan and fry the onion for about 5 minutes until brown and caramelized. Remove, then set aside. Add the remaining oil, and the garlic and ginger to the pan and cook for 1 minute, until softened. Stir in the courgette and peppers and fry for 3–4 minutes, until lightly charred.

Add the cherry tomatoes, garam masala, turmeric, cooked lentils and fresh coriander and heat through. Season. Spoon on to serving plates and top with the caramelized onions. Garnish with the extra coriander and serve with warmed naan bread.

wine suggestion There are plenty of aromatic Indian seasonings in this dish but nothing searingly hot. A light, scented white is the best bet. A varietally labelled Viognier from the Pays d'Oc will add to the overall spiciness, as would a simple Gewürztraminer from Chile or Hungary.

410 g can of brown lentils, drained and rinsed

1 bay leaf

1 teaspoon coriander seeds, lightly crushed

1 teaspoon cumin seeds, lightly crushed

3 tablespoons vegetable oil

1 onion, sliced

1 garlic clove, crushed

2 cm (¾ in) piece of fresh root ginger, finely chopped

1 courgette, cut into chunks

1 red pepper, seeded and sliced

10 cherry tomatoes, halved

1 teaspoon garam masala

½ teaspoon turmeric

a handful of fresh coriander leaves, chopped, plus extra to garnish

salt and freshly ground black pepper

chick-pea curry

preparation time: 10 minutes | cooking time: 15 minutes | serves 4–6

A quick satisfying vegetarian curry. Serve simply with naan bread or poppadums.

Heat the sunflower oil in a large pan, then add the onion, potatoes, carrots and garlic and fry for 3 minutes until golden. Stir in the curry paste, turmeric, chopped ginger, tomatoes, red pepper, chick-peas and vegetable stock, then season well. Bring to the boil, cover and simmer gently for 10 minutes.

Meanwhile, make the raita: mix the cucumber with the mint and yoghurt, then season to taste. Spoon into a small dish and chill until ready to serve.

Top the chick-pea curry with raita. Serve with poppadums and/or rice.

wine suggestion An earthy dish that requires earthy flavours in the accompanying wine, this curry will be best suited by a midweight red from southern Europe. Cahors or Costiè res de Nîmes from the south of France, a big Spanish red from Navarra or Barbera from Piedmont will all work.

1 tablespoon sunflower oil

1 large onion, chopped

450 g (1 lb) potatoes,
   finely chopped

300 g (10 oz) carrots,
   finely chopped

2 garlic cloves, chopped

2 tablespoons mild curry paste

1 teaspoon turmeric

4 cm (1½ in) piece of fresh root
   ginger, peeled and
   finely chopped

400 g (14 oz) tomatoes,
   cut into chunks

1 red pepper, seeded and cubed

2 x 410 g can of chick-peas,
   drained

150 ml (5 fl oz) vegetable stock

salt and freshly ground
   black pepper

4 poppadums, to serve

FOR THE RAITA:

½ cucumber, chopped

2 tablespoons chopped fresh mint

150 g (5 oz) natural yoghurt

chick-pea curry

meat

tenderness is a highly prized quality for meat and most methods of preparing and cooking meat aim to produce tender and succulent results. Meat should also be tasty, but modern methods of intensive agriculture and use of growth promoters and other drugs mean that livestock is brought up to the weight for slaughter younger than ever before. Meat produced from young animals can be tender but it may lack texture. And, in intensive agriculture, animals do not use their muscles – they are mainly sedentary or nearly sedentary. This, their bland diet and their immaturity all have a detrimental affect on the flavour of meat. Moreover, modern butchery does not hang meat to develop flavour. All this means that today's meat is somewhat insipid compared with what meat used to be like. However, as many people are used to this type of meat, and probably do not remember any other type, they can find the stronger and gamier flavours of meat produced organically somewhat surprising, if not off-putting.

what to look for when buying meat

Whichever style of meat you choose to buy, red meat should look fresh and moist and the fat should be creamy white and not dried. The age of the animal, how it was slaughtered and how long it has been hung determine the tenderness of meat. Hanging is a process that relaxes the muscle and allows certain enzymes (proteins that produce chemical changes) to alter the composition of the muscle, to make it more tender. Most meat today is not hung for long, so the emphasis is on buying cuts of meat that are known to be more tender – and these tend to be more expensive. Marinades, together with longer cooking methods such as casseroling, will add flavour and assist in tenderizing less expensive cuts of meat.

When buying meat to roast, allow 100–175 g (4–6 oz) per person for a boneless joint or 225–350 g (8–12 oz) if the meat is on the bone.

roasting meat

Because roasting is a dry method of cooking, it is important to choose the best quality and most tender cuts of meat. Meat on the bone can be moister, have more flavour and less shrinkage, but boned meats cook more evenly, slice more easily and have little wastage. Some cuts of meat (especially beef) benefit from a quick pan-frying first, to seal in the juices and caramelize the surface for extra flavour and colour. It also helps smaller cuts of meat to begin cooking quicker, which shortens the cooking time and prevents them from drying out.

The meat must fit in the pan. If the pan is too large, the juices will burn during cooking. If the pan is too small or too deep, the meat steams. To flavour the gravy and prevent meat from stewing in the fat and juices at the bottom of the pan, place any bones and a quartered onion and carrot under the meat. Alternatively, place the roast on a metal roasting rack. If the juices in the bottom of the pan start to burn, pour in a little water or stock.

what joint to buy for roasting

beef

Fillet Small, very tender joint that cooks quickly. Ideal for Beef Wellington (roasted in puff pastry).
Fore rib Roast on the bone, or have it chined to loosen the bone, or boned and rolled.
Prime rib More expensive, best roasted on the bone.
Sirloin The tenderest cut from the back of the loin – either roast on the bone (chined) or boned and rolled.
Top side Rolled rump, with a good flavour and texture; cheaper but not so tender, so needs to be cooked more slowly.

lamb

Leg or half leg The most popular, tender and flavoursome cut. Choose either the shank/knuckle or fillet from the top end.

roasting times for meat

Meat	Preference	Roasting time	Temperature
beef	Rare	20 minutes per 450 g (1 lb) + 20 minutes	190°C/375°F/Gas 5/ fan oven 170°C
	Medium	25 minutes per 450 g (1 lb) + 25 minutes	
	Well done	30 minutes per 450 g (1 lb) + 30 minutes	
lamb	Medium	25 minutes per 450 g (1 lb) + 25 minutes	180°C/350°F/Gas 4/ fan oven 160°C
	Well done	30 minutes per 450 g (1 lb) + 30 minutes	
pork	Medium	30 minutes per 450 g (1 lb) + 30 minutes	180°C/350°F/Gas 4/ fan oven 160°C
	Well done	35 minutes per 450 g (1 lb) + 35 minutes	

Allow 5 minutes extra per 450 g (1 lb) for boned and rolled joints.

Loin Either the chump end or rib end. Roasted on or off the bone; off, it is rolled and can be stuffed.

Rack of lamb Cut from the best end of neck, this is like a row of cutlets. Very tender meat. Carve between the bones to give individual cutlets.

Shoulder Makes a large roasting joint. Fattier, but often with more flavour. Because it contains the blade bone it is more awkward to carve.

pork

Belly of pork About half fat, half meat, usually boned, stuffed and rolled.

Fillet/Tenderloin Lean, expensive cut bought in one long piece for roasting or cut into steaks for frying.

Leg Either knuckle (cheaper, more bone) or fillet end.

Loin Like large chops. Can be fore loin, from the rib end, or hind loin, which is better for roasting. Choose off the bone, or on the bone, chined to loosen the bone and make it easier to carve.

Shoulder (hand and spring) Can be roasted on the bone or boned, stuffed and rolled.

roasting pork

Pork should never be undercooked – always pierce the meat and check that the juices run clear. In the past, pork was often fatty but new breeds have meat so lean that leg or loin joints need to be basted with the pan juices or roasted in foil or a roasting bag to stop them from drying out. When covering meat with foil or a casserole lid, allow an extra 5 minutes cooking per 450 g (1 lb). If boning and rolling at home, tie the joint with kitchen string at evenly placed intervals.

Pork is often 'chined': the bone is loosened by the butcher (or you) to make it easier to carve.

- A really sharp carving knife and a fork with a safety guard are vital utensils. A board with spikes to hold the meat is helpful.
- All joints benefit from a resting period of at least 10 minutes at the end of cooking, which makes them easier to carve and more juicy. Leave the joint in the switched-off oven, if you like.
- Carve joints off the bone into slices of whatever thickness you prefer. Carve across the grain of the meat (this makes the meat more tender to chew). Lamb is usually cut thicker than pork or beef.
- A leg is usually carved starting with a V down to the bone and then slicing from each side of the V.
- A shoulder is placed meat-side down (skin-side up) on the carving surface and slices are cut straight down (like cutting a cake) to the bone and then lifted off.

frying and grilling meat

Use only the tenderest cuts of meat for these quick-cooking methods. Steaks, chops and cutlets are the most suitable. Excess fat should be removed since it will become tough, but a little gives flavour and helps retain the moisture in the meat. Meat should be no more than 5 cm (2 in) thick. Beef and lamb should be grilled or fried quickly over a high heat, but pork should be cooked more slowly or it will become dry and tough. Pork also benefits from being basted with a sauce to help keep it moist. Only add salt at the last minute or it will draw out the juices and prevent the meat from browning properly. Cubed meat can be threaded on skewers with vegetables before grilling or barbecuing.

cuts for grilling and frying

Beef Fillet, rump, sirloin.

Veal Fillet, loin chops, best end cutlet, rump.

Pork Spare-rib chops, loin chops, chump chops, best end cutlets, spare ribs, fillet, tenderloin.

Lamb Best end cutlets, loin chops, chump chops, steaks from fillet end of leg.

frying times for steaks (time given is total, not per side)

Cut	Rare	Medium	Well done
Tenderloin/fillet/tournedos	4 minutes	5–7 minutes	
T-bone/porterhouse	6–7 minutes	9–12 minutes	12–15 minutes
Sirloin	6–7 minutes	12–14 minutes	16–20 minutes
Rump/minute steak	5–6 minutes	7–10 minutes	10–12 minutes

steaks

Rare and half-cooked meat is tenderer than well cooked meat, because the cooking process, which sets the fibre and dries the juices, will not have toughened the muscle. Chefs often serve steak undercooked to preserve tenderness. *Rump steak* is cut across the grain of the rump and is about 2 cm (¾ in) thick. *Fillet steak* is taken from the back of the beef, between rib and rump where the sirloin joint (or steak) is also situated. *Tournedos* is the name given to a neat round steak cut from a larger fillet steak. *Steak (or beef) medallions* are thinner pieces, also cut from the fillet steak. *Sirloin* steak covers a larger area than fillet steak and can be cut into individual steaks or *T-bone steaks*, when it includes part of the rib. *Porterhouse* steak is a double-sized T-bone steak.

slower cooking methods

stewing meat

Less expensive cuts of meat can be used for stewing, such as beef chuck steak or brisket, lamb breast, knuckles or scrag end of lamb or pork. These cuts are generally less tender and require longer, slower, moist cooking (though more tender cuts of meat can be used to make quicker stews). The meat is cut into evenly-sized cubes and usually fried in the casserole or stew pan until browned, before adding vegetables and stock. The meat is often coated with seasoned flour to thicken the liquid, or cornflour mixed with water can be added at the end.

braising or pot-roasting

This method is generally used for whole cuts of meat, particularly beef. Tougher cuts with plenty of flavour but little fat remain moist, while gristle dissolves to give a syrupy texture to the sauce. The meat can be marinated first. The meat is fried gently in the casserole before adding plenty of vegetables – usually cut into large chunks, since the cooking can be up to 3 hours or more. Often wine is added, plus stock and plenty of herbs. Partially braised meat and vegetables can be used as pie fillings. Transfer the mixture to a cold pie dish containing a pie funnel, then put on a pastry lid and continue cooking in the oven.

cuts for stewing or braising

Beef Chuck, brisket, flank, neck, topside, silverside; also shin (foreleg), shin or leg (hind leg) for pies.
Veal Leg, shoulder, middle neck, scrag, breast.
Lamb Chops, loin, leg, scrag, breast, and knuckle.
Pork Cubed shoulder or leg, hocks.

offal

Offal includes all the edible internal parts of the animal and extremities such as feet. White offal includes brain, sweetbreads, stomach, chitterlings and tripe. Tripe is available from specialist butchers. It is creamy yellow or white if it has been bleached. It needs to be soaked in cold water, rinsed and dried before being cut into pieces for use. Red offal includes head, heart and kidneys. Heart is rich in B vitamins and minerals but also very high in cholesterol. Head is mainly used in sausages. Liver and kidney are usually the only offal cooked at home.

Lamb's, pig's, calf's and ox liver are very rich sources of folates, other B vitamins and vitamin A, due to the intensive feed used in modern farming (a government health warning states pregnant women should not eat liver because too much vitamin A causes birth defects). Liver should be glistening and dark brown. It has a strong, distinctive flavour and is very soft, so that it cuts and minces easily but becomes tough very quickly when cooked. Calf's liver, the most expensive, is paler brown than other kinds and has a much more delicate flavour (with a price to match). Any membrane should be removed before slicing. Ox and pig's liver can be soaked in milk for an hour to reduce the strength of flavour before braising (pig's) or stewing (ox). Calf's liver is usually pan-fried because it is more delicate. Liver is usually dipped in seasoned flour before frying. Chicken livers can be grilled or fried and chopped or used in pâté and terrines.

Lamb's, ox, pig's and veal kidneys are, like liver, low in fat but high in cholesterol; they also contain iron and B vitamins. Kidneys should be plump and moist and from light brown to red-brown in colour. Peel off the outer membrane and halve the kidney; then snip out the white core with scissors. As with liver, veal and lamb's kidneys have a sweeter, more delicate flavour than larger animals'. Soak ox and pig's kidneys in cold water for 30 minutes to mute the flavour; drain and dry well before grilling, sautéing or braising. Ox kidney is the type traditionally used in steak and kidney pies and puddings.

Pig's trotters have become a fashionable food in some restaurants. The pig's feet are rich in gelatine, which is released during long, slow simmering before grilling or baking.

sausages

Fresh sausages are made from chopped, minced or blended meats that are neither cured nor smoked. The meat, usually pork or beef or a mixture, is blended with cereal, spices, seasonings and food additives and usually stuffed into casings. Fresh sausages differ from salamis made from cured and raw meat that is sliced and eaten raw, because they must be cooked thoroughly before eating. Frying and grilling are popular cooking methods and, during cooking, the colour turns from pink to grey-brown. Sausages can also be baked, braised and barbecued and even boiled or added to casseroles, pies and stews.

The addition of different spices, herbs and other ingredients such as onions, leeks and diced apple means a wide variety of sausages is available today. All butchers and supermarkets will have their own recipes and specialities. Almost any meat can be used in sausages and, in commercially prepared sausages, many parts of the animal that we might not think of as meat, such as intestines, fat, gristle, head, skin and so on, are used. Good-quality sausages will contain a high proportion of meat, at least 80% (check the amount on the pack). Cheap sausages contain a lot of additives, to make the low-quality meat tasty and to give texture. Preservatives, colourings and flavourings are commonly added. Natural casings, such as intestines and stomachs (for haggis), have largely been replaced by synthetic casings.

types of sausages

Andouille sausage Contains chitterlings or tripe as the main ingredient, and is like a salami; *andouillette* is

foie gras and haggis

Foie gras literally means 'fat liver'. To make their livers into a delicacy, ducks and geese are force-fed grain. The enlarged liver is pale and creamy and is either eaten raw (rarely available and only in France during the season before Christmas) or bought ready cooked from a delicatessen. Pasteurized and preserved *foie gras* is more widely available in jars and cans. *Foie gras* is an expensive delicacy and used mainly as a garnish or canapé.

Haggis is a mixture of chopped offal and entrails, mixed with cereal and spices and originally enclosed in a sheep's stomach. The basic recipe contains lungs, liver, heart, beef or mutton fat, oatmeal, seasoning and spices such as cayenne pepper and nutmeg. The skin is pricked to prevent it from bursting and the haggis is boiled for about 3 hours. It is ceremonially served with mashed swede (neeps) on Burn's Night, 25 January, when its entry at functions is toasted with whisky and accompanied by a piper and a recitation of the ode *To a Haggis (Great chieftain o' the puddin-race!)*, by Robert Burns.

a small sausage with similar ingredients that is grilled and served hot with beans or cabbage, or bistro-style with mustard and puréed potatoes.

Black pudding A large, circular, black sausage made from fresh pigs' blood, suet and seasonings. It was brought to Britain by the Romans, whose recipes were highly spiced. Traditionally, black pudding is made in the Midlands and north of England. The name varies from region to region and the recipe varies according to local versions. Black pudding is called *boudin noir* in France, where it is traditionally served on Christmas Eve after Midnight Mass. In Spain it is called *morcilla*, in Italy *biroldo* and in Ireland *drisheen*. Black pudding contains high levels of fat (and cholesterol) and is rich in iron, due to the high blood content.

Chipolata A small pork or pork and beef sausage around half the size of a standard sausage. Cooked as for standard sausages but for a shorter time.

Cumberland sausage Made from coarse-cut pork and quite spicy. Instead of being twisted into links, the sausage is sold by length from a long coil.

Frankfurter Originated in Germany. It is sold cooked and can be eaten cold. Made from a mix of beef and/or pork, mildly spiced and usually smoked; either in casing or skinless. Most widely used in hot dogs for which they are reheated by simmering in water for 3–5 minutes. There are many similar German sausages that are part-cooked and heated before serving, for example, *knackwurst* (pork and beef flavoured with cumin), *bierwurst* (pork and beef flavoured with garlic) and eaten with beer, *schinkenwurst* (made from ham).

Glamorgan sausages Show that sausages can be made from ingredients other than meat; some are made of fish but the Glamorgan sausage is made of cheese and leeks and is not in a casing.

Lorne sausages Scottish, they neither have a casing nor are they cylindrical, but square.

Merguez A sausage from North Africa made of pure beef (to comply with Islamic dietary law) coloured with red peppers and seasoned with harissa. Eaten grilled with cous cous. French versions can be made with other meats.

Mortadella sausages Italian and made from pork. They are sold cooked and may be sliced and served or added to sauces.

Morteau sausages French and pure pork, these sausages are usually smoked and intended for poaching and serving with cabbage, lentils or potatoes.

Saveloys Can be made from pork, beef or any part of a pig or cow, which is dried, smoked and then cooked. As saveloy is already cooked, it can be eaten without further cooking, but is often simmered for 5 minutes and served with mustard or tomato sauce in a bread roll – in the north of England it can be served with pease pudding.

Tomato sausages These are popular in the Midlands. They are standard butcher's sausages coloured with tomato purée.

Toulouse sausage A long, fresh, coarsely textured pork and pork-fat sausage, flavoured with pepper, garlic and sometimes wine. It takes its name from the city of Toulouse in France. The sausages are usually longer than standard British sausages and are traditionally coiled and grilled and used in soups and stews, such as the classic French cassoulet.

White pudding or boudin blanc Made from white meat such as pork and mixed with cream, eggs, onions and breadcrumbs – not as high in fat as black pudding and not widely available.

minced meat

Mince is meat that has been ground or minced; the fat content will vary depending on the cuts of meat and fat included but, generally, it will be quite high in fat. Meat regulations stipulate the fat content of mince: not more than 20% for beef; not more than 25% for lamb; and not more than 30% for pork. 'Lean' mince must have not more than 7% fat.

Supermarkets have their own grading system: 'extra-lean' or 'healthy' mince will have the lowest fat content and the exact percentage should be stated on the pack. Economy mince will be higher in fat. Minced poultry tends to be leaner.

uses for minced meat

Beef Cottage pie, burgers, meatballs, stuffings for vegetables, e.g. sweet peppers, vine leaves.
Lamb Kebabs, kofte, kibbeh, shepherd's pie, meatballs, stuffings for vegetables.
Pork Stuffings for vegetables, meatballs.
Veal Pies, meatballs, stuffings for vegetables.
Turkey Burgers, meat balls, vegetable stuffing.

spiced roast beef

serves 8 | preparation time: 10 minutes | cooking time: about 1¾ hours

We've added a mustard, soy and honey glaze to the beef but, if you prefer a classic roast, just omit the extra flavourings.

1.5 kg (3 lb) sirloin of beef
1 tablespoon English mustard
2 teaspoons sea salt
2 teaspoons crushed black peppercorns
a good pinch of freshly grated nutmeg
1 tablespoon soy sauce
1 tablespoon honey
1 onion, peeled and quartered
1 tablespoon plain flour
150 ml (5 fl oz) beef stock or vegetable cooking water
150 ml (5 fl oz) red wine
salt and freshly ground black pepper

Pre-heat the oven to 190°C/ 375°F/Gas 5; fan oven 170°C from cold. Weigh the meat and calculate the cooking time according to the chart on page 98. Mix the mustard, salt, peppercorns, nutmeg, soy sauce and honey together to make a paste. Rub all over the surface of the meat. Place on a rack in the roasting tin. Add the onion to the roasting tin. Roast in the centre of the oven for the required length of time.

Remove the meat from the oven and allow to rest, covered with foil.

Meanwhile, make the gravy. Place the roasting tin on the hob or pour the juices into a small pan. Add the flour and cook for a few minutes, stirring all the time until the flour has browned. Gradually stir in the stock until smooth. Pour in the wine and boil for a minute or two until the gravy has thickened. Taste and season. Strain the gravy into a serving jug and keep it warm.

wine suggestion Choose a red with a good tinge of spice in the flavour if you're using the suggested glaze for this roast. A Portuguese red from Estremadura or the Alentejo would be good, or perhaps a southern Italian red such as Aglianico del Vulture or Primitivo.

menu: sunday lunch 1

prawn cocktail with whisky mayonnaise (page 154)

spiced roast beef and yorkshire pudding (pages 104–105)

perfect roast potatoes (170)

red cabbage with apple and port (page 171)

tarte tartin (page 191)

yorkshire pudding

preparation time: 5 minutes | cooking time: 15–20 minutes | serves 4

The secret to successful Yorkshire pudding is to cook it in a tin with very hot fat. Cooking in china or ovenproof ware will make the batter soggy.

Pre-heat the oven to 220°C/425°F/Gas 7/fan oven 200°C. Sift the flour into a mixing bowl. Add the salt. Make a well in the centre and add the egg. Add half the milk and whisk in the flour until smooth. Gradually add the remaining milk and beat until well mixed.

Spoon a little oil or lard into a four-cup Yorkshire pudding pan or into 10–12 individual bun tins. Place in the top of the pre-heated oven for 5 minutes until the fat shows a haze and is really hot. Pour in the batter and return to the oven. Bake for 15–20 minutes until the batter has risen and is crisp and brown.

50 g (2 oz) plain flour

a pinch of salt

1 egg

150 ml (5 fl oz) milk

2 tablespoons sunflower oil or lard

yorkshire pudding variations

Add a teaspoon of wholegrain mustard to the batter or a few chopped fried onions and some sage or rosemary leaves.

Make double the quantities for a larger pudding cooked in a small roasting tin or an 18–20 cm (7–8 in) shallow tin. Bake for about 40–45 minutes.

peppered steaks with garlic potatoes and red wine gravy

serves 2 | preparation time: 10 minutes | cooking time: 40 minutes

250 g (9 oz) potatoes, cut into
small cubes
6 unpeeled garlic cloves
1 teaspoon olive oil
sea salt and freshly ground
black pepper

FOR THE STEAK AND GRAVY:
2 × 150 g (5 oz) beef medallions
2 tablespoons cracked
black peppercorns
1 tablespoon olive oil
150 ml (5 fl oz) red wine
1 teaspoon chopped fresh
rosemary leaves, plus sprigs
to garnish
1 tablespoon redcurrant jelly

Pre-heat the oven to 200°C/400°F/Gas 6; fan oven 180°C from cold. Put the potatoes and garlic in a small roasting tin. Drizzle with oil, season and shake the pan so the potatoes are tossed in the oil. Cook in the oven for 30–40 minutes, until tender and golden.

Pre-heat a griddle or heavy-based frying pan. Place the pepper on a plate and press both sides of the steak well on to the pepper. Brush the steaks with oil, sprinkle with a little salt and cook on the griddle for 3–4 minutes on each side, until well browned but still a little pink in the centre.

Meanwhile, pour the wine into a pan and bring to the boil. Add the rosemary, redcurrant jelly and vinegar and boil rapidly for 5 minutes, until reduced by half. Season to taste.

Spoon the potatoes on to two serving plates and top with the peppered steaks. Spoon around the red wine gravy, garnish with rosemary and serve immediately.

wine suggestion Bring out your biggest, spiciest red for this dish. The crushed black pepper on the steaks demands it. Northern Rhône Syrah (Crozes-Hermitage or St-Joseph) will cope with it, as will the burliest Australian Shiraz. Don't worry about youthful tannin; it will be thrown into relief by the pepper.

menu: autumn supper party

mushroom and parmesan baked eggs (page 80)

peppered steaks with garlic potatoes and red wine gravy

(page 106)

chocolate mousse cups (page 219)

peppered steaks with garlic potatoes and red wine gravy

beef tortilla wraps

serves 2 | preparation time: 15 minutes | cooking time: about 25 minutes

Minced beef makes a very quick supper. Serve the meat sauce on its own, with rice, or rolled up in these soft flour tortillas. Tortillas are readily available now in supermarkets.

1 tablespoon sunflower oil
2 garlic cloves, crushed
2 green chillies, seeded and chopped
1 red pepper, seeded and chopped
225 g (8 oz) lean minced beef
2 teaspoons ground coriander
2 teaspoons ground cumin
230 g (7½ oz) can of chopped tomatoes
1 beef stock cube
½ bunch of fresh coriander, chopped
1 avocado, peeled, stoned and sliced
salt and freshly ground black pepper

TO SERVE:
4 soft tortillas
4 tablespoons soured cream

Heat the oil in a large saucepan over a medium heat. Add the garlic, chillies, red pepper, mince, ground coriander and cumin. Stir to break up the mince, then add the tomatoes with their juice and crumble in the stock cube. Season to taste with salt and freshly ground black pepper.

Bring to the boil, then leave to simmer for 15 minutes, stirring occasionally. Warm the tortillas for 1 minute in the microwave or as directed on the packet.

Stir the coriander and avocado into the mince mixture, then spoon it along the centre of each tortilla. Add a spoonful of soured cream and roll up like a pancake. Serve immediately.

wine suggestion The minced beef and chillies in these tortillas make them an obvious red wine dish, but you will need a brawny specimen to do them justice. Spanish Garnacha or Argentinian Malbec would suit the mood, but southern-hemisphere Shiraz, or even a strapping California Zinfandel, will meet the challenge too.

roast pork with apricot and pine nut stuffing

preparation time: 20 minutes | cooking time: about 2½ hours | serves 8

A succulent joint of pork with a fruity stuffing and crisp crackling makes Sunday lunch with friends a really special meal.

Make the stuffing: heat the butter and oil in a pan and gently fry the onion until softened. Mix the apricots, pine nuts, sage, garlic and breadcrumbs, then stir in the onion and seasoning. Stir in the beaten egg and mix well.

Pre-heat the oven to 180°C/350°F/Gas 4; fan oven 160°C from cold. Place the joint, skin-side down, on a flat surface and trim away any loose fat or connective tissue to give a good shape. Spoon the stuffing along the centre, roll up the joint and tie with a string at 2.5 cm (1 in) intervals.

Weigh the stuffed joint to calculate the cooking time (see the chart on page 98). Sprinkle the salt evenly over the skin. Place in a roasting tin and then in the oven and cook for the required time.

Remove from the oven, cover in foil and allow it to rest. Meanwhile, make the gravy. Pour off most of the fat from the roasting tin, leaving behind about 5 tablespoons of the juices.

Stir the flour into the juices in the roasting tin and cook for 1 minute, stirring. Slowly stir in the cider or apple juice and the stock until smooth. Boil rapidly for 2–3 minutes, then season. Strain the gravy into a serving jug and keep warm.

Cut the string from the joint and cut through the fat just underneath the crackling. Remove and cut into pieces. Carve the pork into thin slices and serve with gravy, crackling, apple sauce and vegetables.

wine suggestion A red with plenty of aromatic character will cope with the fruit and fresh herbs in the stuffing. One of the sturdier *cru* wines of Beaujolais (Morgon or Moulin-à-Vent) will match it well, or you could go down the Pinot Noir route, via California, Oregon or New Zealand.

1.75 kg (4 lb) boned loin of pork, skin scored (see below) at 5 mm (¼ in) intervals

1 tablespoon salt

FOR THE STUFFING:

25 g (1 oz) butter

1 tablespoon sunflower oil

1 onion, finely chopped

100 g (4 oz) dried ready-to-eat apricots, chopped

25 g (1 oz) pine nuts, toasted

1 tablespoon chopped fresh sage

2 garlic cloves, crushed

100 g (4 oz) fresh white breadcrumbs

1 egg, beaten

FOR THE GRAVY:

2 teaspoons plain flour

150 ml (5 fl oz) cider or apple juice

150 ml (5 fl oz) vegetable or pork stock

salt and freshly ground black pepper

tips and accompaniments

For perfect crackling choose a joint that has a thick, dry skin. Score rind deeply at 5 mm (¼ in) intervals using the tip of a sharp knife.

Do not baste during cooking. If the rind has not crackled, remove it and snip into strips with scissors, then place under the grill.

Apple sauce Place 450 g (1 lb) of chopped cooking apples in a pan with 3 tablespoons of water. Cover with a disc of buttered greaseproof paper. Cook gently for 10 minutes, until softened. Beat apples to a pulp. Add sugar to taste and stir in a knob of butter before serving.

spicy pork stir-fry with sesame noodles

serves 4 | preparation time: 25 minutes | cooking time: 5 minutes

350 g (12 oz) lean pork fillet or stir-fry pork strips
5 tablespoons hoisin sauce
1 garlic clove, crushed
½ a small red chilli, seeded and chopped
1 tablespoon rice wine or sherry
1 tablespoon soy sauce
2 tablespoons sunflower oil
4 spring onions, sliced diagonally
175 g (6 oz) mangetout, cut into strips

FOR THE NOODLES:
250 g (9 oz) pack of egg noodles
1 teaspoon sunflower oil
100 g (4 oz) beansprouts
1 teaspoon sesame oil

Cut the pork fillet into thin slices, then cut into strips and place in a glass or china bowl (or place stir-fry strips in bowl). Mix hoisin sauce, garlic, chilli, rice wine or sherry and soy sauce together. Pour over pork and allow to marinate for 15 minutes.

Heat a wok over a high heat, add the oil and heat to smoking point. Lift the pork out of the marinade using a slotted spoon and add to wok. Stir-fry for 2–3 minutes. Add the spring onions, mangetout and any remaining marinade. Stir-fry for another 2–3 minutes, until the pork is tender.

Cook the noodles according to the instructions on the pack and drain them well.

Fry the beansprouts in the sunflower oil for 1–2 minutes. Add the noodles and sprinkle with sesame oil. Serve with the pork.

wine suggestion A classic match with Chinese food is muskily perfumed Alsace Gewürztraminer, but Pinot Gris, dry Muscat or Riesling from that region are all sympathetic partners. The hoisin marinade here, though, is sufficiently rich and piquant to take a light red. Try lightly chilled Brouilly from Beaujolais.

menu: sunday lunch 2

red pepper, tomato and garlic soup (page 60)

roast pork with apricot and pine nut stuffing (page 109)

vegetables

easy lemon tart (page 192)

spicy pork stir-fry with sesame noodles

sticky ribs

serves 4 | preparation time: 8 minutes | cooking time: 45 minutes

Sweet, sticky and using storecupboard ingredients: everyone will love these. They are great barbecued, too, but beware, they burn quickly. It's best to cook them in the oven and finish off on the barbecue for the last 10 minutes or so.

12–16 (depending on size) pork spare ribs
6 tablespoons tomato ketchup
4 tablespoons Worcestershire sauce
2 tablespoons Dijon mustard
a pinch of chilli powder
4 tablespoons muscovado sugar

Pre-heat the oven to 180°C/350°F/Gas 4; fan oven 160°C from cold. Place the ribs in a single layer in a roasting tin. Mix together the ketchup, Worcestershire sauce, mustard, chilli powder and sugar, then pour the spicy sauce over the ribs.

Bake the ribs for 45 minutes, turning halfway through and brushing them with the sauce occasionally.

Serve with garlic bread and a salad.

wine suggestion This irresistible barbecue dish needs a good, earthy barbecue red. A certain amount of rough-edged rusticity won't go amiss, but aim for ripe, juicy fruit too. California Zinfandel, Pinotage from South Africa, or simple Australian Shiraz or Grenache are the principal runners and riders.

quick and tasty ideas for pork chops or steaks

Honey and ginger glaze Mix 2 tablespoons of honey with a 2.5cm (1 in) piece of peeled and grated fresh root ginger, 1 tablespoon of soy sauce and a crushed clove of garlic. Brush over the pork chops before grilling.

Sticky marmalade glaze Mix together 2 tablespoons of orange marmalade, 1 tablespoon of Dijon mustard and a pinch of ground ginger.

Mushroom, sherry and crème fraîche sauce Dust a pork steak with 1 teaspoon of plain flour mixed with salt, pepper and a pinch of dried sage. Fry in oil and butter until browned. Add ¼ onion, sliced, and fry until it is tender. Add 50 g (2 oz) of sliced mushrooms and fry for 2–3 minutes. Then add about 1 tablespoon of sherry and stir well. Pour in 2–3 tablespoons of crème fraîche or double cream and simmer for 2–3 minutes. Serve with noodles and green vegetables.

traditional baked ham

preparation time: 10 minutes | cooking time: about 3 hours | serves 12–14

A traditional ham is perfect for feeding a large number of people for a special occasion such as Christmas or Easter or for a buffet.

When you buy a gammon, check whether soaking is required; most gammons are mildly cured, which means soaking isn't necessary. If soaking is needed, place the gammon in a large pan, cover with cold water and leave it for at least 6 hours or even overnight; then drain.

Place the gammon in a pan and fill it with water; boil and drain. Return to the pan and pour in half of the wine or cider and enough water to cover. Add the peppercorns, onions, celery and bay leaves. Bring to the boil and skim off any scum; cover and simmer for 2–2½ hours.

Remove the pan from the heat and set aside until cool. Pre-heat the oven to 180°C/350°F/Gas 4; fan oven 160°C from cold. Drain the gammon and carefully cut away the skin, leaving the layer of white fat intact. Using a sharp knife, score the fat diagonally to make a diamond pattern.

Spread the mustard over the scored surface and sprinkle with the sugar. Place the gammon in a roasting tin. Pour the remaining wine or cider into the tin; bake for 30 minutes, basting once.

Remove the cooked ham from the oven and leave to rest for 15 minutes.

3–3.5 kg (7–8 lb) half leg of gammon
a bottle of dry white wine or 750 ml (1¼ pints) dry cider
12 peppercorns
2 onions, quartered
a handful of celery leaves
2 bay leaves
2 tablespoons wholegrain mustard
5 tablespoons demerara sugar

wine suggestion An aromatic white with a touch of residual sweetness and a little gentle acidity is the first-choice wine for baked ham. German or Austrian Kabinett or Spätlese Rieslings are superb.

tips and a variation

Carve slices from one side of the ham, cutting diagonally to achieve an even thickness. When you reach the bone, insert the knife at a flatter angle and slice across the top of the bone. Turn over the leg to carve slices from the other sides.

Alternative glazes for ham Mix 1 tablespoon of Dijon mustard and 3 tablespoons of clear honey, then brush half over the scored fat. Top with sliced oranges and stud with cloves. Bake at 180°C/350°F/Gas 4/fan oven 160°C for 30 minutes.

If half a ham is more than you need, choose a middle cut or corner piece of boned gammon instead and use only half the amount of all the other ingredients. Follow the method as usual, but calculate the total cooking time at 30 minutes per 450 g (1 lb). A 2.25–2.75 kg (5–6 lb) gammon will serve 8–10 people.

gammon with leek and cheese crumb topping

serves 4 | preparation time: 10 minutes | cooking time: about 8 minutes

A quick, tasty supper dish. If you like the sweet combination of pineapple with gammon, add a chopped pineapple ring to the crumb mixture instead of the leek. Serve with grilled tomatoes and new potato salad.

3 slices of white bread
15 g (½ oz) butter
½ a leek, thinly sliced
4 gammon steaks,
about 150 g (5 oz) each
1 teaspoon wholegrain mustard
25 g (1 oz) Parmesan cheese,
freshly grated
freshly ground black pepper

Cut the crusts off the bread and place it in a food processor. Whizz into crumbs, or dice very finely.

Melt the butter in a small frying pan. Add the leek and fry for 5 minutes or until softened. Remove from the heat and stir in the cheese and mustard. Snip any rind on the gammon so that it doesn't curl up.

Pre-heat the grill to high. Grill the gammon for 5 minutes on one side. Then turn over, spread the other side with the leek mixture and scatter over the breadcrumbs and Parmesan cheese. Sprinkle with black pepper. Grill for 2–3 minutes, until golden and bubbling.

wine suggestion The topping in this dish is quite robustly flavoured, and calls for a red with a certain amount of spicy presence but not too much tannin. The southern Rhône or Languedoc will prove happy hunting-grounds for this style – perhaps an oak-aged Corbières.

creamy curried lamb

preparation time: 20 minutes | cooking time: 55 minutes | serves 4

A simple, mild and rich curry. Serve with rice or naan bread for a satisfying supper

Heat the oil in a large saucepan. Add the onion and fry for 3–4 minutes, until tender. Add the lamb and fry until browned. Add the garlic, ginger and all the spices and cook for 2–3 minutes, stirring constantly. Add the tomatoes, tomato purée and salt and enough boiling water just to cover the meat. Bring to the boil, cover with a lid and simmer for 45 minutes, until the meat is tender.

Remove the lid and boil rapidly to reduce the liquid by a third, to make a rich sauce. Remove from the heat and stir in the cream. Heat gently to warm through.

wine suggestion Cabernet Sauvignon or Merlot reds, or blends thereof, are good matches for an Indian red meat dish, and you needn't worry about the hot chilli spice doing them damage. They can cope quite well, especially if there is a little tannin in the wine. Think California or Chile, or a big Rhône red like Gigondas.

3 tablespoons sunflower oil

1 onion, finely chopped

900 g (2 lb) boneless leg of lamb, cubed

1 garlic clove, crushed

2.5 cm (1 in) piece of fresh root ginger, peeled and grated

1 tablespoon ground coriander

2 teaspoons ground cumin

½ teaspoon chilli powder

6 cardamom pods, bruised

1 teaspoon turmeric

1 cinnamon stick, broken

6 cloves

250 g (9 oz) tomatoes, quartered

1 tablespoon tomato purée

½ teaspoon salt

150 ml (5 fl oz) double cream

five-minute gravy and a quick marinade for lamb

Redcurrant and rosemary gravy Lightly fry ½ a sliced onion in 1 tablespoon of olive oil until tender. Stir in 2 tablespoons of redcurrant jelly, 2 tablespoons of orange juice and 1 tablespoon of chopped fresh rosemary. Serve with lamb chops or steaks.

Quick marinade for lamb Finely grate 1 small onion and place in a bowl with 2 cloves of crushed garlic, 1 teaspoon ground cumin, ½ teaspoon cayenne pepper, 3 tablespoons olive oil and the juice of 1 lemon. Add 450g (1 lb) cubed leg or shoulder of lamb and leave to marinate for at least 20 minutes. Thread onto skewers (with onion wedges and chunks of red pepper if liked) and grill or barbecue for about 15 minutes or until tender.

roast lamb with a herb and pine nut crust

preparation time: 10 minutes | cooking time: 2 hours | serves 6–8

Pre-heat the oven to 180°C/350°F/Gas 4; fan oven 160°C from cold. Heat the oil, add the garlic and cook for 2 minutes until well softened. Stir in the breadcrumbs, pine nuts and herbs and cook for a minute or two; season well.

Place the lamb in a roasting tin and press the herb mixture evenly over the skin. Weigh the meat and roast according to the chart on page 98 (about 2 hours for a 2 kg/4½ lb joint).

Check the lamb after an hour and cover loosely with foil if it has become too brown.

When the lamb is cooked, remove from the oven and cover with foil while you make the gravy. Pour 2 tablespoons of the pan juices into a pan and stir in the flour and mustard. Stir over a low heat for 2 minutes until thickened. Gradually add the wine and stock to the pan, stirring until smooth. Bring to the boil, then simmer for 10 minutes.

Stir in the redcurrant jelly, season to taste and simmer for 2 minutes. Serve with the lamb and vegetable accompaniments.

wine suggestion Here is a sumptuous dish for your very best, mature bottles of Cabernet Sauvignon. Roll out the classed-growth claret if you can, but California, Washington or Chile will also do the trick. Otherwise, go for richly oaked Spanish Reserva from Rioja or Ribera del Duero, or Douro or Alentejo red from Portugal.

½ tablespoon olive oil

2 garlic cloves, chopped

100 g (4 oz) fresh white breadcrumbs

50 g (2 oz) pine nuts, finely chopped

a small bunch of fresh parsley, chopped

5 fresh rosemary sprigs, chopped

1 leg of lamb, about 2 kg (4½ lb)

salt and freshly ground black pepper

FOR THE GRAVY:

1 tablespoon plain flour

1 teaspoon wholegrain mustard

150 ml (5 fl oz) red wine

300 ml (10 fl oz) vegetable water or stock

1 tablespoon redcurrant jelly

salt and freshly ground black pepper

roast lamb with herb and pine nut crust

sausages with onion gravy and perfect mash

serves 4–6 | preparation time: 10 minutes | cooking time: 25 minutes

Choose your favourite sausages – pork, beef or venison – and grill or fry to serve with this delicious gravy. Add mash and you have a great tasty supper.

1 kg (2¼ lb) sausages

FOR THE PERFECT MASHED POTATO:
1 kg (2¼ lb) King Edward's or Maris Piper potatoes
150 g (5 oz) butter
300 ml (10 fl oz) hot milk
salt and black pepper

FOR THE ONION GRAVY:
1 onion, thinly sliced
2 tablespoons vegetable oil
2 teaspoons plain flour
2 teaspoons ready-made mustard
2 teaspoons Worcestershire or soy sauce
600 ml (1 pint) chicken stock
salt and black pepper

To cook the perfect mash, choose floury potatoes for the best texture such as King Edward's or Maris Piper. Peel and scrub the potatoes and then boil in lightly salted water for 20–30 minutes, until tender. Drain and mash with the butter. Mash with a potato masher or, for a lighter, fluffier texture, press through a mouli-légumes or potato ricer (like a giant garlic press). Season and beat in the hot milk.

Meanwhile, to make the gravy: fry the onion in the oil for 5 minutes. Stir in the flour and cook for 1 minute. Stir in the mustard, Worcestershire or soy sauce and stock and bring to the boil, stirring. Simmer for 15 minutes, then season.

Grill or fry the sausages, pricking the skins so they don't burst, and serve with the gravy and the mash.

wine suggestion Best pork sausages with creamy mash and this unctuously flavoured onion gravy need a midweight red, say Merlot, Pinot Noir or one of the lighter Cabernet Sauvignons from somewhere like Bulgaria, northern Italy or Portugal. Or maybe a Rioja Reserva.

mash variations

Cheesy mash Stir in 75 g (3 oz) of grated Cheddar, Gruyère, Gorgonzola or Dolcelatte cheese or 50 g (2 oz) of grated Parmesan.

Mustard mash Stir in 2 tablespoons of wholegrain mustard.

Horseradish mash Stir in 2 teaspoons of freshly grated horseradish or 1 tablespoon of creamed horseradish.

Olive oil mash Mash the potatoes with 3 tablespoons of olive oil, 4 tablespoons of hot cream and 2 tablespoons of grated Parmesan.

Root vegetable mash Cook peeled parsnips, swede or carrot in salted, boiling water until tender and mash with the potatoes.

sausages with onion gravy and perfect mash

poultry
and game

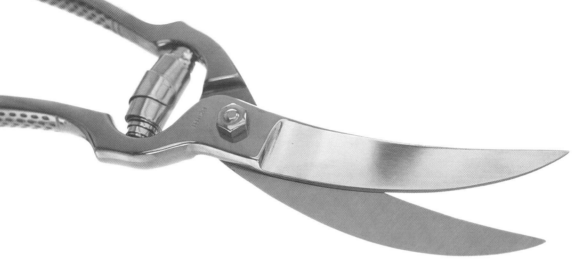

ost poultry and game are lean, giving them a healthy-eating advantage, and they are also excellent sources of B vitamins and some minerals. The term poultry includes all types of domesticated fowl raised for the table: ducks, geese, guinea fowl, quail and turkey as well as chicken. Today, virtually all the poultry we eat is raised by intensive farming methods. The flocks are crowded, which is why antibiotics and other drugs are used routinely to prevent diseases; additional drugs are also used to treat diseases caused by the intensive system. The farming industry (along with medical and veterinary authorities) are subject to requests to reduce the amount and type of antibiotics being used because of the increasing problems of antibiotic resistance leaving doctors with fewer drugs to treat human disease.

chicken

Standard British chickens Kept not in cages but purpose-built chicken houses, on a floor covered with deep litter wood shavings or straw.

Free-range chickens The density of the flock is legally limited and for about half their average life of 56 days the birds must have access to open-air runs and covered vegetation. Access is through 'pop holes' (openings) in the side of the hen house. Free-range chickens must be fed at least 70% cereal. If the packaging claims that a bird has been fed a particular diet, at least one-third of the diet (far less than most consumers would reasonably expect) must comprise that food, except corn-fed birds (see below).

Traditional free-range The houses are similar to free-range but with 12 birds per square metre instead of 13 for free-range. No more than 4888 birds are allowed in each house. Outside, the chickens get two square metres per bird instead of one for free-range. Traditional free-range birds are grown to a maximum of 81 days and the diet is as for free-range.

Free-range total freedom All the previous standards for traditional free-range must be met. In addition there must be free access to pasture without fences.

poultry roasting times and temperatures

When cooked, the dark leg meat at the deepest part of the thigh should reach 75°C/170°F and the breast meat 71°C/160°F, in order to destroy any salmonella bacteria present.

Bird	Cooking time	Temperature
Chicken	45 minutes/kg or 20 minutes/lb (even small chickens take 1 hour to cook)	190°C/375°F/Gas 5; fan oven 170°C from cold
Guinea fowl	1 hour and 10 minutes	190°C/375°F/Gas 5; fan oven 170°C from cold
Duck up to 2.5 kg (5 lb)	45 minutes/kg or 20 minutes/lb	190°C/375°F/Gas 5; fan oven 170°C from cold
Duck over 2.5 kg (5 lb)	55 minutes/kg or 25 minutes/lb	180°C/350°F/Gas 4; fan oven 160°C from cold
Goose	55 minutes/kg or 25 minutes/lb	180°C/350°F/Gas 4; fan oven 160°C from cold

Organic These chickens live in groups of between 100 and 500. They do not have permanent indoor housing but constant access to outside pasture during normal daylight hours. They are not debeaked (the other systems do this because of overcrowding); a minimum of 80% of their feed is organically produced and all must be free from genetically modified organisms (within five years, 100% of the feed must be organic). Routine administration of prophylactic (preventive) antibiotics (necessary for intensive systems) is banned. However, antibiotics are allowed to treat specific illnesses, during which time and for a period afterwards the chickens cannot be sold as organic.

Corn-fed chickens Can be produced from a standard or free-range system; the packaging will state which. Half their food must be maize and it is the natural colourings in the maize (corn) that produces the yellowish colour of the flesh and fat on corn-fed birds.

Poulet noir A black-legged French chicken that looks more like guinea fowl than the standard British chicken. This breed of bird, popular in France, has more leg meat than breast meat (the opposite of UK chicken). The speciality *poulet noir* sold in the UK is usually free-range.

types of chicken

Poussins Four to six weeks old, they serve one person. They do not have a lot of flavour and benefit from basting or marinating. *Double poussins* are six to ten weeks old and serve two people. Butterflied or spatchcocked poussin has been split in half and flattened. These are popular for barbecuing as they cook in 20–30 minutes.

Spring chicken Also called poulet; ten to twelve weeks old and serves two people.

Boilers or boiling fowl Not seen very often. They are old laying hens and tougher than younger chickens, but with more flavour for casseroles.

Chicken pieces are available on and off the bone, with or without skin. Breasts are usually boneless and they can be skinless, they are sometimes called fillets. Other widely available chicken pieces include thighs, drumsticks, quarters and wings. Thigh and drumstick together is sometimes called a Maryland. Breast and wing together is called a supreme.

storing chicken and giblets

Unwrap poultry from any plastic wrappings and if it contains giblets, remove them as soon as possible. Wipe the outside and the inside of the bird with kitchen paper and place on a deep plate or tray in the bottom of the fridge. Cover the chicken lightly with greaseproof paper or freezer film, allowing the bird to 'breathe'. Store the giblets separately in a container in the fridge for up to a day.

turkey

While chicken has become an everyday food, turkey has retained its link with festivities, particularly Christmas and Thanksgiving in the US. A roast turkey is perfect for a special occasion because it can feed a large gathering and still provide cold meat. The majority of turkey production is conducted under intensive conditions but there are free-range and organic birds. 'Traditional' turkeys are usually special breeds such as Norfolk Black and Cambridge Bronze, which are bred and reared for more flavour and hung for longer to develop flavour. Traditional turkeys do not have water added during processing to increase the weight. They can be raised intensively or free-range.

Pieces of turkey include drumsticks, thighs and breasts. They can be quite large; one cut will probably serve two people. Boneless breast steaks, escalopes and fillets offer single servings. A whole breast on the bone without the legs and wings is called a crown roast; the number of servings depends on weight.

Minced turkey is also available all year as a lower-fat alternative to red meat for making sauces, lasagne, burgers, meat balls and so on.

Thaw in the coolest room of the house. Remove the plastic wrap and place on a tray or deep plate to collect liquid. While the bird is thawing, cover it loosely with greaseproof paper or a plastic bag. Check regularly and, when thawed, remove all packaging. Remove the giblets and store separately in the fridge. Wipe the inside and outside of the bird with kitchen paper. Store in the fridge until ready to cook.

Stuff the neck end only. Allow the turkey to rest for 20–30 minutes after roasting and before carving. Do not re-heat the bird on the carcass. If you wish to re-heat leftover meat, cut into slices, cover with gravy and then re-heat. Freeze turkey slices covered with gravy for up to one month.

what size turkey?

Weight	Number of servings
1.5–2.25 kg (3–5 lb)	4–6
2.25 kg–3 kg (5–7 lb)	6–8
3.5–4 kg (8–9 lb)	8–10
4.5–5 kg (10–11 lb)	12–14
5.5–6 kg (12–13 lb)	16–18
6.5–7.5 kg (14–17 lb)	20–24
8–9 kg (18–20 lb)	28–34

thawing times for frozen turkey

Weight	Thawing time (room temperature)	Thawing time (in the fridge)
3.5–4.5 kg (8–10 lb)	22 hours	65 hours
5–6 kg (11–13 lb)	25 hours	70 hours
6.5–7.25 kg (14–16 lb)	30 hours	75 hours
7.5–9 kg (17–20 lb)	40 hours	80 hours
9.5–11 kg (21–24 lb)	48 hours	96 hours

turkey roasting times

Oven-ready weight, stuffed or not	Cooking time at 180°C/350°F/Gas 4; fan oven 160°C from cold
1.5–2.25 kg (3–5 lb)	1 hour 20 minutes–2 hours
2.75–3 kg (6–7 lb)	2 hours 20–40 minutes
3.5–4.5 kg (8–10 lb)	3 hours–3 hours 20 minutes
4.5–5.5 kg (10–12 lb)	3 hours 40 minutes–4 hours
5.5–6 kg (12–13 lb)	4 hours 30–40 minutes
6.5–7.5 kg (14–17 lb)	5–6 hours
8–9 kg (18–20 lb)	6 hours 20 minutes–7 hours
9.5–11 kg (21–24 lb)	7 hours 20 minutes–8 hours 20 minutes

Small turkeys up to 6 kg (13 lb) can be cooked at a higher temperature, 200°C/400°F/Gas 6; fan oven 180°C from cold, for 25 minutes per kg or 12 minutes per lb. Be careful the bird does not dry out. Cover well during roasting and remove the cover for the last hour or so, to let it brown.

turkey rescue remedy

If the turkey has not cooked on time, bend the legs away from the breast and return to the oven to allow the heat to penetrate.

other poultry

guinea fowl

Guinea fowl is smaller than chicken and has less breast and more leg meat. The meat is darker than chicken; it has a slightly gamy flavour and needs careful cooking so that the lean meat does not dry out. Guinea fowl are raised for the table using intensive farming methods.

duck

Duck contains more fat than chicken and the meat is darker. There is less meat to the pound of duck on the bone than there is for chicken. Allow about 750 g (1½ lb) raw weight per person when buying whole duck or duckling. Most of the fat is found just below the skin and is easy to remove before cooking, if liked. For roasting, prick the skin all over, allowing a lot of the fat to drain away.

Duckling refers to a bird slaughtered up to six months of age. Ducklings weigh between 1.5 kg (3 lb), which feeds two to three people, and 3 kg (7 lb), which feeds six people.

Cuts of duck include legs and boneless breast; the legs tend to be tough and are best used in stews and casseroles. Breast can be grilled, pan-fried or barbecued; allow one per person.

goose

Goose is a lot fattier than chicken and turkey and has rich, dark meat. Visible fat can be removed, as for duck. Use the same technique of pricking the skin to remove excess fat. Goose weighs 3–5.5 kg (7–12 lb). There is not a lot of meat on a goose, so allow 750 g (1½ lb) raw weight per person when buying goose or gosling.

Goslings are sold at six to eight months and are tenderer and less fatty than goose. Goslings weigh up to about 2.25 kg (5 lb).

Fewer geese are raised than ducks and chickens and they tend to be bred on smaller, often free-range farms. Most are raised for Christmas and they are not widely available at other times of the year.

game

Game has become popular for its flavour and because it is a lean meat. Several types of game are available fresh during their seasons, or can be purchased frozen.

Grouse Lives on moors in northern England and Scotland. The 'Glorious Twelfth' (of August) marks the start of the shooting season, which ends on 10 December. The birds feed on heath shoots, berries and insects. Their meat is dark red and very gamy. A grouse weighs about 750 g (1½ lb) and feeds one person.

Partridge About the same size as a grouse. The meat is paler with less flavour. A bird serves one.

Pheasant Intensively reared but shot during the season from 1 October to 1 February. The meat is gamy and most pheasant in supermarkets will not be hung, so the flavour will not be strong. A pheasant weighs about 1.5 kg (3 lb) and will serve two to three people. Unless it is very young, it should not be roasted because it can be tough. Generally the female (hen) birds are plumper and tenderer than the cocks (males).

Pigeon Whether squab (the farmed bird) or wild, pigeon is available all year. Even though it is small, pigeon is quite meaty. The meat is dark and well flavoured.

Quail A game bird that is now bred for the table. It is very small with a delicate flavour and often two birds are served per person.

Rabbit Will have been bred for the table, unless it is sold as wild rabbit. The two are quite different. Intensively reared rabbit is a white meat similar to chicken and without much flavour and texture. Wild rabbit is darker and sinewy with a gamy flavour. Both are low in fat and need careful cooking so that they do not become dry and tough. Braises, casseroles and stews give the best results with wild rabbit, but reared rabbit can be cooked as if it were chicken.

Wild duck Available August to March. The commonest type of wild duck is mallard. They are quite large and one will serve two to three people. Widgeon is considered to have a better flavour than mallard and is smaller, serving just two people.

game roasting times and temperatures

Pigeon	35 minutes	200°C/400°F/Gas 6; fan oven 180°C from cold
Grouse	30 minutes	190°C/375°F/Gas 5; fan oven 170°C from cold
Partridge	25 minutes	190°C/375°F/Gas 5; fan oven 170°C from cold
Pheasant	1 hour	190°C/375°F/Gas 5; fan oven 170°C from cold
Quail	20 minutes	190°C/375°F/Gas 5; fan oven 170°C from cold
Wild duck	45 minutes	200°C/400°F/Gas 6; fan oven 180°C from cold

take a chicken breast

A quick tasty sauce or topping can jazz up a plain chicken breast and turn it into a classy supper dish.

parmesan and pesto crust

Slash a boneless, skinless chicken breast lightly with a knife. Spread with 1 tablespoon of pesto sauce. Sprinkle with 1 tablespoon of grated Parmesan cheese, mixed with 1 teaspoon of plain flour and plenty of black pepper. Bake at 200°C/400°F/Gas 6; fan oven 180°C from cold, for about 20–25 minutes or until cooked right through.

lemon and tarragon sauce

Roast two boneless chicken breasts at 190°C/375°F/Gas 5; fan oven 170°C from cold, for about 20 minutes. Chop the leaves from a small bunch of tarragon and sprinkle over the chicken, with the juice of 1½ lemons, and return to the oven for another 10 minutes. Transfer the chicken to a warm plate and pour the chicken juices into a pan (or cook the sauce in the roasting tin). Add a 200 ml tub of crème fraîche and 2 teaspoons of dijon mustard. Bring to simmering point and then pour over the chicken.

orange and sherry casserole

Dust 4 boneless chicken breasts with a little flour and salt and freshly ground black pepper. Fry in a large pan with a little olive oil, until golden. Add 2 sliced onions and 1 deseeded, sliced red pepper and cook for another 5 minutes, until the onion has softened. Add 300 ml (10 fl oz) of chicken stock, the grated zest of 1 orange and the juice of 2 oranges. Add 150 ml (5 fl oz) of sherry and a tablespoon of Worcestershire sauce. Bring to the boil and then simmer for 25 minutes.

Stir in 250 g (9 oz) of sliced mushrooms and cook for a further 5 minutes. Sprinkle with chopped fresh parsley and serve with mashed potatoes or rice.

quick peanut satay

Thread cubed chicken breasts on skewers. Sprinkle with a little chilli powder and drizzle with lemon juice before grilling for about 20–25 minutes or until cooked through. Mix together 3 tablespoons of crunchy peanut butter,1 teaspoon of sugar, ½ teaspoon of chilli powder and 4 tablespoons of lemon juice. Spread over the chicken breasts, grill for a further 4–5 minutes and serve hot or cold.

chicken breast with parmesan and pesto crust

coq au vin

serves 6 | preparation time: 30 minutes | cooking time: 1½ hours

This classic dish cannot be beaten for a warming, entertaining menu. It can be made in advance and re-heated in the oven for 35–40 minutes. Use whole chicken legs or breast quarters for this recipe.

2 tablespoons plain flour, seasoned
6 chicken portions
25 g (1 oz) unsalted butter
1 tablespoon vegetable oil
350 g (12 oz) button onions
175 g (6 oz) unsmoked streaky bacon, chopped
4 tablespoons brandy
a bottle of red wine
2 garlic cloves, crushed
2 teaspoons fresh thyme leaves
2 bay leaves
225 g (8 oz) chestnut mushrooms
salt and freshly ground black pepper
fresh thyme sprigs, to garnish

Place the flour in a large plastic bag, season with plenty of salt and freshly ground black pepper, add the chicken and shake until lightly coated on all sides.

Heat the butter and oil in a large flameproof casserole dish. Add the onions and fry until they are just beginning to brown, then add the bacon pieces and fry until lightly browned. Transfer the bacon and onions to a plate, using a slotted spoon.

Fry the chicken in batches in the casserole until golden brown on all sides. Pour in the brandy and wine and stir well to scrape up the browned juices from the bottom of the pan.

Return the bacon and onions to the casserole, add the garlic, thyme and bay leaves and bring to the boil. Cover and simmer gently for 1½ hours, until the chicken is tender. 15 minutes before the end of cooking stir in the mushrooms.

Transfer the chicken to a serving dish and spoon around the onions and mushrooms; keep warm. Boil the pan juices for about 15 minutes until they have reduced by one-third and are thick and glossy; season to taste. Pour the sauce over the chicken, garnish with thyme and serve with a selection of seasonal vegetables, if you like.

wine suggestion Since it originates from Burgundy, there is no more impeccable match for coq au vin than the best red burgundy you can afford. Three or four years' bottle-age will help. Otherwise, look to California, Oregon or New Zealand for equally good Pinot Noir.

chicken tikka with mint raita

This recipe uses cubes of chicken breast but you can marinate joints of chicken, if you prefer. We've also included a recipe for garam masala. Keep the remainder in an airtight jar for up to 6 months, or use 2 teaspoons ready-made garam masala. Chicken tikka is traditionally served with naan bread and mango chutney.

To make the garam masala: place the cardamom seeds, cinnamon, peppercorns, cloves, bay leaf, cumin and coriander seeds in a coffee grinder and whizz until it grinds to a powder.

To make the marinade: grate a tablespoon of the onion and set aside. Roughly chop the remaining onion and place in a food processor, with the garlic cloves, ginger, chilli and lemon juice. Whizz the mixture to a paste and then transfer to a large bowl.

Stir in 300 g (11 oz) of yoghurt, 2 teaspoons of garam masala, the chopped coriander, salt and paprika. Cut the chicken breasts into equal-sized cubes and add to the bowl. Mix well, cover and chill for at least 2 hours or overnight.

Meanwhile, make the mint raita. Mix the reserved onion, the remaining yoghurt, the honey, vinegar and mint in a small serving bowl; chill. The raita will keep for up to 2 days in the fridge.

Remove the chicken from the marinade and thread on to skewers. Cook the chicken under a hot grill for 15 minutes, turning several times, until the outside is crisp and the chicken is cooked through. Serve hot with mint raita, mango chutney and warm naan bread.

wine suggestion A crisp and exotically scented white wine will marry well with the spices. Viognier, Gewürztraminer or an Argentinian white called Torrontés are all good. Alternatively, drink well-chilled Indian beer to fit the mood of the dish.

1 onion

2 garlic cloves, chopped

2.5 cm (1 in) piece of fresh root ginger, peeled

1 green chilli, seeded

2 tablespoons fresh lemon juice

450 g (1 lb) low-fat natural yoghurt

2 tablespoons chopped fresh coriander

1 teaspoon salt

3 tablespoons paprika

750 g (1½ lb) skinless, boneless chicken breasts

2 teaspoons clear honey

1 teaspoon white wine vinegar

3 tablespoons chopped fresh mint

FOR THE GARAM MASALA:

8 cardamom pods, split and the seeds extracted

4 cm (1½ in) cinnamon stick, broken into small pieces

1 teaspoon black peppercorns

1 teaspoon whole cloves

1 bay leaf, torn in half

1 teaspoon cumin seeds

2 tablespoons coriander seeds

herb and lemon roast chicken

serves 4–6 | preparation time: 15 minutes | cooking time: 1½ hours

A delicious roast chicken is one of life's simple pleasures but not if you use bland, battery-farmed birds. A roasted free-range and/or organic chicken will have so much more flavour and remind you just how good roast chicken can be. Serve with green vegetables or braised celery and beetroot.

1.75 kg (4 lb) free-range and/or organic chicken
1 lemon
25 g (1 oz) butter, softened
3 tablespoons chopped fresh parsley
1 tablespoon chopped fresh oregano or 1 teaspoon dried oregano
4 streaky bacon rashers
2 onions
salt and freshly ground black pepper

FOR THE GRAVY:
2 teaspoons plain flour
300 ml (10 fl oz) white wine or apple juice
300 ml (10 fl oz) stock or vegetable cooking water
1 teaspoon mustard
salt and freshly ground black pepper

Pre-heat the oven to 190°C/375°F/Gas 5; fan oven 170°C from cold. Using your fingers, loosen the skin from the breast of the chicken.

Finely grate the zest of the lemon and beat with the butter and herbs. Spread the butter mixture between the flesh and skin of the chicken.

Cut the lemon in half and place inside the cavity of the bird. Season the chicken. Lay the bacon rashers across the top of the breast. Cut the onion into wedges and place in the roasting tray. Place the chicken on top and roast for about 1½ hours (or 20 minutes per 450 g (1 lb) plus 20 minutes: see roasting chart on page 98) or until tender.

Pierce between the chicken breast and thigh with a knife. If the juices run clear, it is cooked. Transfer the chicken and onion wedges to a warm serving dish and cover with foil.

To make the gravy: pour off all the fat and leave about 4 tablespoons of the pan juices. Re-heat the roasting tin on the hob, stir in the flour and cook for 1 minute. Stir in the wine or apple juice and stock or vegetable cooking water and bring it to the boil, de-glazing the pan by scraping up and incorporating all the browned juices from the base of the pan. Add the mustard and seasoning and simmer for 5 minutes, until smooth and glossy. Pour through a sieve into a gravy boat and serve.

wine suggestion An immensely versatile dish, this will be as much at home with a richly buttery Chardonnay from Burgundy, Australia, California or Chile as with a medium-bodied red such as Pinot Noir from Burgundy or California, or Corbières or Minervois from the Languedoc.

herb and lemon roast chicken

roast turkey with fresh herb stuffing

serves 10–12 | preparation time: 15 minutes | cooking time: about 4 hours

For the perfect Christmas dinner, serve this succulent turkey with Bread Sauce (see opposite) and/or Cranberry and Orange Sauce (see page 134) and Lemon Roasted Potatoes (see page 172).

5.6 kg (12 lb) turkey, thawed if frozen
75 g (3 oz) butter, melted
salt and freshly ground black pepper
bay leaves and fresh rosemary, to garnish

FOR THE STUFFING:
75 g (3 oz) butter
2 onions, finely chopped
8 rindless streaky bacon rashers, chopped
150 g (6 oz) white breadcrumbs
225 g (8 oz) sausagemeat
3 tablespoons chopped fresh sage
3 tablespoons chopped fresh parsley
3 tablespoons chopped fresh thyme
1 egg, beaten
salt and freshly ground black pepper

FOR THE GRAVY:
175 ml (6 fl oz) pan juices
3 tablespoons plain flour
1 litre (1½ pints) turkey stock (see page 58)
300 ml (10 fl oz) dry white wine
salt and freshly ground black pepper

Pre-heat the oven to 180°C/350°F/Gas 4; fan oven 160°C from cold. Remove the turkey giblets and use to make the stock. Wash the turkey inside and out and dry well with kitchen paper.

Make the stuffing: melt the butter in a pan; add the onions and bacon and fry gently for about 8 minutes, until softened and golden. In a bowl, combine the breadcrumbs, sausagemeat, herbs and egg; season with salt and freshly ground black pepper. Add the onion, bacon and their cooking juices and mix well. Leave until cold.

Stuff the neck end of the turkey, pushing the stuffing up between the flesh and breast. Weigh and calculate the cooking time, allowing 20 minutes per 450 g (1 lb), plus 20 minutes extra (see chart on page 100).

Place the turkey in a roasting tin, brush the breast and legs with the melted butter and season well. Cover loosely with foil and roast for the calculated time.

To test whether the turkey is cooked, insert a skewer into the thickest part of the thigh – the juices should run clear. If they do not, separate the legs from the breast and return to the oven for a little longer. Transfer to a platter, cover with foil and allow to rest in a warm place for 15 minutes.

Make the gravy: pour off any excess fat and re-heat the remaining pan juices; add the flour, stir well to pick up all the browned juices and cook for 2 minutes, until it begins to turn golden. Gradually add the stock and bring to the boil, stirring until thickened and smooth; season to taste. Pour through a sieve into a warmed gravy jug. Serve the turkey garnished with bay leaves and rosemary sprigs.

wine suggestion This is normally a festive dish and requires a lot of effort, so be sure the wine suits the occasion, whether it be red or white. Fine claret or burgundy, premium California Pinot Noir or Merlot are best. Otherwise, big Chardonnays from Burgundy or the New World won't let the side down.

bread sauce

preparation time: 5 minutes | cooking time: 25 minutes | serves 10–12

To make this sauce richer, stir in some single cream at the end.

In a pan, preferably a non-stick, heavy-based one, simmer the milk, butter, onion, cloves, bay leaf and thyme for about 20 minutes, until the onions are soft. Strain then pour back into the pan. Add the breadcrumbs and simmer for 3–4 minutes more. Season well with salt and freshly ground black pepper. Stir in the single cream, if using. Serve warm.

600 ml (1 pint) full-fat milk
50 g (2 oz) butter
1 onion, finely chopped
6 whole cloves
1 bay leaf
3 fresh thyme sprigs
100 g (4 oz) white breadcrumbs
salt and freshly ground
    black pepper
4–5 tablespoons single cream
    (optional)

menu: christmas dinner

smoked salmon and avocado pots (page 65)

roast turkey with fresh herb stuffing (page 132)

bread sauce (page 133)

cranberry and orange sauce (page 134)

perfect roast potatoes (page 170)

or lemon roasted potatoes (page 172)

sweet and sour carrots (page 171)

brussels sprouts with chestnuts (page 173)

christmas pudding (page 232)

boozy butter (page 233)

honey-glazed duck salad with cherries

serves 4 | preparation time: 5–10 minutes | cooking time: 15–20 minutes

The cherries give a nice fruitiness to this salad. You can use canned cherries, well drained, or omit them altogether and use orange segments instead. The honey-glazed duck is delicious with this salad but you could also serve it with hot vegetables.

2 tablespoons clear honey
2 tablespoons dark soy sauce
4 duck breast fillets
1 teaspoon Dijon mustard
1 tablespoon orange juice
3 tablespoons walnut oil
1 teaspoon red wine vinegar
350 g (12 oz) red cherries, stoned
mixed salad leaves, such as
frisée, rocket and oakleaf
salt and freshly ground
black pepper
2 tablespoons snipped fresh
chives, to garnish

Pre-heat the oven to 200°C/400°F/Gas 6; fan oven 180°C from cold.

Mix the honey and soy sauce, brush over the duck and roast on a rack in the oven for 15–20 minutes, until crisp but still pink inside.

Mix together the mustard, orange juice, oil and vinegar. Add the cherries, season to taste and toss thoroughly.

Slice the duck, arrange on a bed of salad leaves and spoon over the cherries and dressing. Garnish with the chives and serve with warm crusty bread.

wine suggestion The piquancy and fruitiness of this salad work best with a light, perhaps slightly chilled, red. *Cru* Beaujolais wines like Fleurie or Morgon or a Cabernet Franc red from the Loire (Bourgueil or Chinon) will cope with its complexities.

cranberry and orange sauce

serves 8–12 | preparation time: 5 minutes | cooking time: 10 minutes

A refreshing alternative to the traditional bread sauce with the festive turkey, or why not make both?

225 g (8 oz) cranberries
1 teaspoon grated orange zest
3 tablespoons fresh orange juice
75 g (3 oz) light muscovado sugar
2 tablespoons port

Place all of the ingredients in a small pan, with 3 tablespoons of water. Bring to the boil, reduce the heat and simmer, uncovered, for 10 minutes, stirring frequently until the cranberries are tender. Serve warm or cold.

venison and chestnut casserole

preparation time: 45 minutes + pre-cooking | **cooking time: 2½ hours** | **serves 8**

This large and hearty casserole is an ideal dish for winter entertaining. The dried chanterelles give a rich flavour but you can use fresh flat mushrooms instead and just fry them with the shallots.

Pre-heat the oven to 160°C/325°F/Gas 3; fan oven 140°C from cold. Cover the chanterelles with warm water and leave to soak for 20 minutes, then drain.

Meanwhile, put the flour into a large plastic bag and season with plenty of salt and freshly ground black pepper. Add the venison and shake well to flour the meat.

Fry the bacon in a dry frying pan for about 3–4 minutes, then transfer to a large (2-litre/3½ pint) casserole. Add the butter, oil and shallots to the frying pan, fry gently to brown and add to the casserole. Lightly brown the venison in batches and transfer to the casserole. Add the drained chanterelles.

Pour the red wine into the hot frying pan and stir to incorporate all the browned juices from the base. Transfer to the casserole, with the stock, plenty of salt and black pepper, the juniper berries, bay leaves and vinegar. Cover and simmer in the oven for 2 hours.

Scoop out the bay leaves and add the chestnuts. Cover and cook for a further 20–30 minutes. Serve with jacket or mashed potatoes and a green vegetable.

wine suggestion The dense, gamy meat, the piercing flavour of juniper, mealy-textured chestnuts and the long cooking here require a towering red. Spanish and Portuguese reds from native grape varieties would be good (go for a minimum 13% alcohol), as would Grenache from Australia or Châteauneuf-du-Pape.

50 g (2 oz) dried chanterelles

2 tablespoons plain flour

1 kg (21/2 lb) chopped venison

225 g (8 oz) unsmoked streaky bacon rashers, snipped into small pieces

25 g (1 oz) butter

1 tablespoon olive oil

300 g (10 oz) shallots

300 ml (10 fl oz) red wine

600 ml (1 pint) vegetable stock

12 juniper berries, crushed

3 bay leaves

1 tablespoon red wine vinegar

100 g (4 oz) peeled, canned or vacuum-packed chestnuts

salt and freshly ground black pepper

fish and shellfish

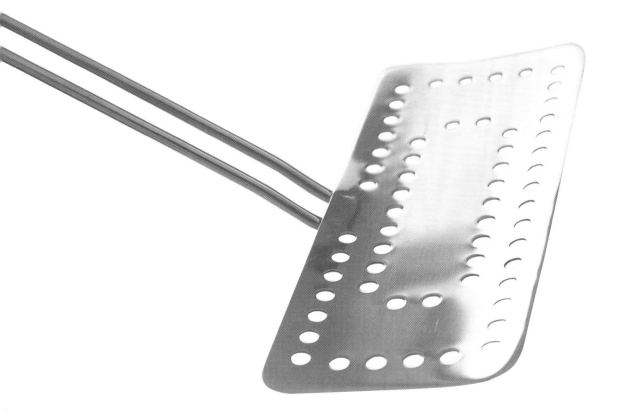

as the nation that invented one of the original fast foods – fish and chips – we have continued to show a preference for deep-fried fish coated in batter or breadcrumbs. It is only recently that we have become enthusiastic about the wide range of fresh fish from around the world that is now more widely available through fishmongers and supermarkets. This section is full of inspiration and confidence-boosting preparation tips and cookery techniques to help you make more of fish.

Fish is one of the quickest and easiest foods to cook. All types of fish are an excellent low-fat protein food. White fish (e.g. cod, haddock, and plaice) is especially low in fat and rich in minerals, including iodine. And oily fish contain special beneficial fats (for more details, see page 11).

You don't have to be an expert cook with special skills to enjoy fish because the fishmonger or super-market has already done much of the preparation (de-scaling, cleaning, filleting and skinning). But in case you are lucky enough to be given a fresh catch by a fisherman, we have included instructions on how to clean and prepare fish.

white fish

White fish includes small flat fish such as *flounder, plaice, dab* and *sole*, which are often the right size for an individual serving on the bone. To pan-fry, simply score the skin with a sharp knife and fry in a little butter or olive oil. Grilling is possible, too. Oil the grill pan or rack to facilitate turning the fish once during cooking. Be careful not to scorch or dry out the fish during grilling. On a barbecue, best results are achieved by putting the fish in a special basket that holds it in position over the coals. *Dover sole* are larger than the flat fish mentioned above and are more usually filleted, which provides more servings.

Larger flat fish, such as *brill, halibut* and *turbot*, are available whole or in steaks and fillets. *John Dory* is, technically, not a flat fish but looks like one and is usually filleted as if it were.

Monkfish has a huge ugly head and a disproportionate amount of flesh on its 'tail', the part of the body that is cut into two large boneless fillets from the piece of cartilage that runs down the centre. The fish is chewy in texture and mildly flavoured and before it became a sought-after fashionable and expensive fish in its own right, it was passed off as lobster and scampi in breaded recipes.

Rock salmon, also called huss or dogfish, is a type of shark and is commonly sold in fish and chip shops. The advantage is that it has no bones but a cartilaginous skeleton; its flesh is quite soft and not to everyone's taste.

Shark steaks are very meaty in texture and dark in colour. They are increasingly popular marinated and grilled on barbecues, cubed and used in kebabs or cooked in Thai-style sauces and stir-fries. Shark can also be braised.

Skate, and ray, the name sometimes given to small skate, appear to fly through the water on 'wings', and it is their large wings that are skinned and sold whole or cut into smaller pieces. The skate has a cartilaginous skeleton, which means it is free from fine fish bones; it produces a gelatinous texture when cooked. Skate is often served with black butter or herbed butters. The white 'meat' can be cut from the main part of the body and is sold as skate 'knobs'; these are similar in texture to monkfish, but slightly softer. They can be pan-fried or cooked in a sauce or used in fish stews.

Tuna, swordfish and marlin are very meaty fish usually sold as steaks. Tuna is also available as fillets. Swordfish and marlin are more likely to have been previously frozen than tuna. Sometimes these fish are compared with veal and they can be cooked as for veal escalopes. Their firm texture makes them suitable for the barbecuing, grilling and kebabs, or they can be baked and braised in a variety of sauces, particularly tomato-based.

Exotic white fish from subtropical waters are increasingly available because of air freighting and transporting at near-freezing temperatures. *Snapper, grouper, orange roughy* and *mahi mahi* (or *dorado*) are firm-fleshed white fish available whole or filleted, or in the case of mahi mahi in steaks. Red snapper is often steamed to retain its flavour and these fish can also be grilled and barbecued (with or without marinating) baked and braised. Snapper is traditionally used in the Spanish-influenced Caribbean dish Escabèche – a dish in which fish is marinated, cooked and served cold.

Bass, grey mullet and red mullet have a finer flesh that is flakier than other exotic white fish. There are several varieties of bass, both freshwater and sea, but the sea bass is the most sought after. Mullet are sold whole or as fillets and sea bass whole or as steaks. The grey mullet looks a little like a trout. The red mullet is usually cooked whole with the skin on and without being cleaned (gutted) – which accentuates its already gamy flavour. *Cod, haddock, hake, pollack* and *whiting* are mild in flavour and have firm white flesh that flakes into large pieces. Fillets and steaks are the most usual and deep-frying in batter, for fish and chips, is the most common way of serving cod and haddock. However these fish are far more versatile and can be grilled, sautéd, steamed and baked with or without sauces. Cod and haddock are often used in fish cakes and can also be minced to make quenelles and mousselines.

Sea bream, either red or black, are sold whole or in fillets. They are good stuffed and baked.

oily fish

Salmon Used to be a delicacy but extensive fish farming has brought the price down so that it is now an everyday fish. Most salmon is farmed, but small amounts of wild and organic salmon are available. These are paler, leaner and firmer because the flesh has not been coloured with (natural) dyes added to food and the fish have exercised more than farmed fish.

Salmon trout is a name dreamt up by supermarkets and used to describe either very large rainbow trout (see below) or sea-grown rainbow trout. Rainbow trout is the main breed of trout that is farmed commercially on a wide scale (and originated as a native of north American lakes and streams). It is farmed in fresh water and can be recognized by a broad purple or violet band along the flanks and black spots on the tail fin. Small-scale fish farming of golden trout (another native American fish) has recently begun at a couple of fish farms in the UK, but it is not yet widely available.

Brown trout is the native European freshwater trout. The colour varies but is most commonly brownish with lots of black and rusty red spots – saltwater versions are known as sea trout.

Salmon and trout can be poached whole and served hot or cold; steamed, baked, sautéed, pan-fried, grilled, cooked *en papillote*, braised, made into pâtés, terrines and mousses.

French *truite au bleu* (blue trout) is fresh rainbow trout dipped in vinegar to turn the skin blue and then simmered for a very short time in a *court-bouillon* (an aromatic fish stock).

Herring, mackerel, sardine, shad are all oily fish with soft flesh. Oily fish should be gutted, refrigerated and used as quickly as possible. They have fine bones, making them very difficult to fillet, and most fillets still contain some bones. Traditionally, mackerel and herring were soused and mildly pickled with vinegar solutions to counteract the oiliness. Today, they are more popular grilled and barbecued, cooking methods in which much of the oil drains from the fish. To counteract the oiliness, coat herring in oatmeal and serve sardines with tomatoes and mackerel with gooseberries. Serving with potatoes (as in Scandinavian cuisine) has a similar effect.

buying fish

All the above fish can be bought fresh from fishmongers and supermarkets' wet-fish counters, or pre-packed from chiller cabinets. On average, allow 150–225 g (5–8 oz) per person for steaks, fillets and cutlets and 350–450 g (12 oz–1 lb) for whole fish on the bone. Fresh fish is always best used on the same day it is bought but it will store in the fridge at 4°C (40°F) for up to 3 days.

Pre-packed fresh fish will probably keep longer (be guided by use-by dates on the packs) because the pack has been flushed with a mixture of gases that slow bacterial growth. If the fish has not been previously frozen (which packs and labels on the wet fish counter will state), it can safely be frozen at home. Previously frozen fish is unsuitable for freezing. Gas flushing does not affect freezing quality but, obviously, the best freezing results are obtained from freezing very fresh fish, which is why frozen-at-sea frozen fish is the best.

how to freeze fresh fish at home

This needs to be done carefully so that ice crystals do not form and break up the texture of the flesh. Use the booster control on the freezer to ensure it is at its coldest. Thaw fish slowly (overnight) in the refrigerator to retain its texture. Fish will store for three months in a properly maintained freezer

scaling fish

Whole fish and unskinned fillets need to have the scales removed. Do this over the sink or cover a flat surface with newspaper. Lay the fish down and hold it by the tail. Using a blunt knife, scrape away the scales working from the tail towards the head. From time to time, rinse the scales off the knife under cold running water.

cooking salmon

A 2.25 kg (5 lb) salmon serves 8–10; while a 4 kg (9 lb) salmon will serve 16–18. It can be eaten oven-baked (see page 143) or poached. For more information on how to prepare and serve salmon, see page 143.

Cooking times will depend on the size of the fish. When poaching salmon in the oven, allow 8–10 minutes per 450 g (1 lb). Do not overcook salmon or it will become dry and chewy.

To cook salmon in a fish kettle stuff with lemon slices and parsley and then add a sliced onion, 2 bay leaves, 8 black peppercorns and enough water to cover the fish. Bring slowly to the boil. Time the cooking from this point: allow 10 minutes per 450 g (1 lb). If serving hot, carefully remove the salmon at the end of cooking time. If serving cold, cool the salmon completely in the liquid.

cleaning (gutting) fish

Round fish, e.g. herring, mackerel and trout Slit the fish along the belly from behind the gills to just above the tail. Scrape out the entrails. Rinse the gut cavity under the cold tap and rub away any black skin. Cut off the gills below the head and the fins from the body. If the recipe calls for it, cut the head off just below the gills and slice off the tail. If you leave the head on (for grilling whole fish or barbecuing), take out the eyes, as they may pop during cooking.

Flat fish, e.g. plaice and sole Open the cavity containing the entrails by placing the fish, dark-side up, on a flat surface and making a slit behind the gills. Scrape out the entrails and wash under a cold tap. Cut off the fins and cook the fish whole or fillet it.

skinning fish

Round fish Make a slit in the skin around the head on one side and loosen the skin, then pull it down towards the tail and cut it off. Repeat for the other side.

Flat fish Work with the dark skin uppermost and slit above the tail. Loosen the skin and pull the skin towards the head and cut it off. The white skin on the other side is usually left on.

filleting fish

Round fish After the head has been removed, cut along the backbone, working towards the tail, gently easing the flesh from the bone. Once the whole fillet is free, open out the fish and cut off the fillet at the tail. Repeat for the other side.

Flat fish Place the fish dark-skin uppermost on a flat surface and cut along the backbone, working from the head to the tail. Make a semi-circular cut below the head to the backbone and work the knife along the bone to separate and lift the fillet off the bone. Repeat with the second fillet and then turn the fish over and repeat to produce two more fillets from the other side.

boning cooked fish, e.g. salmon and trout

After the fish has been poached and drained, place it on a board and snip the skin below the head and above the tail; then peel off the skin. Now snip the backbone at the head and tail and insert the blade of a sharp knife along the backbone. Gently ease the bone out from the back.

cooking fish

Oily fish are more suited to barbecuing, grilling, roasting and baking, because they have 'built-in' oils that baste the fish as it cooks. White fish are more delicate and so better suited to poaching and other methods. As a rough guide, these are the most successful methods of cooking for different cuts of fish.

Baking/roasting Suitable for fillets, steaks and whole fish. Lay the fish in a buttered dish. Make four diagonal scores through the skin on each side. Cover. Bake in a pre-heated oven at 180°C/350°F/Gas 4; fan oven 160°C from cold for approximately 10 minutes for fillets, 20 minutes for steaks and 30 minutes for whole fish. Fillets will need regular basting.

Pastry case Whole small fish and large fillets can be baked in a puff-pastry case or an enriched dough. Favourite fish for this method are trout, salmon, mullet and sea bass. Roll out the pastry and cut a base and top roughly to the shape of the fish or fillets. De-scale and oil the fish and lay on the pastry or dough; seal the edges well. Scale patterns can be marked on the 'fish', which is then glazed with egg or milk and baked.

En papillote Baking fish in a baking parchment (paper) or foil parcel prevents it from drying out, seals in the juices and allows the flavours of other ingredients to permeate the fish. The method can be used for oily or delicate white fish. Herbs and a julienne of mixed vegetables can be put in the package around, beneath or inside the fish.

Sautéing and pan-frying The traditional way to cook fillets of cod and haddock, whole round fish such as herring or trout, flat fish such as sole and fish steaks such as salmon. For shallow-frying, first dip the fish in beaten egg and seasoned flour and/or breadcrumbs; then put into hot oil or butter (or a mixture of both) and fry until golden brown, allowing about 10 minutes each side, depending on the thickness of the piece of fish.

Deep-frying Small fish like sardines and whitebait are usually deep-fried. To check that the oil is at the right temperature for deep-frying, drop in a 2.5 cm (1 in) bread cube, which should become golden brown in 1 minute. Coat the fish in a milk and flour batter before deep-frying.

Grilling Has become more popular because it adds less, or no, fat, which is better for health. Grilling is versatile and suited to fillets, steaks and whole fish. Baste white fish and fillets with olive oil and/or lemon juice during grilling. Oily fish, such as sardines, trout, herring and mackerel, need no basting. Pre-heat the grill to a high temperature and cook the fish quickly. Fillets take 5–6 minutes and do not need to be turned. Steaks take around 12 minutes and are turned halfway through cooking, as are whole fish.

Griddling Griddles with raised ridges are popular with chefs, because a cross-hatching effect can be achieved on fish (and meat). Only firm fish can be cooked in this way, for example, swordfish, shark, salmon or tuna.

Poaching Especially good for small, delicate fillets and steaks that might break up under a grill or in a frying pan. The fish is only just covered in water or stock or a mixture of water and wine, to which seasoning and herbs are added. The liquid is brought to simmering point and kept at that point until the fish is cooked. Poaching can be done in the oven or on the hob. Large fish, such as salmon and salmon trout, are usually poached whole in *court-bouillon*.

Steaming Probably one of the healthiest methods of cooking fish, as it cooks quickly, does not leach nutrients (vitamins and minerals) into cooking liquid and does not add fat. Fillets, steaks and whole fish can be steamed over hot water, stock or *court-bouillon*.

Stir-frying Cooks fish quickly, retaining the flavour. It is suitable for fish and for shellfish. There are endless permutations of mixtures of fish and vegetables cooked with different spices and herbs.

shellfish

Shellfish should be used as soon as possible, preferably on the day it is bought. Do not keep in the refrigerator for more than a day. If the shellfish is live, make sure it is alive and moving. The shells should be shut tight; discard any that are broken. To store, place in a container and cover with a tea towel soaked in cold, salted water while storing in the fridge. Change the cloth after 12 hours. If bought cooked, shellfish should be heavy for its size.

boiling live lobster, crab, shrimps, prawns and crayfish
A large, deep pan is needed, with enough salted water to cover or a *court-bouillon* flavoured with herbs. Bring the water to the boil and, if flavourings are used, simmer for 5 minutes. Make sure the water is at a rolling boil before adding the shellfish, which will die in a few seconds. Boil for 5 minutes or as instructed in the recipe.

types of shellfish
Clams Come in many sizes; the meat is less firm and distinct in shape and flavour than that of scallops. Open as for oysters.

Crab Crabs can be bought live or cooked. To remove the meat from a cooked crab: first, twist the claws and legs off the body. Crack the shell with a small hammer or the back of a heavy knife and pick the meat out with a skewer. Twist the body off from the back of the shell.

Discard the soft gills and cut the body section in half with a sharp knife. Pick out the meat with a skewer. Scoop the soft brown meat out of the shell. Dressed crabs have had their meat packed back into the cleaned shell.

Soft-shelled crabs or blue crabs are eaten whole, after the tail, eyes and gills have been removed. They are, in fact, crabs that have been caught after shedding their shells and before growing a replacement. Sauté in butter.

Crayfish Looks like a miniature lobster but is the size of a large prawn and lives in fresh water. Crayfish need to be cleaned if they are bought live. The intestine is in the tail and is removed by grasping the end of the tail and twisting while pulling gently – this is done either before or after cooking.

Save the shells of crayfish, prawns and lobsters for making into stock and sauces; simmer in water, strain and then reduce the liquid by at least half.

Mussels Usually sold cleaned, but it is still advisable to immerse in cold water just before use and scrub the shells to remove debris. Discard any that do not close when put in cold water. Scrape off any barnacle shells, for the sake of appearance, but not necessary for cooking. Pull off the 'beard' (bysuss) threads. The easiest way to open mussels is to steam them in a large, covered pan with *court-bouillon*, water or white wine for 5 minutes, shaking the pan occasionally. The mussels will open; discard any that have not opened after 5 minutes. Serve the mussels in their shells, on the half shell or out of their shells.

Oysters Usually farmed and graded according to their size, from 1 to 4, with 1 being the largest. Oysters are often served raw. Some have a creamy flesh and some a more opaque, firmer flesh. Raw oysters can be served with lemon juice, vinegar or chilli sauce – and wholemeal bread and butter.

Short oyster knives have a shield between handle and blade so the hand is not pushed in to the tough shell during opening. A short, pointed knife will do instead.

Hold the oyster in the other hand against a thick cloth or an oyster glove. Insert the point of the knife next to the hinge and twist the knife to open the shell. Cut the muscle that holds the oyster to the top half of the shell and loosen the oyster from the lower, hollow shell. Put the oyster on ice and serve.

Oysters can also be grilled or wrapped in bacon and cooked as kebabs for 'angels on horseback', or deep-fried. Stuffed into a steak, they make 'carpet bag steak'.

Prawns Can be bought raw but are usually sold cooked and shelled. Raw prawns are grey; they turn pink on cooking. There are various types of prawn, including langoustine, also called scampi or Dublin Bay prawn, large prawns and common prawns. Tiger prawns are very large and sometimes 'butterflied (as are large prawns and scampi). Shell the prawn, make a full-length cut along the back, about halfway through the flesh. De-vein the prawn (see below) and then open it out to a butterfly shape before cooking.

The dark intestinal vein should be removed from the back of large raw prawns before they are cooked. This can be done after cooking, or before if the prawns are to be cooked and served immediately, for example, if they are barbecued on skewers. Leave the shells and heads on, if you like, when the prawns are served. But they will have to be removed if de-veining is done before cooking; the very end of the tail can be left in place when the vein is removed

Scallops Have a pretty fluted shell that has inspired everything from Botticelli's *Birth of Venus* to garden ornaments. Scallop shells are opened in a similar way to oysters (above), holding the convex shell in one hand with the flat top uppermost and inserting a knife blade between the top and bottom. Instead of twisting the knife, slide the blade around the shell to sever the muscle, and discard the top shell. Loosen the scallop from the bottom shell and tip the scallop and the orange 'coral' (actually, the roe) into a bowl ready for cooking. The coral should remain intact as it is edible – in fact, a delicacy.

oven-poached whole salmon

preparation time: 15 minutes | **cooking time: about 40 minutes** | **serves 8 as a main course**

Pre-heat the oven to 180°C/350°F/Gas 4; fan oven 160°C from cold. Using the back of a knife held at an angle, scrape the scales from the whole fish, working from the tail to the head. Rinse the salmon under cold water and then pat dry with kitchen paper.

Using a very strong knife or a strong pair of scissors, cut off the salmon's fins and remove the head. Weigh the fish and calculate the cooking time, allowing 8–10 minutes per 450 g (1 lb).

Line a shallow roasting tin with a double layer of foil and brush the base with a little oil. Sprinkle the inside of the salmon evenly with salt and freshly ground black pepper, then lay the fish on the foil and tuck the lemon slices and parsley sprigs into the cavity. Scatter over the peppercorns and pour over the wine or water.

Gather the foil together and seal at the top to form a very loose parcel, so the fish can poach inside. Place in the oven and bake for the required time. To test if the salmon is done, press a knife into the thickest part; the flesh should flake easily. The fish should also feel firm to the touch.

Using two fish slices, carefully lift the salmon from the tin, allowing it to drain, then place on a board to cool. Using a small knife, slit the skin down the length of the back and peel off. Turn over and repeat, then cut off the tail. With the back of a small knife, scrape along the back ridge to remove the fin bones, then gently scrape off any dark flesh, without disturbing the pink flesh. Transfer to a serving platter and garnish. Serve at room temperature.

To serve: the cooked fish will lift easily off the bone. Cut the flesh off one side of the fish at a time. Either slide a knife along the backbone and lift the whole fillet carefully off the bone with a palette knife, or break into portions following the flakes of the fish. Remove any small bones. When you have removed all the flesh from one side, remove the backbone and cut up the bottom fillet.

wine suggestion Salmon is very obliging when it comes to wine, happily partnering either a densely textured white, such as Pinot Gris, Semillon or Chardonnay (with or without oak), or even a lightish red such as New Zealand Pinot Noir or Beaujolais. Or then again, champagne …

1.8 kg (4 lb) fresh whole salmon, gutted
a little oil, for brushing
1 small lemon, sliced
5–6 fresh parsley sprigs
5 black peppercorns, coarsely crushed
100 ml (3½ fl oz) white wine or water
salt and freshly ground black pepper

TO GARNISH:
fresh watercress or dill sprigs
lemon slices

take a salmon steak

Salmon steaks and fillets take only a few minutes to cook and make a great last-minute supper.

to cook salmon steaks or fillets

Fry in a little olive oil and butter for 2–3 minutes each side, depending on thickness. Or bake in a buttered dish, covered with foil or greaseproof, for 15–20 minutes at 200°C/400°F/Gas 6; fan oven 180°C from cold. Or microwave in a covered dish on medium for 4–5 minutes and then leave to stand for 1–2 minutes before serving.

seared honey soy salmon

Mix together 1 tablespoon of wholegrain mustard, 2 teaspoons of honey and 1 tablespoon of soy sauce. Fry salmon steaks or fillets in a little oil for 2–3 minutes on each side until tender. Brush with the sauce. Pour over the sauce and bring to the boil. Serve with new potatoes and salad.

salmon with orange and parsley butter

Beat 50 g (2 oz) of butter until softened. Beat in the grated zest of half an orange, 1–2 tablespoons of chopped fresh parsley and 1 teaspoon of wholegrain mustard. Chill the butter until firm. Bake or fry the salmon and top with slices of the butter just before serving.

salmon with lime and coriander butter

Beat 50 g (2 oz) of butter with a pinch of chilli powder, the grated zest and juice of 1 lime and 2 tablespoons of chopped fresh coriander. Chill butter until firm. Season with salt and freshly ground black pepper. Bake or fry the salmon and top with slices of the butter just before serving.

seared honey soy salmon steak

griddled tuna with tomato salsa

serves 4 | preparation time: 20 minutes | cooking time: 15 minutes

The mild hint of chilli in this tomato salsa is delicious served with grilled fish such as tuna, or with lamb steaks, on top of burgers or with barbecues. Serve the tuna with a green salad or lightly cooked vegetables.

FOR THE SALSA:
6 tomatoes, skinned, seeded and finely chopped
1 red chilli, seeded and finely chopped
1 garlic clove, finely chopped
4 tablespoons olive oil
1 tablespoon red wine vinegar
5 basil leaves

FOR THE GRIDDLED TUNA:
4 × 175 g (6 oz) tuna steaks
olive oil, for brushing
salt and freshly ground black pepper

To make the salsa: place the tomatoes, chilli and garlic in a bowl. Whisk together the oil and vinegar with a fork and pour over. Tear the basil leaves and add just before serving, with a good shake of salt and freshly ground black pepper.

Sprinkle the tuna steaks with black pepper. Heat a griddle or heavy-based frying pan. Brush the tuna with a little extra olive oil. Cook for 3–4 minutes on each side for a rare steak or 5–6 minutes for a firmer fish. Serve with the tomato salsa spooned on top.

wine suggestion A white wine with a fair amount of citric flavour, such as an Australian Riesling or Semillon, works well with tuna, but the tomato and chilli in that salsa might even more happily lead you to a light red – something like Côtes du Rhône-Villages.

trout with spring onion and ginger

preparation time: 30 minutes | cooking time 10–12 minutes | serves 4

*Trout is very quick to cook, just pan-fried in a little butter and olive oil.
Add a few flaked almonds at the end of cooking and a squeeze of lemon
juice. For a more exotic entertaining recipe, try this gingered trout.*

Cut several deep crosses on both sides of the fish. Mix the spring onion
with the ginger, garlic, soy sauce, sherry and sugar. Spread the mixture
over the fish, rubbing it into the cuts; reserve the excess. Leave to
marinate in a cool place for 20 minutes.

   Line a grill pan with foil; lightly grease with the vegetable oil and then
place the trout on top. Grill under a medium heat for 4–5 minutes on
each side until lightly browned and cooked through; drizzle with any
reserved soy sauce mixture during cooking.

   To make the sauce: place the spring onions in a pan and add the
vinegar. Boil rapidly to reduce the liquid to 1 tablespoonful; then remove
the pan from the heat and beat in the butter, one piece at a time; return
to a gentle heat if the sauce becomes too thick. Season to taste.

   Place the trout on serving plates and spoon over a little sauce.

wine suggestion Go for those aromatic Alsace grape varieties again
here, or the equivalent wines from Austria. The drier German Rieslings
would be fine, too. If you've a taste for it, warm sake would make an
unimpeachable match for this dish.

4 × 225 g (8 oz) whole trout
1 spring onion, finely chopped
1 tablespoon finely chopped fresh
   root ginger
1 garlic clove, crushed
1 tablespoon light soy sauce
1 tablespoon dry sherry
½ teaspoon caster sugar
vegetable oil, for greasing

FOR THE SAUCE:
2 spring onions, finely chopped
3 tablespoons white wine vinegar
100 g (4 oz) butter, chilled
   and cubed
salt and freshly ground
   black pepper

classic fish pie

serves 6 | preparation time: 30 minutes | cooking time: 45 minutes

A classic fish pie is brilliantly versatile, great for a lunch with good friends, nutritious and filling for the kids and always rich and comforting! Best of all, it can be made in advance and re-heated the next day. The classics are cod and salmon, but vary the fish according to what's available. Cod, haddock and coley are all good, or add mussels or prawns, or a can of drained tuna, and hard-boiled eggs or vegetables. Top with cheese or not and, if you want a lighter version, use all milk instead of the cream. (If you want to freeze the pie, it is best made with milk.)

1 kg (2¼ lb) potatoes

450 g (1 lb) salmon fillet

450 g (1 lb) cod fillet

450 ml (15 fl oz) milk

1 bay leaf

75 g (3 oz) butter, plus extra for greasing

50 g (2 oz) plain flour

284 ml carton of single cream

175 g (6 oz) large cooked peeled prawns, thawed if frozen

3 tablespoons chopped fresh parsley

150 g (5 oz) mature Cheddar, grated

salt and freshly ground black pepper

Peel the potatoes and cut into quarters. Boil for 20 minutes, until tender. Drain and mash.

Meanwhile, put the salmon and cod, skin-side up, in a wide pan, pour over the milk and add the bay leaf. Bring to the boil and then simmer for 5 minutes or until the fish is just cooked. Using a slotted spoon, remove the fish and place on a plate. Strain and reserve the cooking liquid.

Pre-heat the oven to 200°C/400°F/Gas 6; fan oven 180°C from cold. Butter a 1.5–1.75-litre (2½–3-pint) casserole dish. Flake the fish into large chunks, removing the skin and any bones, and put in the dish, together with the prawns.

Melt 50 g (2 oz) of the butter in a pan. Stir in the flour and cook for 1 minute. Gradually stir in the reserved cooking liquid and the cream and cook, stirring, until thickened, smooth and just boiling. Remove from the heat and stir in the parsley. Season and pour over the fish.

Beat the remaining butter into the potatoes, along with 100 g (4 oz) of the cheese; season. Spread the potatoes over the fish so it is well covered. Sprinkle over the remaining cheese. Chill in the fridge for up to 24 hours until ready to cook, or bake for about 30 minutes, until golden and bubbling.

To make in advance: chill quickly, before baking in the oven, and then refrigerate overnight or freeze, wrapped in freezer film, for up to 3 months. Thaw overnight in fridge before cooking. Bake at 200°C/400°F/Gas 6; fan oven 180°C from cold for 45–50 minutes.

roasted monkfish with mediterranean vegetables

preparation time: 20 minutes | cooking time: 40 minutes | serves 6

Monkfish is a moist, succulent fish, ideal for kebabs or served whole for a great supper dish. Wrap in prosciutto, Parma ham or bacon to prevent the fish from drying out. Serve with new potatoes.

Pre-heat the oven to 190°C/375°F/Gas 5; fan oven 170°C from cold. To make the stuffing: heat the olive oil and gently fry the garlic and onion for 5 minutes, until softened. Stir in the breadcrumbs and parsley; season.

Arrange the prosciutto or Parma ham slices, overlapping, to make a rectangle big enough to wrap the stuffed fish. Season the fish on both sides and place on top, cut-side up.

Spoon the breadcrumb stuffing all along the length of the cavity and then bring the two halves of the fish together to sandwich the filling. Wrap the ham round the fish and tie with string at 2.5 cm (1 in) intervals. If the fish does not cover the stuffing completely at the tail end, wrap the ham round it tightly.

Place the peppers, courgettes, red onion and garlic in a large, shallow ovenproof dish and then top with the fish. Mix together the oil, red wine and balsamic vinegar, herbs and seasoning; drizzle over the fish and vegetables. Bake for 35–40 minutes, until the fish is firm and the vegetables are cooked, stirring the vegetables and basting the fish with the juices occasionally during cooking.

Remove the string and slice the fish into thick pieces. Spoon the vegetables on to plates and arrange the fish on top.

wine suggestion You could opt for one of the more characterful Italian whites, such as Vernaccia di San Gimignano or Verdicchio dei Castelli di Jesi, but the prosciutto wrapping and the robust stuffing here might better suggest a red. Good Chianti Classico or other Tuscan Sangiovese should do it.

150 g (5 oz) very thinly sliced prosciutto or Parma ham
1.5 kg (3 lb) monkfish tail, centre bone removed
1 red and 1 yellow pepper, seeded and thickly sliced
4 medium courgettes, thickly sliced
1 red onion, roughly chopped
6 garlic cloves
4 tablespoons olive oil
1 tablespoon red wine vinegar
2 teaspoons balsamic vinegar
1 tablespoon chopped fresh thyme
1 tablespoon chopped fresh rosemary
salt and freshly ground black pepper

FOR THE STUFFING:
1 tablespoon olive oil
2 garlic cloves, crushed
1 onion, finely chopped
25 g (1 oz) fresh breadcrumbs
1 tablespoon chopped fresh parsley
salt and freshly ground black pepper

crispy cod with parmesan mash

serves 4 | preparation time: 5 minutes | cooking time: 20 minutes (total)

Creamy cod, cooked in minutes, with a rich and flavourful mash, is a great combination for relaxed entertaining or a mid-week supper.

750 g (1½ lb) floury potatoes, peeled and chopped

2 tablespoons olive oil

50 g (2 oz) butter

4 thick pieces of cod, about 175 g (6 oz) each

1 teaspoon English mustard

50 g (2 oz) Parmesan, grated

1 tablespoon snipped fresh chives and a few whole chives to serve

a drizzle of olive oil

grilled cherry tomatoes to serve

Boil the potatoes in a pan of salted water for about 20 minutes, until they are tender.

In a large frying pan, heat the oil with 25 g (1 oz) of the butter and then add the cod, skin-side down, and cook for 5 minutes. Turn the fish over and cook for about 5 minutes more or until cooked through.

Drain and mash the potatoes. Mix the mustard into the potato with the remaining butter and the cheese and snipped chives. Spoon on to plates. Serve with the cod, skin-side up, and grilled tomatoes. Drizzle with a little olive oil.

wine suggestion You'll need quite a gutsy white wine to cut through the bite of mustard in the mash. Old-style white Rioja Reserva or barrel-fermented Chardonnay from California, Chile or Burgundy will handle the firm texture of the cod as well.

crispy cod with parmesan mash

smoked haddock fish cakes

makes 4 | preparation time: 25 minutes | cooking time: 10 minutes

A great family meal. The fish cakes can be made in advance and chilled before cooking. They can also be made with cod, haddock or salmon instead of smoked haddock.

450 g (1 lb) potatoes
450 g (1 lb) smoked haddock
1 hard-boiled egg, shelled and chopped
grated zest of 1 lemon
2 tablespoons chopped fresh parsley
1 egg
100 g (4 oz) fresh white breadcrumbs
salt and freshly ground black pepper
4 tablespoons vegetable oil, for frying

Peel and quarter the potatoes. Cook in boiling, salted water for about 20 minutes, until tender. Drain and mash well.

Place the fish in a frying pan with just enough water to cover. Bring to the boil and then cover and simmer for 5 minutes, until just cooked. Drain and allow it to cool or place the fish between two ovenproof plates and microwave on high for a minute or two, until it is just tender. Break the fish into flakes.

Mix the fish, potato, hard-boiled egg, parsley and a good shake of salt and freshly ground black pepper together. Shape into four rounds, using floured hands.

Beat the egg on a plate, and put the breadcrumbs on another plate. Dip each cake in egg and then in breadcrumbs. Chill until firm, if possible.

Heat the oil in a frying pan and fry the fish cakes gently for 5 minutes on each side until golden.

wine suggestion Smoked fish always means a lavishly oaked white, and a tinge of delicate sweetness in the wine won't go amiss, either. An Australian Chardonnay made in this style is a racing certainty with these fish cakes, or you could try an oak-matured Sauvignon from New Zealand or Bordeaux.

grilled lemon sole with bacon

preparation time: 5 minutes | cooking time: 5 minutes | serves 2

Ever so easy to cook when you get home from work, and light on the calories, too. Look for small sole or dabs in the supermarket or fishmongers: they are just the right size for supper. Serve with boiled new potatoes, a wedge of lemon and some seasonal vegetables.

Pre-heat the grill. Line a grill pan with a sheet of foil and butter it lightly. Arrange the fish on the foil in one layer and season with salt and freshly ground black pepper. Cut the bacon into thin strips and scatter over the fish. Top each with a knob of butter and squeeze over some lemon juice and then grill for 4–5 minutes until the fish is just cooked. Transfer to plates, spoon over the cooking juices and parsley and serve.

wine suggestion A light-textured, refreshing white with appetizing acid bite is what's needed with this unusual combination. Muscadet de Sèvre-et-Maine *sur lie*, a snappy Italian white like Frascate Superiore, or Pouilly-Fumé or Sancerre from the Loire are all appropriate.

a knob of butter

4 plaice or sole fillets, or dabs

3 smoked back bacon rashers

1 lemon

1 tablespoon chopped fresh
   parsley

salt and freshly ground
   black pepper

---

menu: thirty-minute supper

goats' cheese salad with cranberry dressing (page 63)

grilled lemon sole with bacon (page 153)

new potatoes and green beans

bowl of fresh fruit

prawn cocktail with whisky mayonnaise

serves 4 | preparation time: 5 minutes

This is really the basic prawn cocktail recipe but with whisky added to perk it up. Some people use sherry instead or, if you prefer, add no alcohol at all, just a dash of Worcestershire sauce.

175 ml (6 fl oz) mayonnaise
5 tablespoons tomato ketchup
2 tablespoons whisky
4 tablespoons natural yoghurt
a bag of mixed salad leaves
250 g (8 oz) extra-large cooked prawns, peeled
salt and freshly ground black pepper
a handful of fresh basil leaves, to garnish

Place the mayonnaise, tomato ketchup, whisky and yoghurt in a bowl and whisk well together. Season to taste. Place salad leaves on individual plates or in one serving bowl. Pile the prawns in the centre and drizzle with dressing. Scatter with basil leaves.

wine suggestion This isn't going to be especially kind to any wine. If you've used sherry in the recipe, drink a chilled *fino* or *manzanilla* with it; if you're feeling particularly bold and have used whisky in the sauce, perhaps a nip of watered lowland malt Scotch might do the trick.

thai prawn salad

serves 4 | preparation time: 10 minutes

This lively dressing takes prawn cocktail to a new level. You could add a little fresh crabmeat, mussels or cooked squid to the salad, too.

1 lime
1 lemon grass stalk, roughly chopped
½–1 red chilli, seeded and chopped
2 spring onions, sliced
1 tablespoon chopped fresh coriander
1 tablespoon fish sauce (*nam pla*)
a bag of mixed salad leaves
225 g (8 oz) large cooked peeled prawns

Grate the lime zest and squeeze the juice. Place in a mixing bowl and mix in the lemon grass, chilli, spring onions, coriander, fish sauce and 4 tablespoons of cold water. Arrange the salad leaves in a bowl. Place the prawns on top and drizzle with the dressing. Serve immediately.

wine suggestion Keep it light, unoaked, delicately fruity and perhaps a little off-dry, and this salad will present no problems for a white wine. Sauvignon Blanc, Chenin Blanc or Riesling are the favourite grapes, France, Germany and Austria the best sources for the dish.

pan-cooked prawns with garlic and ginger

preparation time: 10 minutes | cooking time: about 6 minutes | serves 2

A spicy supper dish for two. Try to use raw prawns but, if you have to use a bag of frozen cooked prawns, just heat through for a minute or two or they will become tough and chewy.

Place the butter in a frying pan over a medium heat, add the garlic, ginger and chilli and cook gently for about 2 minutes, stirring until the ginger and garlic are softened; take care not to burn the garlic or it will become bitter.

Add the cream, stirring quite quickly to make a creamy consistency, and then stir in the coriander.

Add the prawns and grind in some black pepper. If using raw prawns, cook for 1–2 minutes until they change from blue-grey to pink. If using ready-cooked prawns, simply stir until heated through.

Serve the prawns with crusty bread or noodles.

wine suggestion Perfumed, oak-free whites are best with the oriental seasonings in this dish. Gewürztraminer, Riesling, Argentinian Torrontés or, if you see it, a central European varietal called Irsay Oliver are going to be the best shots. Avoid anything too rich or alcoholic.

50 g (2 oz) butter

4 garlic cloves, crushed

2 teaspoons grated fresh root ginger

1 teaspoon seeded and finely chopped green chilli

4 tablespoons single cream

4 tablespoons chopped fresh coriander

250 g (8 oz) raw headless king prawns, thawed if frozen

freshly ground black pepper

moules marinière

preparation time: 10 minutes | cooking time: 3–4 minutes | serves 4

This classic dish is simplicity itself and very satisfying to eat. Mop up the delicious juices with lots of crusty bread. Or serve with chips and mayonnaise!

Scrub the mussels, remove the beards and scrape off any barnacles. Discard any mussels that do not close when tapped.

Place the mussels in a large pan with the butter, onion, wine and 1 tablespoon of the parsley. Cover with a lid and cook over a high heat for 3–4 minutes, giving a quick stir halfway through cooking. As soon as all the mussels are open, remove from the heat or they will overcook.

Using a large slotted spoon, scoop the mussels into serving bowls, discarding any that have not opened. Strain the juices through a sieve to remove any grit and pour over the mussels. Scatter with more parsley.

1.5 kg (3½ lb) mussels

50 g (2 oz) butter

1 onion, chopped

50 ml (2 fl oz) dry white wine

2 tablespoons chopped fresh parsley

speedy mediterranean fish stew

serves 6 | preparation time: 30 minutes | cooking time: 30 minutes

A quick and simple rich fish stew that is perfect for relaxed entertaining, served with rouille a garlicky, chilli-flavoured paste and lots of warm crusty bread.

FOR THE ROUILLE:

50 g (2 oz) fresh breadcrumbs

1 red chilli, seeded and finely chopped

3 garlic cloves, crushed

1 tablespoon sun-dried tomato paste

2 egg yolks

about 150 ml (5 fl oz) olive oil

salt and black pepper

FOR THE FISH STEW:

3 tablespoons olive oil

2 onions, chopped

3 celery sticks, chopped

2 garlic cloves, crushed

750 ml (1¼ pints) passata

2 tablespoons tomato purée

2 fresh parsley sprigs

1 bay leaf

1 fresh oregano or marjoram sprig

1 thin strip of orange peel and juice of 1 orange

450 ml (15 fl oz) fish stock

1 kg (2¼ lb) mixed fish, such as cod, haddock, monkfish, red mullet, skinned and boned

225 g (8 oz) shelled mussels or prawns

225 g (8 oz) whole mussels

a few saffron strands, soaked in 1 tablespoon warm water

salt and black pepper

To make the rouille: place all ingredients, except the olive oil, in a food processor or liquidizer and whizz until smooth. With the machine running, gradually add the oil, a few drops at a time, until the mixture begins to thicken; then increase to a thin stream of oil. Add enough to give the consistency of mayonnaise. Season and transfer to a bowl.

In a large pan, heat the olive oil and fry the onions and celery for 10 minutes, until softened. Add the garlic, passata, tomato purée, herbs, orange peel and juice and fish stock. Bring to the boil.

Cut the fish into large chunks. Add the fish and saffron (with the soaking liquid) to the pan and simmer, covered for 5–6 minutes or until the fish is tender and cooked. Add the mussels, both shelled and whole, and prawns if using. Cook for a further 3–4 minutes. Do not over cook. Season to taste and serve with rouille.

wine suggestion Choose a southern European white to accompany the richness and robustness of this dish. Light Portuguese whites, unoaked Rueda or Rias Baixas from Spain, or Chardonnay or Pinot Grigio from Italy's Alto-Adige region will all work well.

---

menu: spring supper party

classic caesar salad (page 52)

speedy mediterranean fish stew (page 156)

raisin and vanilla cheesecake (page 226)

---

speedy mediterranean fish stew

vegetable dishes

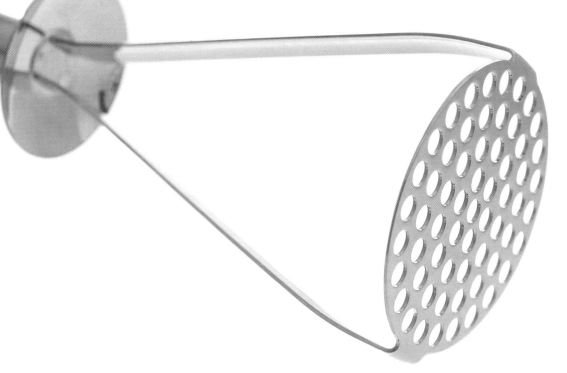

I t is estimated there are nearly three million vegetarians in Britain today (4.5% of the population), with twice as many vegetarian women as men. A lot of people are also cutting down on meat, especially red, and are interested in eating more meat-free meals.

balancing the vegetarian diet

Strictly speaking, vegetarians eat no fish, flesh or fowl. Most eat eggs and dairy produce but vegans eat no animal produce at all. There are lots of reasons for being a vegetarian but, for the diet to be healthy, animal protein has to be replaced with vegetable protein.

Protein in animal foods is made up of amino acids (protein building blocks). In meat, fish, dairy food and eggs, the eight essential amino acids that cannot be made in the body are in the right proportions. Vegetarians need to eat a combination of two of the three plant-protein food groups listed below to get the right proportions. The three groups of vegetable protein foods are: *pulses* (beans, peas and lentils); *nuts and seeds*; and *grains* (rice, bread, pasta and other wheat products, rye, barley, oats).

Dairy foods enhance the available protein in vegetable foods, so vegetarians who eat milk, yoghurt, cheese and eggs will obtain enough protein very easily. However, vegans need to combine vegetable proteins.

If that all sounds rather complicated, reassuringly familiar, everyday foods contain suitable vegetarian protein, for example: beans on toast; pitta bread and hummus; peanut butter sandwiches; *dhal* (lentil curries) or bean curries with rice or Indian breads; Mexican tacos and re-fried beans; and pasta and bean salads.

Other vegetarian protein foods include textured vegetable protein (TVP), tofu, tempeh and Quorn (see below). With the exception of tempeh, most are available from supermarkets and health-food shops. Quorn has no flavour, but will absorb flavours from other foods with which it is cooked. It is also sold in ready meals and pies. With so many alternatives on offer, it is easy to avoid the pitfall of relying too much on any one food, for example, high-fat cheese or eggs.

A well-balanced vegetarian diet can offer health benefits. Studies show that vegetarians are less likely to develop heart disease or cancer.

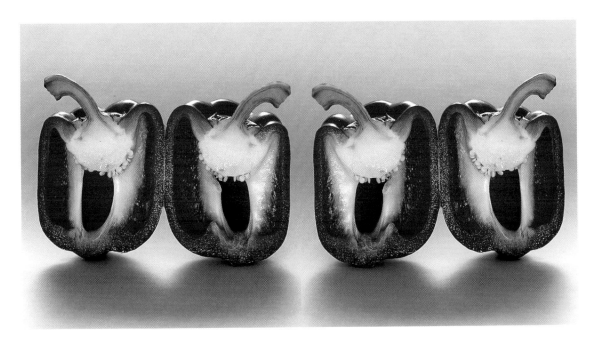

ironing out some vegetarian problems

The body more easily uses the iron in meat and fish. The same is true for zinc, another important mineral found mainly in shellfish and meat. Anaemia occurs as a result of low iron intake (and sometimes because of low folic acid and vitamin B12 intakes). Iron-rich vegetarian foods include green leafy vegetables, pulses, dried fruit, wholemeal bread and fortified breakfast cereals; food or drink rich in vitamin C (citrus fruit/juices; other fruit and vegetables) eaten with vegetarian sources of iron improves the body's uptake of iron.

Vegetarian sources of zinc (which is also better absorbed when taken with vitamin-C-rich food) include pulses, brown rice and wholemeal and rye bread. Zinc is also found in cheese and eggs, carrots and peanuts. Eat them regularly to benefit.

To prevent osteoporosis (demineralization of bones, which can lead to fractures and breaks later in life), vegans in particular need a good calcium intake (as well as adequate exercise and avoidance of cigarette smoking). Good sources of calcium (in addition to dairy food and eggs) are whole-grain cereals, muesli, oatmeal, pulses, nuts and seeds, dark green vegetables and dried fruit. Hard water, and some mineral waters, are also good sources of calcium. White bread is fortified with calcium, so alternate it with wholemeal, if you like.

vegetarian protein alternatives

Quorn A vegetarian protein food made from myco-protein, a microscopic fungus that occurs naturally in soil. The myco-protein is grown in large vats under controlled conditions and is processed and cut into slices or chunks or made into various meat substitute shapes and textures. Quorn is not suitable for vegans because it contains albumen from eggs.

Quorn is a versatile ingredient because it does not have much flavour and will absorb flavour during cooking. It is extruded into different forms to provide a substitute for meat in home-cooked dishes and ready meals.

Tofu (soya bean curd) Made by soaking, grinding and boiling soya beans. The resulting soya milk is then turned into a curd by adding a mineral coagulant and the curd is pressed into blocks. Tofu can be plain, flavoured or smoked. It contains around 8% protein and 3.5% fat.

Firm tofu can be baked, barbecued, grilled and steamed – and marinated to improve the flavour. Soft tofu can be scrambled and used in dressings, sauces and dairy-free cheesecakes.

Tempeh Made by boiling soya beans and then packing them in containers with a starter called *Rhizophus oligosporus*. The beans are then incubated and left until a fluffy white layer forms around the beans, holding them together as a solid cake. Tempeh smells a bit like mushrooms and the cake of beans can be sliced.

It can be cut into burger shapes and cooked as vegetarian burgers. It can also be sliced into strips and is used in lots of vegetarian and vegan recipes. It is a good source of vitamin B.

nuts

Nuts are concentrated sources of energy, vitamins and minerals, providing all the 'stuff of life' (like seeds) to nourish a new plant. The majority are a good source of NSPs (fibre) and the fat they contain is unsaturated (except for coconut). Salted nuts are not good news for people with high blood pressure, and their high calorie content is a problem for the overweight. When eaten as part of a balanced diet, though, nuts are nutrient-dense foods.

To remove the skins from nuts, blanch them. Place them in a bowl, cover with boiling water and leave to stand for 3 minutes. Drain, cover with cold water and then remove the skins by pressing the kernel between thumb and forefinger. Dry on kitchen paper.

All nuts and seeds should be stored in an airtight container in a cool place for maximum freshness and flavour and to prevent the nut oils from becoming rancid.

Almonds Small, flattish oval nut with a creamy-white flesh and amber-brown skin. Available in their shells in the late summer and autumn, otherwise sold whole in their skins, whole and skinned, chopped, slivered, flaked and ground. For use in savoury dishes, cakes, biscuits, confectionery and as a garnish.

Marzipan is a paste made from ground almonds, sugar and egg white. It is available coloured (pale yellow) or uncoloured.

Brazil nuts Very hard three-edged triangular nut with firm white flesh. Buy in the shell in autumn and winter and store in a cool place. Shelled nuts are available all year and are served as a dessert or with fruit or cheese. They can be used in vegetarian savoury cutlets, roasts and burgers. Often they are used whole to decorate cakes and are sold covered in chocolate, but are not commonly used in confectionery or cakes and biscuits.

Candlenuts Used in Indonesian and Malaysian cookery. They are a round and flat nut available from ethnic stores.

Often roasted and mixed with shrimp paste and chillies to make curry pastes or accompaniments for curries, they were originally used to make candles, hence their name.

Cashew nuts Kidney shaped with a cream-coloured flesh and a characteristic flavour. Always sold shelled, either whole, halved or in pieces, or, most frequently, salted as a popular bar and party snack. Unsalted nuts can be used in vegetarian savoury cutlets, roasts and burgers or be added to stir-fries. Good toasted in salads and stuffing.

Chestnuts Roasted on the streets in winter, these nuts are associated with Christmas in Britain and are available fresh during autumn and winter. On the continent they are popular in confectionery or processed as *marrons glacés* and preserved in liqueurs. Sold vacuum-packed and in cans, either whole or puréed for use mainly in desserts and confectionery. There's more carbohydrate than protein in chestnuts, which have quite a different (non-oily) texture to other nuts.

Coconut Familiar fruit of a palm tree with its thick, fibrous brown shell and layer of white flesh and liquid in the centre. Available imported all year and processed as desiccated coconut and creamed coconut (see page 67). The flesh is made into coconut milk for use in Indonesian, Malaysian and Indian dishes. Shredded coconut flesh is used in confectionery, biscuits, cakes and ice-cream

Gingko nuts These are unusual among nuts in providing vitamin C. Used in Chinese, Japanese and Korean cuisine – roasted as a snack.

Hazelnuts A small, round nut with a brown skin. Also known in Britain as cob nuts and filberts. The season for hazelnuts, grown in Kent in the UK, starts at the end of August, but they are available from imports all year, both in their shells and shelled. Use whole, chopped or ground in savoury and sweet dishes. Hazelnuts are quite sweet and most often used in cakes, petits fours, confectionery, yoghurt, ice-creams and desserts.

Macadamia nuts Native to Australia, with a very high unsaturated fat content and a good source of fibre. They are round and waxy and look quite similar to a less wrinkled chick-pea. Very hard – use chopped and whole in desserts and confectionery and ice-cream or salted as a snack.

Peanuts Also called groundnut, monkey nut and goober. Strictly speaking, they are a pulse and not a nut. Peanuts are a basic staple food in parts of Africa, where they are ground into sauces and made into stews. Sold raw in their thin, straw-coloured pods, which break easily without nutcrackers to reveal red-skinned nuts. However, peanuts are more familiar in the UK as a salted snack or as peanut butter, made by roasting skinned peanuts and grinding to a paste with palm (saturated) oil and salt. Roasted or salted peanuts can also be used in salads and in sauces with rice and pasta and are popular in cookies and ice-cream. Ground nuts make the basis of satay sauce.

Pecan nuts Thin, elliptical nuts with a ridged kernel, like narrow, less wrinkled versions of walnuts. They are

sold in their shells in autumn and winter or shelled and whole at other times. The most famous pecan recipe is pecan pie, similar to a nutty treacle tart. Used in biscuits, cakes, breads, and confectionery and ice-cream – pecans also make good praline.

Pine nuts or kernels Small, waxy, cream-coloured kernels that are the seeds of mature pine cones. Available all year round, they can be roasted or grilled until golden to enhance the flavour. Useful in stuffing, salads and savoury dishes.

Pesto is made from ground pine nuts mixed with basil, olive oil and Parmesan cheese.

Pistachio nuts Have an attractive green flesh encased in a red-purple papery skin and tight, round shells. Available in the shell and shelled or blanched all year round. Salted pistachios are sold in the shell, which is partially opened. Unsalted pistachio can be used in meat terrines, can stud joints of cured pork and can be cooked in, or garnish, pâtés.

Walnuts Look like little brains encased in a brown skin. Nutritionally valuable for their essential fatty acid content – particularly valuable for vegetarians who do not eat oily fish. Walnuts have a distinctive rich flavour and varieties sold in the UK have a yellow-brown flesh. Available in the shell imported from around the world most of the year, but particularly plentiful in autumn and winter. Sold shelled as halves and pieces for use in breads, cakes and biscuits, pastries and confectionery. Good in salads (particularly the classic Waldorf) and salad dressings served with cheese and as a dessert nut. Green (unripe) walnuts are pickled and served with cold meats and cheese.

Walnut oil is made from toasted walnuts to bring out its wonderfully aromatic quality.

healthy nuts
Two major medical studies have shown that people who eat nuts frequently, have a lower risk of heart

disease, and lower death rate than those who do not eat nuts. Including as little as 25 g (1 oz) of walnuts per day in your diet can have a beneficial effect within a month.

seeds

Linseed The seed of the flax plant. It is added to cereals and breads and sold in health-food shops, because the oils in the seed are rich in omega-3 fatty acids (protective against heart disease) and phytoestrogens (naturally occurring plant hormones thought to be beneficial to health).

Poppy seeds Tiny, slate-blue seeds most familiar as a decoration on white bread and bread rolls and in poppy-seed cakes. Popular in Turkish, Eastern European and Jewish cuisine; poppy-seed oil is widely used in Turkey.

Pumpkin seeds Flat, oval seeds in a whitish shell. A rich source of iron and zinc. Available from health-food shops and supermarkets. Can be toasted before eating as a snack and in salads, on muesli, in vegetarian savoury dishes and in breads and biscuits and granola bars and flapjack-style slices.

Sesame seeds Small, flat, cream-coloured seeds (although brown ones are available in oriental stores). Rich in unsaturated oils and calcium, plus vitamin E and minerals. Familiar as the topping to prawn toasts in Chinese cuisine and as an addition to snack bars and confectionery. Can be roasted or eaten raw. Mix with breadcrumbs for coating food before frying.

Sesame seed paste is called tahini. It is used as a butter or spread in the Middle East and is the key flavour in hummus and halva. Sesame oil has a rich flavour and is used in stir-fries and salad dressings.

Sunflower seeds A good source of iron, zinc and vitamin C; they are rich in polyunsaturated oil. Flat and oval, with a familiar black-striped shell. Once shelled, they can be used as a snack and added to cakes, biscuits, bread and other baked products. An ingredient in health bars and in savoury vegetarian dishes. Add to stir-fries, rice dishes and pasta. Toasted, they can be tossed over fruit salads.

peanut allergy

A rise in potentially life-threatening peanut allergies among babies and children has left many parents wondering whether it is safe to give their children foods such as peanut butter. Nuts should never be given to babies and children under three years because they could choke on them. However, for non-allergic children, smooth peanut (and other nut) butter is a good source of minerals, unsaturated fats, and protein, but it should not be introduced until around one year of age. The delay is because peanuts have long been recognized as a common allergen (along with egg, gluten in wheat and cows' milk). Infants' immature digestive systems make them most susceptible to developing food allergies in the first few months of life.

Babies born into families with a history of allergic disease, such as asthma, hay fever and allergy-related eczema, are most at risk of allergy. It might be sensible to delay introduction until age five for 'at risk' children.

As peanuts are legumes, it might seem logical that baked beans, peas and lentils could also cause allergies, but it is very rare to be allergic to pulses.

tandoori tofu skewers

serves 4 | preparation time: 45 minutes, | cooking time: 10 minutes

*These tasty tofu kebabs are quick to cook but are best marinated for
30 minutes, to allow the flavours to be absorbed by the tofu. Serve with
naan bread and a crisp salad.*

2 tablespoons tandoori paste
200 ml (7 fl oz) Greek yoghurt
275 g (10 oz) plain tofu, cubed
1 tablespoon sunflower oil
10 cm (4 in) piece of cucumber
1 tablespoon chopped fresh mint

Mix together the tandoori paste and 2 tablespoons of the yoghurt.
Add the tofu and stir until well coated. Leave to marinate for at least
30 minutes.

Pre-heat the grill until glowing hot. Thread the tofu on to skewers,
brush with oil and grill for 3–4 minutes on each side, until golden.

Grate the cucumber, mix with the mint and remaining yoghurt and
serve with the kebabs.

wine suggestion The strong marinade in this recipe calls for either a
high-acid white or a light red. Austrian or Alsace dry Riesling would make
a sympathetic match, as would Beaujolais or Italian Dolcetto from
Piedmont. Red or white, serve it chilled.

polenta with mushroom and mascarpone

preparation time: 10 minutes | cooking time: 10 minutes | serves 4

Traditional polenta takes a long time to cook, so use a quick-cook variety for this tasty supper. When cooked, polenta is delicious sliced and grilled with a topping of blue cheese, roasted vegetables, tomato sauce or these creamy mushrooms.

Pour the stock into a pan and bring to the boil. Sprinkle in the polenta and cook for 2–3 minutes, stirring constantly until thickened. Stir in the olive oil and season well. Spread out in a greased 15 cm (6 in) square cake tin and allow to cool.

Pre-heat the grill to high. Cut the polenta into triangles, place on a baking tray and grill until just golden.

Meanwhile, melt the butter in a small pan, add the mushrooms and fry for 3–4 minutes, until softened. Stir in the garlic and cook again for a minute or two. Remove from the heat and sprinkle with parsley.

Place two triangles of polenta on each plate, pour over the mushrooms and top with a good dollop of mascarpone.

wine suggestion Go for a richly constituted Italian red to suit this dish. Southern-region wines, such as Salice Salentino or Aglianico del Vulture, will make for a successful marriage, or try one of the Californian versions of Italian grapes such as Barbera or Sangiovese.

500 ml (17 fl oz) vegetable stock
125 g (4½ oz) quick-cook polenta
1 tablespoon olive oil
50 g (2 oz) butter
225 g (8 oz) mushrooms, sliced
1 garlic clove, crushed
2 tablespoons chopped
  fresh parsley
150 ml (5 fl oz) mascarpone
salt and freshly ground
  black pepper

broccoli and filo flan

serves 6 | preparation time: 20 minutes | cooking time: 35–40 minutes

*This modern version of the quiche will be liked by everyone and is ideal
for a light lunch, picnic or buffet menu.*

1 red pepper, halved and seeded
275 g (10 oz) broccoli florets
8 filo pastry sheets
25 g (1 oz) butter, melted
1 tablespoon olive oil
200 g (7 oz) packet of feta cheese,
crumbled
3 tablespoons fresh basil leaves,
shredded
150 ml (5 fl oz) double cream
150 ml (5 fl oz) milk
3 medium eggs
1 teaspoon Dijon mustard
salt and freshly ground
black pepper

Place the pepper halves under a hot grill, skin-side up, and grill until the
skin has blistered and is blackened. This will take 10–15 minutes. Place
in a plastic bag, knot the end and leave until cool enough to handle; then
peel off the skin and cut the flesh into strips.

Cook the broccoli florets in boiling, salted water for 5 minutes, until
just tender. Drain and rinse with cold water until cold. Set aside.

Pre-heat the oven to 180°C/350°F/Gas 5/fan oven 160°C. Lightly
grease a 23 cm (9 in), loose-based, straight-sided, shallow flan tin.
Lightly brush one sheet of filo pastry with the melted butter mixed with
the olive oil. Line the flan tin with the filo, overlapping the edges. Repeat
with the remaining filo pastry sheets, overlapping the pastry equally all the
way round. Scrunch the pastry around the sides.

Arrange the broccoli, red pepper and crumbled feta cheese in the flan.
Mix together the basil, cream, milk, eggs and mustard. Season well, pour
into the flan and bake for 35–40 minutes, until the custard is just set and
the pastry is golden. Serve warm or cold.

wine suggestion Sauvignon Blanc will make a peerless match here,
to complement the green veg as well as the salty feta cheese and to cut
the creamy richness of the filling. Sancerre or Pouilly-Fumé would be the
first choices, but wines from New Zealand or Chile are more than
capable of fitting the bill.

menu: vegetarian dinner

warm cous cous, vegetable and feta salad (page 54)

broccoli and filo flan (page 166)

green salad and baked potatoes

crème brûlée (page 223)

broccoli and filo flan

chestnut, stout and stilton stew

serves 6 | preparation time: 15 minutes | cooking time: 20 minutes

This rich and satisfying stew is delicious served with jacket potatoes, mash or even dumplings.

50 g (2 oz) butter
2 tablespoons olive oil
2 onions, sliced
2 carrots, diced
750 g (1½ lb) button mushrooms, halved if large
225 g (8 oz) cooked peeled chestnuts, fresh, canned or vacuum-packed
2 garlic cloves, finely chopped
150 ml (5 fl oz) stout or dark ale
1 tablespoon black treacle
2 teaspoons light muscovado sugar
1 tablespoon chopped fresh thyme or 1 teaspoon dried thyme
175 g (6 oz) Stilton, grated or finely sliced
salt and freshly ground black pepper

Melt the butter with the oil in a large pan. Add the onions and carrot. Fry gently for 4–5 minutes. Add the mushrooms and fry for 5–7 minutes, until the juices begin to run. Add the garlic, chestnuts, stout or ale, treacle, sugar and thyme and simmer for 10 minutes, stirring occasionally. Add the Stilton and stir constantly for about 4 minutes, to prevent it from sticking to the bottom of the pan. Serve hot, with mashed potatoes and a green vegetable.

wine suggestion Nothing less than a thoroughly sturdy red wine will suit the complex and satisfying flavours of this dish. Big Shiraz or Zinfandel reds from Australia or California, or perhaps one of the muscular Spanish reds like Priorato, will keep up with the pace.

spiced nut pilaf

preparation time: 15 minutes | cooking time: 15 minutes | serves 4

This Turkish style pilau (pilaf) makes a filling supper dish. Use the basic recipe to experiment: use any nuts you prefer; vary the dried fruits, using dates or figs instead; or you could add canned chick-peas, or chunks of roasted vegetables such as pumpkin, courgette, red pepper or carrot. You could even ring the changes by flavouring with curry paste instead of the Middle Eastern spices.

Heat the oil in a large pan and then stir-fry the nuts until golden; remove with a slotted spoon.

Fry the onions for 10 minutes and then add the ginger, garlic, rice and spices and stir-fry for a few seconds. Stir in the stock, apricots and honey, season, and then cover and simmer for 10–12 minutes, until the rice is tender and most of the stock has been absorbed.

Stir the orange zest into the rice and serve the rice scattered with the nuts.

wine suggestion The fruits and spices in this recipe will need a full-fruited, spicy red. That means Grenache/Syrah reds from the Languedoc and southern Rhône (Châteauneuf-du-Pape, Minervois, Corbières) or the equivalent blends from California or Australia.

2 tablespoons olive oil
100 g (4 oz) mixed nuts, such as
    pine nuts, peanuts, almonds,
    pistachios, pecans, cashews
    (not salted, dry roasted, etc.)
2 red onions, chopped
5 cm (2 in) piece of fresh root
    ginger, peeled and chopped
2 large garlic cloves, chopped
225 g (8 oz) basmati rice
8 green cardamom pods, bruised
2 cinnamon sticks
8 whole cloves
100 g (4 oz) ready-to-eat
    dried apricots, chopped
900 ml (1½ pints) hot
    vegetable stock
1 tablespoon clear honey
grated zest of 1 orange
salt and freshly ground
    black pepper

perfect roast potatoes

serves 6 | preparation time: 10 minutes | cooking time: 50 minutes

1 kg (2¼ lb) King Edward,
Maris Piper or
Desiree potatoes
4–6 tablespoons olive oil

Pre-heat the oven to 190°C/375°F/Gas 5; fan oven 170°C from cold.
Peel the potatoes, cut into chunks and parboil for 5 minutes. Drain well.
Then shake the potatoes in the pan so the outsides are roughened,
which gives them a crisper surface. Spread the potatoes in a roasting tin
in a single layer and drizzle with enough olive oil to coat. Season and
cook (above the joint, if you are serving them with a roast dinner) for
about 45 minutes, until golden and crisp.

spicy roast parsnips

serves 6–8 | preparation time: 10 minutes | cooking time: 30 minutes

750 g–1 kg (1½–2 lb) parsnips,
trimmed and quartered
lengthways
2 tablespoons sunflower oil
2 teaspoons mustard seeds
2 teaspoons cumin seeds
1 teaspoon paprika
½ teaspoon turmeric
salt and freshly ground
black pepper

Cut out the tough cores from the parsnips. Toss with the oil, mustard
seeds, cumin seeds, paprika, turmeric and seasoning until evenly coated.
Roast around the joint or in a small roasting tin at 190°C/375°F/Gas 5/
fan oven 170ºC for 30 minutes.

red cabbage with apple and port

preparation time: 10 minutes | cooking time: 1¼ hours | serves 10–12

A delicious sweet and sour accompaniment for roast chicken, turkey or pork. Make ahead and re-heat if you like.

Cut the red cabbage into quarters. Remove the central core. Slice the cabbage thinly. Melt the butter in a large pan. Add the onion and fry until soft. Add the cabbage and stir-fry for 2 minutes; then stir in the remaining ingredients. Cover and cook over a very low heat for about 1¼ hours.

450 g (1 lb) red cabbage
25 g (1 oz) butter
1 small onion, chopped
1 apple, peeled, cored and sliced
50 ml (2 fl oz) red wine vinegar
150 g (5 oz) redcurrant jelly
75 ml (3 fl oz) port
25 g (1 oz) light muscovado sugar
**salt and freshly ground
   black pepper**

sweet and sour carrots

preparation time: 10 minutes | cooking time: 15 minutes | serves 4–6

A delicious and unusual accompaniment that can be served with most meats and poultry.

Peel and slice the carrots lengthways and cut into 5 cm (2 in) lengths. Place them in a pan into which they will just fit. Add all the remaining ingredients and enough water just to reach the top of the carrots. Bring to the boil and then simmer for 10 minutes, until the carrots are almost tender. Turn up the heat and fast boil for 5–10 minutes, until all the water has evaporated and a sticky glaze is produced. Take care not to let it burn. Remove the star anise and serve.

450 g (1 lb) carrots
1 tablespoon butter
1 tablespoon lemon juice
1 tablespoon brown sugar
1 tablespoon soy sauce
**2 pieces of star anise or
   a pince of Chinese
   five spice powder**

braised celery and beetroot

serves 6 | preparation time: 10 minutes | cooking time: 25 minutes

1 head of celery
400 g cooked beetroot
50 g (2 oz) butter
1 onion, chopped
1 bay leaf
4–5 fresh thyme sprigs
300 ml (10 fl oz) vegetable or
chicken stock
salt and freshly ground
black pepper

Cut the celery and beetroot into short sticks.

Melt the butter in a pan with a tight-fitting lid. Add the onion and fry gently for 5 minutes, until softened. Add the celery, bay leaf and thyme; season with salt and freshly ground black pepper. Stir well and then cover and gently cook for 10 minutes.

Add the stock, bring back to a simmer, then cover and cook for 10 minutes more until the celery is just tender. Stir in the beetroot and warm through.

lemon roasted potatoes

serves 10–12 | preparation time: 10 minutes | cooking time: 1–1½ hours

These are the perfect accompaniment to a roast dinner.

1 kg (2¼ lb) potatoes, peeled
2 tablespoons olive oil
1 red onion, cut into wedges
1 lemon, cut into 6 wedges
coarse sea salt and freshly
ground black pepper

Pre-heat the oven to 190°C/375°F/Gas 5; fan oven 170°C from cold. Cut the potatoes into equal-sized pieces. Dry them well with kitchen paper, then toss in the olive oil until evenly coated. Arrange in a roasting tin in one layer, then toss in the onions and lemons and season well with salt and freshly ground black pepper. Roast for about 1–1½ hours, until crisp and golden brown.

cabbage with caraway seeds

preparation time: 5 minutes | cooking time: 10 minutes | serves 6

Fry the caraway seeds in a dry pan for a few seconds to release therir aromas. Tip onto a plate to cool. Heat the oil in a shallow pan and add the cabbage. Stir well over a high heat for a couple of minutes, then add the stock and bring to the boil. Cook until the cabbage has just wilted but still remains crisp. Add the caraway seeds and season well.

1 teaspoon caraway seeds
3 tablespoons olive oil
750g (1½ lb) Savoy cabbage, shredded
6 tablespoons vegetable stock
salt and freshly ground black pepper

brussels sprouts with chestnuts

preparation time: 10 minutes | cooking time: 10 minutes | serves 6

Traditionally served with roast turkey (see page 132), these are good with other meats, too. Try walnuts or hazelnuts instead of chestnuts, or simply serve with chopped crisp bacon.

Trim the stalks off the sprouts and discard any tough outer leaves. Cut a cross in the base. Boil in salted water for 10 minutes until just tender. Drain. Add the butter and chestnuts and heat through for 2–3 minutes.

450 g (1 lb) brussels sprouts
25 g (1 oz) butter
100 g (4 oz) chestnuts, peeled and cooked, or tinned or vacuum-packed

bread
and pizza

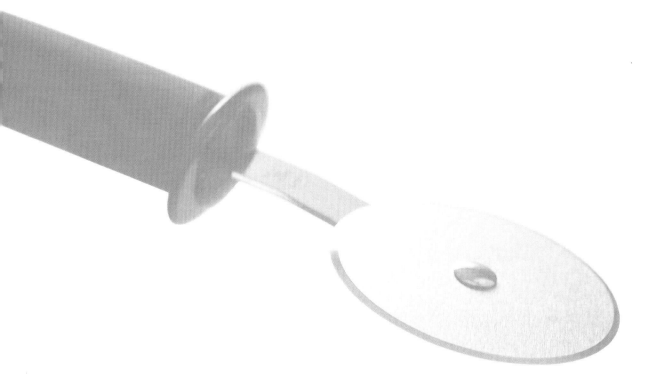

making bread at home is not difficult and yet many people feel intimidated and do not develop a skill that is simple to master and very satisfying. Once you have the basics, you can create your own versions of a wide variety of commercially baked breads and other recipes made from yeast dough, such as hot cross buns, rum babas, croissants, brioches, wholemeal bread and many more. Some breads are made without yeast, including soda bread and corn bread. Sourdough breads are made using a piece of dough from the previous batch as a raising agent.

bread tins

If using a baking tray for bread or rolls, make sure it is a heavy tray that will not buckle in the high temperatures used for baking. Select your loaf tin according to the size and shape of loaf required. It is important to grease the sides of the tin well because bread dough is sticky stuff (too much liquid in it makes it very difficult to get off the hands after kneading – the perfect amount of liquid will not leave a sticky residue on your hands, but be careful that your dough is not too dry or the bread will be too). Non-stick tins can be used for baking bread, but they are not as good at conducting heat or browning a loaf as a heavy, good-quality steel loaf tin. Incidentally, commercially baked sandwich bread is baked in tins with lids to prevent the dough rising – that's why the slices are always square!

flour for bread-making

'Strong' flour is used for bread-making. The 'strength' of a flour is the amount of a particular type of protein, called gluten, in it. Wheat, rye, barley and oats all contain gluten. Gluten enables flour to be elastic and strong enough to hold in the carbon dioxide released by yeast and sourdough starters to form the structure of a loaf, allowing the dough double in size.

Barley flour Dark brown-grey and with a distinctive nutty flavour, it is usually whole grain and has not been refined like white flour. It is coarser than wheat flour and, although it contains gluten, there's not enough to make bread entirely from barley. Up to one-third of the quantity of wheat flour in bread recipes may be substituted with barley flour.

Cornmeal or polenta Made by grinding maize to a meal, it is not rich in protein and does not contain gluten; corn 'bread' is raised, like cake-type tea 'breads', using raising agents such as baking powder.

Malted and mixed-grain flour Made from grains such as barley and wheat that are soaked and softened and allowed to germinate. During germination, the starch in the grains converts to sugars. After this, the grain is dried and milled into flour. Often, malted flour also contains some whole, cracked, malted grains.

Oat flour Can be made by grinding oat flakes or rolled oats and you can substitute it for a small proportion (try about a quarter) of wheat flour but, again, it doesn't have enough gluten to be used on its own.

Rye flour Very popular for bread-making in Germany, Eastern Europe and Russia, rye flour can be 100% wholemeal, which is dark and heavy. Lighter rye flours have had some of the bran and germ extracted.

Soya flour Made from ground soya beans, this has a creamy colour and is more like fine semolina in texture than wheat flour. It is used in gluten-free bread-making, with other gluten-free flours. You can replace up to one-third of the quantity of wheat flour in bread recipes with soya flour. It tends to give baking goods a short texture – useful in biscuits and pastry.

White flour White flour has had the bran and wheat germ removed after the grain has been milled. It can be unbleached or bleached; assume it is bleached unless the packaging states otherwise. Both have a similar nutrient content. White flour for bread-making is often labelled 'strong' or it has a specific reference to suitability for bread-making (as opposed to cake-making) on the pack. Self-raising flour is not suitable for traditional bread recipes that use yeast or sourdough starters. All white flour is fortified with calcium and has had 4 teaspoons of baking powder added to each 400 g (14 oz) of flour.

Wholemeal flour None of the bran or wheat germ is removed during milling, grinding and sieving. It contains the same nutrients as existed in the whole grain and so is nutritionally superior to white flour – except that white flour contains more calcium due to fortification. Wholemeal flour can be used in any recipe instead of white flour but the results will be very different, as wholemeal flour makes heavy cakes and biscuits. When substituting wholemeal for white flour, add more liquid because the bran in the flour absorbs a lot.

glazes for bread

Even loaves that look as if they do not have a glaze have been given some kind of finish before baking, to help the crust brown. To get a matt, unglazed look, loaves are brushed with water before baking and dusted with flour or rolled oats. For a more 'polished' or glossy look, brush savoury bread with milk, melted butter, beaten whole egg or lightly beaten egg yolk or white. Egg glazes can also be used on sweet doughs; or brush them with a sugar syrup, or dust with icing sugar (this gives a caramelized look).

toppings and flavourings for bread

The crust can be flavoured with salt crystals (focaccia is famous for this), rolled oats, chopped nuts, chopped or whole seeds such as poppy, sesame and cumin, a herb such as rosemary, or even grated cheese. Cheese and herbs are more suited to rolls, which cook more quickly and so are less likely to dry out or burn.

Nuts, seeds, herbs, spices, dried fruit, sun-dried tomatoes and olives can all be added to bread. Cooked vegetables such as onions can also be added. Either follow a recipe specifically designed around these added ingredients or experiment with your own additions. Remember, added ingredients can require adjustments to liquid levels in recipes if they absorb some of the liquid. They will also affect storage: onion bread will go soft and mouldy quite quickly; however, a loaf with added dried fruit, nuts and seeds will keep for its normal shelf life of two to three days.

Wheatgerm is added to some breads to make soft bread rich in vitamin E from the germ (embryo) of the wheat. Because of its high fat content, wheatgerm should always be stored in an airtight container in the fridge

making bread

The basic ingredients for bread are very simple (see opposite): just flour, yeast, water and salt – the salt is optional. If dried yeast is used, it is dissolved in lukewarm water, which means a temperature of 37°C (98°F). Dough is kneaded to develop the gluten, the protein in wheat that supports the structure of bread. It is then left to rise (once or twice depending on the type of yeast used, see opposite) before baking.

making bread in a machine

Home-made bread is a joy, but quite labour-intensive. Bread-making machines take absolutely all of the effort out of the task: all the ingredients are weighed into the baking tin; the machine then mixes, kneads, proves and bakes the dough. Most machines will bake white, wholemeal or flavoured doughs. Some can be set so that raisins, fruit or nuts can be added at a later stage, to avoid them being broken up during the first mixing, and many can be pre-set so that the bread can be baked at specific times, allowing you, for example, to come downstairs to the smell of freshly baked bread at breakfast time. The size and shape of the loaf varies with each machine and, if you want to make pizzas or bread rolls, the dough can be removed after proving and then shaped and baked in a conventional oven. Many machines can also be set to bake cakes, too.

basic ingredients for bread

Flour

Choose strong white or brown bread flour for yeasted doughs. It contains a high proportion of gluten, the protein which gives the dough its elasticity. Kneading stretches the dough, increasing the elasticity, which helps to give the bread a good rise.

Yeast

Easy-blend dried yeast is easy to obtain and use, and gives consistently good results. As a general rule, the bread needs only one rising.

If using fresh yeast, replace one sachet of easy-blend yeast with 25 g (1 oz) of fresh. Blend the yeast into the warm liquid and add a teaspoon of sugar. Leave to stand until the liquid is frothing. Add to the flour and continue as usual, but give the bread two risings. After the first rising, knock back the dough and knead again. Shape and place in the baking tin. Allow to rise until doubled in size. Bake as opposite.

Liquid

Use water for plain doughs and milk for enriched breads. The liquid should be hand-hot, too hot and it will kill the yeast. Mix one-third boiling liquid to two-thirds cold.

white bread

makes 1 loaf | **preparation time: 20 minutes + rising** | **cooking time: 30 minutes**

This plain bread recipe is the key to a range of yeasted bakes. Once you have mastered the basic technique, you'll be able to make the recipes on these pages with absolute confidence. This is a quick bread recipe using fast-action yeast, which only requires one rising.

675 g (1½ lb) strong white flour
2 teaspoons salt
1 sachet easy-blend dried yeast
2 tablespoons oil or
25 g (1 oz) butter
450 ml (15 fl oz) hand-hot water
flour, for dusting, or beaten egg,
to glaze

Mix together the flour, salt and yeast in a bowl. If you are using oil, add it to the water. If you are using butter, cut it into small pieces and rub into the flour.

Tip the liquid into the flour all at once, mixing quickly to form a rough ball. Draw together with your hands and then turn out on to a lightly floured surface.

Knead the dough. Fold the dough in half towards you, then push down and away from you, using the heel of your hand to do this. Give the dough a quarter turn and repeat the folding and pushing action, developing a rocking rhythm. Continue kneading for about 5–8 minutes, until the dough is smooth and elastic and no longer sticky.

Thoroughly oil or butter a 1 kg (2 lb) loaf tin. Press out the dough to the length of the tin and three times the width. Fold the long sides to the centre, then drop carefully into the loaf tin, with the join underneath. This will give a good shape to the top of the loaf.

Place the loaf tin in a large, oiled and loosely tied polythene bag and leave to rise for about 1 hour or until doubled in size. The dough will spring back when gently pressed when it is ready.

Pre-heat the oven to 220°C/425°F/Gas 7/fan oven 200°C. Dust the top of the loaf with flour for a soft crust or brush with beaten egg for a shiny crust.

Bake for 30–35 minutes, until the loaf is golden and the base sounds hollow when tapped. If the dough is undercooked, return to the oven, out of its tin, for a few minutes. Cool on a wire rack.

to make bread rolls

Divide the dough into sixteen pieces and shape into balls using the palm of your hand, or roll into sausage shapes. Cut a cross in the top or sprinkle with seeds. Bake for 15–20 minutes, depending on size.

what went wrong?

- If the dough does not rise well, the yeast might have been stale or the liquid used to dissolve it too hot. The flour could have been too soft or too much salt could have killed the yeast. The dough might not have been kneaded enough or the oven temperature could have been too low.
- Heavy bread usually occurs because there was too much liquid in the recipe. It could also be that the dough was left to rise for too long before knocking back. Alternatively, it might not have been left to rise for long enough during the second rising.
- Loaves with big holes in them are caused by one of the following: too high a temperature; too much yeast; over-rising (see above).
- A yeasty taste is, as you would expect, caused by using too much yeast.
- Leave space in the oven for bread to rise – you don't want the top of the loaf touching a higher shelf.
- Do not open the oven door until the dough has risen and started to go brown; it will then be set enough not to collapse and you can safely turn the tin or tray to brown the loaf evenly.
- Steam creates a good crust. Commercial ovens are equipped with steam jets. At home, a shallow tin of boiling water in the bottom of the oven, or spraying the loaf with an atomizer during baking, once it has risen and set, or putting ice cubes on the oven floor at this point, will produce enough steam to make a good crust.
- Bread should fall easily from a loaf tin when it is baked. The base of the loaf should sound hollow when gently knocked with the knuckles.
- Always remove bread from its tin to a wire cooling rack so that the steam can escape and not spoil the crust and make the bread go soggy as it cools.
- Home-made bread freezes well. Once it is completely cold, wrap in a freezer bag and freeze. Once defrosted, yeasted breads can be re-heated in a low oven, if you like.

brown bread

makes 1 loaf | preparation time: 20 minutes + rising | cooking time: 30 minutes

450 g (1 lb) wholemeal bread flour
225 g (8 oz) strong white bread flour
2 teaspoons salt
1 sachet easy-blend dried yeast
2 tablespoons oil or 25 g (1 oz) butter
450 ml (15 fl oz) hand-hot water

Make and bake following the instructions for white bread, allowing 30–45 minutes for rising.

white soda bread

makes 1 loaf | preparation time: 10 minutes | cooking time: 30–35 minutes

Soda bread is incredibly simple and quick to make. Buttermilk gives the characteristic moistness and sweetness but, if it's hard to find, use half natural yoghurt, half milk.

350 g (12 oz) plain flour
½ teaspoon salt
½ teaspoon bicarbonate of soda
300 ml (10 fl oz) buttermilk or half milk, half yoghurt

Pre-heat the oven to 200°C/400°F/Gas 6/fan oven 180°C. Mix the flour, salt and bicarbonate of soda in a bowl and then stir well to distribute the bicarbonate of soda evenly. Make a well in the centre and tip in the buttermilk (or milk and yoghurt), mixing quickly and lightly with a large fork to form a soft dough.

Turn out on to a lightly floured board and knead into a soft dough; the more gently the dough is handled, the lighter the result will be. Don't worry if your dough is craggy – it adds character to the loaf.

Liberally sprinkle a baking sheet with flour and place the dough on top; press out to form a 20 cm (8 in) round. Cut a cross on the top and bake for 30–35 minutes or until the loaf is risen and golden brown. As soon as the loaf comes out of the oven, wrap it in a clean tea towel to keep the crust soft.

hot cross buns

preparation time: 2 hours | cooking time: 12–15 minutes | makes 16

Even if you've never made bread in your life, don't be deterred from making these hot cross buns as they're foolproof and they only need one rising before baking. To speed up the dough even more, use a bread machine. The flour and water paste makes a very decorative cross but, if you like, simply cut a cross with a knife.

In a large bowl, mix the flour, salt, mixed spice, yeast and sugar; then stir in the raisins, candied peel and lemon zest. Gently warm the milk and butter until it is just hand hot and the butter has melted. Pour the milk and beaten egg into the flour, stirring constantly, to make a soft dough. (It should be quite soft, but if you find it too sticky, add a little extra flour.)

On a lightly floured surface, knead the dough for 10 minutes until it's less sticky, and smooth and elastic. Put in a lightly oiled bowl, cover with oiled plastic film and leave in a warm place until it has doubled in size (45 minutes–1 hour). To test, press the dough lightly; it should spring back.

Pre-heat the oven to 220°C/425°F/Gas 7/fan oven 200°C and grease two baking sheets. On a lightly floured surface, knead the dough for 3 minutes and then cut into 16 equal pieces. Roll each piece into a ball, place the balls on the baking sheets, well apart, and flatten slightly with the palm of your hand. Gently score a cross on top of each with a knife.

Blend the plain flour with four tablespoons of cold water to make a smooth, thin paste. Spoon into a small plastic bag and, very carefully, snip off a corner to make a tiny hole. Pipe a cross over the marks on each bun. Bake for 12–15 minutes until golden; transfer to a wire rack.

Meanwhile, boil the milk and sugar in a small pan for 30 seconds until the sugar has dissolved. Brush over the buns while warm.

600 g (1 lb 5 oz) strong white flour

a large pinch of salt

2 teaspoons ground mixed spice

2 × 7 g sachets easy-blend dried yeast

3 tablespoons light muscovado sugar

100 g (4 oz) raisins

50 g (2 oz) candied peel, finely chopped

finely grated zest of 1 large lemon

350 ml (12 fl oz) milk

50 g (2 oz) butter

1 egg, beaten

vegetable oil, for greasing

4 tablespoons plain flour, plus extra for dusting

FOR THE GLAZE:

2 tablespoons milk

2 tablespoons caster sugar

perfect pizza

A pizza base is very quick to make using fast-action yeast. Or you can speed it up even further by using a pizza-base mix made according to the packet instructions. This recipe makes 2 x 25–30 cm (10–12 in) thin-crust pizzas, or 1 x 25–30 cm (10–12 in) thick-crust pizza.

For the best results, top the pizza with the basic tomato sauce and then bake for 7–10 minutes before adding the topping of cheese or vegetable. This ensures that the base doesn't end up soggy.

225 g (8 oz) strong white flour
2 teaspoons easy-blend dried yeast
1 teaspoon sugar
½ teaspoon salt
1 tablespoon olive oil
175 ml (6 fl oz) warm milk and water, mixed

Place the flour, yeast, sugar and salt in a large mixing bowl. Add the olive oil to the warm milk and water mixture and then stir into the flour with a wooden spoon. Mix to a soft dough.

Knead for 5 minutes on a lightly floured surface. The more you knead, the better the result. The dough should be soft and smooth to the touch; add a little more flour if the dough is too soft and sticky.

Lightly oil one or two 30 cm (12 in) baking trays. Roll out the dough to make one 25–30 cm (10–12 in) thick-crust pizza or cut in half and roll into two thin-crust pizzas. Cover with oiled cling film and place somewhere warm until the dough has risen and looks soft and bubbly; this will take 20–30 minutes.

Meanwhile, make the topping and pre-heat the oven to 220°C/425°F/ Gas 7/fan oven 200°C. Spread the topping over the dough and bake following the instructions opposite.

margherita topping

Top with a 400 g (14 oz) can of chopped tomatoes, well drained. Bake for 7–10 minutes and then arrange 8 plum tomatoes, thinly sliced, and 225 g (8 oz) of mozzarella, also thinly sliced, on top. Sprinkle with a handful of basil leaves, drizzle with olive oil and bake for a further 7–10 minutes.

prosciutto and mushroom topping

Top with a 400 g (14 oz) can of chopped tomatoes, well drained, and 225 g (8 oz) of mozzarella, finely chopped. Bake for 7–10 minutes and then top with 225 g (8 oz) of sliced mushrooms, 4 garlic cloves, finely sliced, and 100 g (4 oz) of prosciutto, thinly sliced. Bake for a further 7–10 minutes.

five-cheese topping

Top with a 400 g (14 oz) can of chopped tomatoes, well drained. Add 150 g (5 oz) of chopped mozzarella. Cook for 7–10 minutes and then top with 100 g (4 oz) of Red Leicester or Cheddar, thinly sliced, 50 g (2 oz) of Parmesan, thinly sliced, 100 g (4 oz) of Dolcelatte, thinly sliced, and 100 g (4 oz) of mascarpone. Bake for a further 7–10 minutes.

spinach and bacon topping

Top with a 400 g (14 oz) can of chopped tomatoes, well drained. Bake for 7–10 minutes. Meanwhile quickly fry 225 g (8 oz) washed spinach in 1 tablespoon of olive oil for just a minute until wilted. Arrange on top of the pizza with 6 rashers of snipped bacon, 1 finely sliced clove of garlic and 75 g (3 oz) crumbled Stilton. Bake for a further 7–10 minutes.

tuna and anchovy topping

Top with a 400 g (14 oz) can of chopped tomatoes, well drained. Bake for 7–10 minutes. Drain a small can of tuna and flake it on top of the pizza with 6–8 salted anchovy fillets, 1 sliced red pepper and 50 g (2 oz) black olives. Bake for a further 7–10 minutes.

focaccia

makes 1 loaf | preparation time: 15 minutes + rising | cooking time: 25 minutes

450 g (1 lb) strong white flour

1½ teaspoons easy-blend dried yeast

3 teaspoons coarse sea salt

3 tablespoons olive oil, plus extra for greasing

350 ml (12 fl oz) hand-hot water

FOR THE TOPPING:

1 tablespoon extra-virgin olive oil, plus extra for drizzling

2 garlic cloves, finely chopped

2 fresh rosemary sprigs, leaves removed and finely chopped

In a large bowl, mix the flour, yeast and a teaspoon of the salt. Make a well in the centre and pour in the oil. Gradually add the water, mixing until you have a soft dough.

Place the dough on a lightly floured work surface and knead gently for 10 minutes, until smooth. Place in a large, lightly oiled bowl and cover with a tea towel or plastic film; leave in a warm place for 45 minutes–1 hour, or until doubled in size.

When the dough has risen, turn it on to a work surface. Knead four or five times very gently so that you don't knock out the air, tucking the dough under to encourage more bubbles. Cover with oiled plastic film. Leave for 10 minutes.

Pre-heat the oven to 200°C/400°F/Gas 6/fan oven 180°C and lightly oil a large baking sheet. On a lightly floured surface, roll out the dough to about 1 cm (½ in) thick and 30 cm (12 in) diameter. Place on the baking sheet, cover with a tea towel and leave for 20–30 minutes, or until doubled in size.

Just before baking, make holes over the surface with your fingers. Brush with the oil and sprinkle over the remaining salt, garlic and rosemary. Bake for 25 minutes. Drizzle over a little virgin olive oil and transfer to a wire rack to cool.

To freeze: cool and place in a polythene bag. Freeze for up to 1 month. (All of the following variations can be frozen as above.)

focaccia topping variations

Omit the rosemary. Top the bread with strips of roasted red and yellow peppers and bake as before.

Top with lightly fried onions and sprigs of oregano before baking.

Top with pitted black olives and chopped sun-dried tomatoes before baking.

focaccia

pastry and biscuits

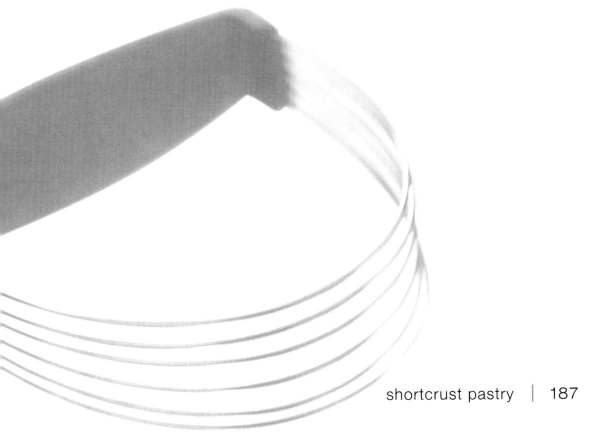

For many of us, the time needed to make pastry is time we'd rather spend doing other things and, since fresh and frozen ready-made pastries are now so good, there seems little point in making your own. However, shortcrust pastry is very easy and quick to make using storecupboard ingredients, and brilliant for making everyday meals such as quiches, pies and tarts. Choux pastry is even easier and profiteroles or éclairs can be knocked up in no time for a treat that will leave friends admiring your cookery skills. Here's a run down of the types of pastry available and their uses.

shortcrust pastry

See the recipe on page 190. The most popular and easy to make pastry, used to make scrumptious quiches, fabulous flans and golden pie toppings.

For a risen, crumblier pastry, use self-raising flour; this is often used for mince pies or pasties but is not advisable for quiches or larger pies, as it is fragile to handle especially when baked.

sweet shortcrust pastry
For sweet flan and tartlet cases, add up to 50 g (2 oz) of caster sugar to every 225 g (8 oz) of flour. For even more richness, bind the fat and flour with egg yolks or a mixture of egg yolks and water or milk or cream. The sugar makes a crisp pastry and the egg yolks give it a yellow colour and rich flavour.

using a food processor
Sift the salt and flour into a mixing bowl or a food processor with a pastry-making attachment, add the fat and whizz until crumbly; then add the water and whizz quickly until bound together.

lining a flan tin or ring
Roll out the pastry in a circle about 5 cm (2 in) wider than the diameter of the ring or tin. Put the ring on a baking sheet. Lift the pastry on to the rolling pin and lower it carefully into the flan ring or tin. Gently shape the pastry against the smooth or fluted side of the ring. Trim the pastry at the rim edge. You can either do this by running a short knife around the top of the rim or by rolling a rolling pin over the top of the pastry-lined ring to cut the pastry level with the top.

baking blind
Sometimes, pastry cases need to be partially baked before the filling is put in, or baked to take a filling that is not cooked in the pastry case. Line the flan ring as above. Line the pastry case with greaseproof paper cut to shape and weigh it down with dried beans or purpose-bought baking 'beans'. Without the weight of the lining and beans, the pastry base would bubble and the pastry case would lose its shape. Bake the pastry case in a pre-heated oven at 200°C/400°F/Gas 6/fan oven 180°C for 15 minutes. Remove the beans and paper and bake for a further 5 minutes or until the base is dry and light brown.

tips for success with pastry

- Keep utensils and hands cool and work in a cool kitchen, if possible.
- Follow recipes carefully because good pastry is reliant on the correct proportion of fat to flour.
- Work quickly with a light touch and keep handling to a minimum.
- Observe any 'rest' periods in the recipe. If you do not, the fat may leak out of pastry, such as flaky or puff, and shrinkage can occur during baking. Pastry is usually covered in the fridge, during 'resting'.
- When rolling pastry out, work on a cool, lightly floured surface. Use short, light strokes and work from the centre of the pastry outwards.

choux pastry

See the recipe on page 194. Equal amounts of fat, flour and eggs are used to make choux pastry. It is piped through a plain nozzle to make éclairs, profiteroles and gougères. The shells can be filled with sweet or savoury mixtures.

other pastries

Filo pastry Wafer-thin, crisp filo pastry is used to make strudels and pastries such as *baklava* from Greece, Turkey, Lebanon and Syria. It is also used in savoury Middle Eastern *mezze*, which are pastries filled with savoury mixtures such as cheese and spinach rolled or folded into fingers and triangles. Filo, or phyllo (from the Greek for leaves) pastry is extremely time-consuming and difficult to make. It takes years of practice to be successful with this pastry which is supposed to be so thin that it can be read through. Luckily, good-quality filo sheets are widely available, either chilled or frozen in supermarkets, and very easy to use.

Allow bought frozen filo pastry to defrost completely in its unopened packet, for 2 hours at room temperature or overnight in a fridge. Once thawed, remove as many sheets as needed and stack them on the work surface. Keep covered to prevent the pastry from drying out. Wrap any unused filo in cling film and chill until needed. Filo will stay fresh in the fridge for 2 days, wrapped in film.

If cutting shapes, stack the pastry and work from the top to prevent it from drying out. Brush with melted butter or margarine as soon as the shape has been prepared. Never wrap filo in a damp tea-towel because the pastry will absorb the liquid and become sticky and unusable; always protect the pastry from damp.

Hot-water crust pastry Raised pies, such as pork or veal and ham, are made with a hot-water crust; this is made with water and, usually, lard brought to the boil and then added to the flour. The dough is kneaded and

moulded while still warm; then either moulded into a cake or raised-pie tin, or around pie moulds or jam jars, and filled with a meat filling while still hot.

Kataifi pastry is also from the Middle East and used to make syrup-soaked desserts. It is a tangled mass of fine strands of dough and is made from batter that is piped onto a heated copper plate. After drying or cooking it is scooped up and packed.

Puff and flaky pastries are deliciously rich and, as the name implies, flaky. Use to make very simple canapés, topped with goats' cheese and tomatoes, simple apple tarts (cut circles of pastry, top with thin apple slices and glaze with apricot jam); use to wrap fillets of salmon, to top a sweet or savoury pie, to make *mille feuilles* or sausage rolls. The fat has to be cut up and dotted over the dough, which is then folded and rolled several times, chilling in between each rolling to make it easier to work with. The fat is trapped in many layers of dough, making the delicious flakes. Such pastry must be baked at a high temperature, 230°C/450°F/Gas 8/fan oven 210°C, to allow the dough to rise and bake into golden flaky layers. Ready-made, fresh or frozen flaky and puff pastry is now readily available in supermarkets, some even already rolled out so that all you have to do is add a filling or topping and bake. Ready-made frozen vol-au-vent cases are also available. You can use either puff or flaky for most recipes.

Rough puff pastry A cross between flaky and puff pastry, this is easier to make but is only as light and flaky when hot; it becomes heavy when cold so is not suitable for pâtisserie.

Suet-crust pastry This pastry is used for traditional British sweet puddings such as spotted dick and jam roly-poly, and savoury puddings such as steak and kidney. It also makes dumplings. Beef suet is traditionally used but vegetarian alternatives made from hardened white vegetable fats are available. Despite the high fat content, the pastry is light in texture.

biscuits

Biscuits can be made using several methods: rubbing in, similar to shortcrust pastry; melting, as for ginger snaps or creaming in (the method used to make a Victoria sponge).

Although some contain raising agents that make them more crumbly, most biscuits are flat and compact. Often the basic flour, butter and sugar dough has added ingredients that define the character of the biscuits: dried fruit, chocolate chips, nuts, seeds or flavouring such as spices, coffee and vanilla.

British biscuits tend to be harder, flatter and more compact than American cookies, which are often risen, chewy and more crumbly and cake-like in texture.

Biscuits should be baked on a greased and floured baking sheet or tin in a hot oven. They need careful watching during cooking because they can quickly over-brown or scorch. Those nearest the hottest part of the oven are in danger of burning first, so trays of biscuits usually need to be turned during cooking. Biscuits should be cooled quickly, to prevent further cooking. Many crisp quickly as they cool and so need to be taken off the baking tray before they become too brittle to move. Slip a palette knife with a flexible blade beneath the bases to loosen the biscuits.

Biscuit dough can be sticky and difficult to roll if it has a high fat content. Rolling out between sheets of greaseproof paper helps. Chill biscuit dough before moulding by hand, to prevent it from becoming sticky.

The dough for sliced biscuits also benefits from chilling, which makes it easier for the knife to go through the roll of dough.

shortcrust pastry

makes 350 g (12 oz) | **preparation time: 15 minutes**

Made with or without sugar, shortcrust pastry can be used to make sumptuous quiches, fabulous flans and golden pie coverings. This recipe makes enough to line an 18–20 cm (7–8 in) flan tin.

225 g (8 oz) plain flour
a large pinch of salt
1 tablespoon caster sugar
(for sweet shortcrust)
100 g (4 oz) cool butter or
margarine, cut into even-
size pieces

Sift the flour, salt and sugar (if using) into a large mixing bowl. Add the butter or margarine.

Rub the fat into the flour with your fingertips until it resembles large breadcrumbs. Keep your hands cool and trickle the mixture between your fingers to incorporate air.

Add 4 tablespoons of cold water (ice-cold if possible) and stir with a table knife until the pastry is loosely combined.

Turn the contents of the bowl out on to a lightly floured work surface and press the mixture together with your fingers to form an even pastry. Handle it as little as possible to retain lightness.

Wrap the pastry neatly in plastic film and, if possible, allow to rest in the refrigerator for at least 1 hour before using. This will help to prevent it from shrinking as it cooks.

wholemeal shortcrust

Try either half wholemeal and half plain flour or all wholemeal.

The amount of water required will vary: use 4 tablespoons to start and then add enough extra to bind the dough.

shortcrust pastry: what went wrong?

Too hard Too much liquid, too little fat or over-handling.

Too soft and crumbly Too much fat or too little water. Also a common fault with pastry made inappropriately from self-raising flour.

Shrunk from sides Excessive handling and rolling out or too little or no resting time before rolling out.

Soggy pastry Filling too wet or pastry case not blind-baked long enough.

Sunken pie Oven too cold, or cold pastry put over hot filling, or too much liquid in filling.

tarte tatin

preparation time: 30 minutes | cooking time: 15 minutes | serves 6

Oozing with caramel sauce, this buttery apple tart is always a winner. Serve warm with ice-cream.

Roll out the puff pastry to a circle 30 cm (12 in) in diameter and 3–4 mm (⅛–¼ in) thick. Place on a board, cover and chill the pastry in the fridge.

Meanwhile, peel, core and halve the apples and toss them well in lemon juice. Take a medium, heavy-based, ovenproof frying pan (about 25 cm/10 in diameter) and, using a spatula, spread the butter evenly all over the base of the pan. Sprinkle over the sugar. Pack the apple halves, cut-sides up, as closely as possible in the pan. Place over a medium heat and cook gently until the apples are just tender and the butter and sugar mixture has all turned golden and caramelized. This should take about 10–15 minutes.

Pre-heat the oven to 200°C/400°F/Gas 6/fan oven 180°C.

Carefully lay the chilled pastry circle on top of the apples. Tuck the edges down the sides of the pan so that, when it is inverted, the edges will create a rim that will hold in the apple, juices and caramel. Place the pan in the oven for about 12–15 minutes to cook the puff pastry and to finish cooking the apples.

Remove from the oven and loosen round the edges of the tart with a knife. Place a plate or tray that is larger than the pan on top and quickly turn the pan upside-down, so that the tart inverts on to the plate. Leave to cool until sticky. Serve warm, with clotted cream.

wine suggestion A very rich, sticky, fortified Muscat wine, such as one of the traditional *vins doux naturels* of southern France, is best with this caramelized tart. Muscat de Beaumes-de-Venise is the star amongst these wines. Washington State also has fine examples of this genre.

250 g (9 oz) puff pastry

6–8 firm Granny Smith or Cox's apples

juice of 2 lemons

150 g (5½ oz) unsalted butter, at room temperature

175 g (6 oz) caster sugar

easy lemon tart

serves 8 | preparation time: 25 minutes | cooking time: 25–30 minutes

A rich tangy dessert that is very quick to make (quicker still if you use a bought pastry case, or 350 g/12 oz of ready-made pastry). Professional chefs and cooks often caramelize the icing sugar on top with a cook's blow torch. A grill does not work so successfully.

FOR THE RICH SHORTCRUST PASTRY:
100 g (4 oz) butter, cut into small pieces
175 g (6 oz) plain flour
25 g (1 oz) caster sugar

FOR THE FILLING:
4 eggs
100 g (4 oz) caster sugar
150 ml (5 fl oz) double cream
finely grated zest and juice of 3 lemons
icing sugar, for dusting

Pre-heat the oven to 200°C/400°F/Gas 6/fan oven 180°C. Make the pastry (see page 190 for full details). Rub the butter into the flour until the mixture resembles breadcrumbs. Stir in the caster sugar, then add about 2 tablespoons of cold water and mix to a firm dough. Wrap in plastic film and chill for 20 minutes, if you have time.

Roll out the dough thinly and use to line a deep 20 cm (8 in) flan tin; press on to the base and against the sides. Trim off the excess pastry. Line with a circle of greaseproof paper and a layer of baking beans. Bake for 15 minutes.

Remove the beans and paper and return to the oven for a further 5 minutes. Reduce the oven temperature to 160°C/325°F/Gas 3/fan oven 140°C.

To make the filling: beat together the eggs and sugar and then stir in the cream. Stir in the lemon zest and juice and pour into the tart case immediately as the mixture will thicken. Bake for 25–30 minutes, until just set. Don't worry if the tart mixture cracks as it cooks. This often happens.

Leave to cool. Dust with icing sugar just before serving.

wine suggestion The citric bite in this classic dessert means that you won't need a massively sweet wine to accompany it. Unfortified late-picked Muscat, from Australia, California or Alsace, would be a winner.

easy lemon tart

choux pastry

You will find that this is the quickest and easiest pastry to make. It is piped or spooned on to baking sheets and then baked in the oven to make profiteroles, larger cream buns or elegant éclairs. You can also fill choux pastry with pâté or cream cheese for delicious savoury dinner party canapés.

65 g (2½ oz) plain flour, sifted
50 g (2 oz) butter or margarine
150 ml (5 fl oz) water
2 eggs, beaten

Sift the flour on to a sheet of greaseproof paper. Gently heat the fat and water until melted. Bring to the boil and remove from the heat.

Tip the flour into the hot butter/water mixture and beat thoroughly with a wooden spoon until the dough binds together. Then return the pan to the heat.

Beat until the mixture forms a smooth, dry ball and leaves the sides of the pan. Cool for 2 or 3 minutes, otherwise the eggs will cook before they are blended.

Gradually beat in the eggs. It will look like scrambled eggs at first but continue beating until the mixture becomes shiny and smooth. Place a 2.5 cm (1 in) plain nozzle in a piping bag and fill with choux paste. Pipe and bake according to recipe.

Choux pastry can be made in advance and kept in the fridge for a day before baking. When it is cooked, the buns can be stored in a tin for 2–3 days, or frozen: re-crisp in the oven.

choux pastry: what went wrong?

Mixture too soft to pipe Insufficient cooling of mixture before adding eggs, or eggs added too quickly.

Pastry did not rise Oven too cold; baking time too short; self-raising flour used; too much glaze spilling from sides of the pastry to the baking tray.

Pastry sinks when taken from oven It has probably not been baked for long enough; put it back immediately and it might rise and set again.

profiteroles with chocolate sauce

preparation time: 30 minutes | cooking time: 15–20 minutes | serves 4–6

Pre-heat the oven to 220°C/425°F/Gas 7/fan oven 200°C. Pipe the choux paste into walnut-sized rounds on to baking sheets. Bake until risen, golden and crisp: 15–20 minutes. Slit the bases to let steam escape. Return to the oven for another minute or two to crispen.

Using a piping bag, pipe whipped cream through the slit in the base of each bun. Pile on to a serving plate.

Melt the chocolate, butter and syrup in a pan. Stir in the cream and, just before serving, pour the sauce over the profiteroles.

1 quantity choux pastry
   (see page 194)
300 ml (10 fl oz) double
   cream, whipped
200 g (7 oz) plain chocolate
25 g (1 oz) butter
25 g (1 oz) golden syrup
2 tablespoons double cream

chocolate éclairs

Pipe sausage shapes 7.5 cm (3 in) long. Bake for about 30 minutes. Then slit along one side (not in the base). Crisp in the oven. Just before serving, fill with whipped cream sweetened with vanilla and a little icing sugar, and ice with melted chocolate or chocolate glacé icing.

mince pies with an almond orange pastry

preparation time: 30 minutes + chilling | cooking time: 20 minutes | makes 12

Since mince pies are so often bought, we've included a rich, luxurious version for a treat.

Rub the butter into the flour. Add the almonds, sugar, almond essence, orange zest, egg yolk and 2 tablespoons of (preferably ice-cold) water and mix to a firm dough. Knead briefly on a floured surface and then wrap and chill for 30 minutes.

Pre-heat the oven to 200°C/400°F/Gas 6/fan oven 180°C. Roll out the pastry thinly and stamp out twelve 7.5 cm (3 in) rounds; use to line 12 bun tins. Spoon in the mincemeat to come two-thirds of the way up the bun tins.

Stamp out holly leaves or slightly smaller circles for lids from the remaining pastry. Place over the mincemeat. Brush with egg white and dredge with caster sugar. Bake for 20 minutes, until crisp and golden brown. Serve with cream or brandy butter.

150 g (5 oz) butter, cut into pieces
225 g (8 oz) plain flour
50 g (2 oz) ground almonds
25 g (1 oz) caster sugar
a few drops of almond essence
grated zest of 1 orange
1 egg yolk
225 g (8 oz) mincemeat
1 egg white, lightly beaten
caster sugar, for sprinkling
Boozy Butter (page 233) or cream,
   to serve

double chocolate chunk cookies

makes about 14 | preparation time: 15–20 minutes | cooking time: 10–12 minutes

100 g (4 oz) butter or margarine,
softened
100 g (4 oz) light muscovado
sugar
25 g (1 oz) caster sugar
1 egg, beaten
1 teaspoon vanilla extract
150 g (5 oz) plain flour
½ teaspoon baking powder
90 g (3½ oz) porridge oats
100 g (4 oz) plain chocolate,
broken into large chunks
100 g (4 oz) white chocolate,
broken into large chunks

Pre-heat the oven to 180°C/350°F/Gas 4/fan oven 160°C and grease two large baking sheets. Beat the butter or margarine and sugars until light and fluffy and then beat in the egg and vanilla extract. Sift in the flour and baking powder and then add the porridge oats and chocolate chunks; mix well.

Using a dessertspoon, space 14 heaped spoonfuls well apart on the baking sheets and flatten slightly with a fork.

Bake for 10–12 minutes or until pale golden and slightly soft in the middle. Leave to firm slightly and then transfer to a wire rack to cool.

fruity flapjacks

makes 14 | preparation time: 10 minutes | cooking time: 35 minutes

Perfect for packed lunches, these moist cake bars are very hard to resist and very simple to make. You can add any dried fruits, nuts or even sunflower seeds to vary the recipe.

250 g (9 oz) unsalted butter
250 g (9 oz) caster sugar
175 g (6 oz) golden syrup
425 g (15 oz) porridge oats
100 g (4 oz) sultanas
100 g (4 oz) ready-to-eat dried
apricots, roughly chopped

Pre-heat the oven to 180°C/350°F/Gas 4/fan oven 160°C. Oil and base-line a 20 × 30 cm (8 × 12 in) shallow cake tin with greaseproof paper.

In a large pan, heat the butter, sugar and golden syrup together over a low heat, stirring occasionally, until the sugar has dissolved. Remove from the heat and stir in the oats, sultanas and apricots. Spoon into the prepared tin. Level the surface and bake for 20–25 minutes, until golden.

Mark into 14 bars and then leave to stand in the tin until almost cold. Turn out, cut into bars and store in an airtight tin for up to 1 week.

pesto and goats' cheese canapés

preparation time: 15 minutes | cooking time: 15 minutes | makes 32

Ready-to-roll puff pastry is perfect for making small savoury tartlets or canapés for a drinks party. They take minutes to make, are very simple and yet look very impressive. Vary the topping by using tapenade (black olive paste), red pesto, chopped roasted vegetables, salami, sliced black olives, anchovies – any combination you fancy.

Pre-heat the oven to 220°C/425°F/Gas 7/fan oven 200°C. Unroll the pastry and cut into eight pieces crossways and four lengthways. Arrange the squares on two dampened baking sheets, allowing a little space between them.

Spoon a little pesto in the centre of each square, top with slices of tomato and cheese and sprinkle with basil leaves. Bake for 12–15 minutes until puffed and golden. Serve warm or cold.

These can be made the day before use and re-heated at 220°C/425°F/Gas 7/fan oven 200°C for 5 minutes. Or cook, freeze and re-heat for 6–8 minutes.

375 g (13 oz) packet ready-to-roll puff pastry, thawed if frozen
3 tablespoons pesto
350 g (12 oz) cherry tomatoes
100 g (4 oz) firm goats' cheese, sliced
a few basil leaves, shredded

cakes

here are so many different varieties of cake that it is hard to imagine how they can be achieved using a few basic ingredients – sugar, eggs and flour, and often some kind of fat – and three basic methods: whisking, creaming and melting. The rubbed-in method produces buns and scones. Whichever type of cake you make, always stick to the recipe because the correct proportion of ingredients is crucial for success.

types of cakes

creamed cakes

The classic example of a creamed cake is the Victoria sandwich. Creamed cakes have a lovely, soft, rich crumb with a delicious flavour of butter (although margarine can be used). The standard quantities are 100 g (4 oz) butter, 100 g (4 oz) caster sugar, 100 g (4 oz) self-raising flour and 2 eggs.

Remove the fat from the fridge at least 30 minutes beforehand to bring it to room temperature, or warm it slightly. This makes it easier to cream with the sugar to produce a lighter result. Do not use soft-tub or reduced-fat margarine or spreads (see all-in-one method, below). To cream the butter or margarine and sugar put them in a bowl and beat with a wooden spoon or electric whisk, until the mixture becomes pale in colour and very creamy and fluffy in texture. The more you beat the

mixture, the more air you will incorporate and the lighter the cake will be.

Make sure the eggs are at room temperature because, if they are cold, they can make the fat coagulate and curdle. Add the eggs very gradually, beating between additions to make an emulsion. If it curdles, add a spoonful of the measured flour.

Sift the flour before folding it into the cake mixture. To fold in the flour, spoon the mixture from the bottom of the bowl and fold it up over the top. Do this in a figure-of-eight movement, cutting through the mixture to make sure there are no pockets of flour. A slotted draining spoon or tablespoon is ideal for folding in. Bake in a 20 cm (7 in) round, shallow cake tin at 180°C/350°F/Gas 4/fan oven 160°C for about 18 minutes.

all-in-one cakes

These have a crumbly, fine texture. Baking powder is used as a raising agent. They are simple to make, because all the ingredients are beaten together in a bowl at once, but they are only successful if you use soft-tub margarine. DO NOT USE butter (as this is too hard) or low-fat and reduced-fat margarines or spreads as they contain too much water: they make the mixture separate and affect the finished texture. Check the small print on the tub to ensure that the margarine can be used for baking. Sunflower margarine has a good

flour and eggs

flavour. A bland vegetable oil, such as sunflower or rapeseed, can also be used in all-in-one cakes.

Do not overbeat the mixture; too much air can make the sponge rise too much and collapse when it comes out of the oven. It also causes the oils to separate out of soft margarine, which makes the sponge sticky on the surface and the cake tough. If you use a wooden spoon, beat only for 1–2 minutes.

whisked cakes

Whisked sponge cakes are very light in texture and used to make Swiss rolls, angel food cake, gâteaux and dessert cakes.

Whisk the eggs and sugar until they hold a definite trail when the whisk is lifted. You should be able to write the letter 'M' on top and count to six before it sinks back into the mixture. Either use an electric hand-held whisk and whisk the eggs and sugar together in a large heatproof bowl over (but not touching) a saucepan of gently simmering (not boiling) water, or whisk them together in the bowl of an electric table-top mixer. It will take about 10 minutes.

Having whisked in all that air, it is then vital not to knock it all out when the flour is added. Gently fold in the sifted flour with a large metal spoon; gently spoon the mixture from the bottom of the bowl up over the top in a figure-of-eight pattern.

melted cakes

These are probably the simplest and most foolproof cakes to make. Butter or margarine and sugar or syrup are warmed in a pan and then the flour and eggs are beaten in. A raising agent such as baking powder or bicarbonate of soda and cream of tartar is usually added, to make the dough rise and give a moist crumb. This method is usually used for gingerbread, parkin and boiled fruit cakes.

rubbed-in cakes

These tend to be plain or lightly fruited cakes, such as rock buns or a date cake. Butter or margarine is rubbed into the flour rather like making pastry, then sugar, eggs and milk are added together with any fruit or nuts. The cakes have a moist but slightly denser quality than cakes made by other methods and keep well.

selecting cake tins

Always use the size and shape of tin specified in the recipe because the baking time is worked out accordingly and the final size and shape of the cake depends on this. A springform cake tin or one with a loose bottom makes removing the cake easier. Long-cooking cakes, such as fruit cakes, need a tin with thick sides, to prevent the sides burning or drying out; tying several layers of newspaper around the outside of the tin helps prevent this.

lining cake tins

Lining a tin properly takes a little time but it ensures the cake will not stick in the tin and gives a smooth surface to the cake. Line the base of a tin with a circle of greaseproof paper or baking paper, drawn using the tin as a template.

The sides only need lining when baking a rich cake that needs long, slow baking, such as fruit cake. To line the sides of a deep, round cake tin or a springform tin, measure the circumference and cut one or two strips the correct length and 2.5 cm (1 in) higher than the tin. Fold up 2.5 cm (1 in) along one long edge. Make slanting cuts every 2.5 cm (1 in) along this edge up to the fold. Grease the tin with melted butter, margarine or vegetable oil and press the strip against the inside with the slashed edges in the base. This will help the paper lie flat, which is difficult to do correctly in a round tin.

what went wrong?

Under-baked The oven was not heated to the specified temperature before the cake was placed in the oven. Putting the raw mixture in the oven instantly reduces the temperature and it then takes time to come back up to the correct temperature. If the oven was too cool to start with, the cake's texture may be adversely affected. Baking at the correct temperature is particularly important with large, rich fruit cakes, as they are so dense and can take a lot longer to bake if the oven is not pre-heated correctly.

If a smaller tin than the one specified is used, the mixture will be deeper and require longer baking.

Ovens vary and there can be as much as 10 to 20 degrees difference between the actual temperature and what the temperature gauge indicates. Buy an oven thermometer to remove any doubt.

Over-baked The oven temperature might have been too high. If the cake was baked in a fan-assisted or fan oven, were the temperature and timing adjusted according to the manufacturer's instructions? Was the cake tin too large so that the mixture spread out too thinly?

Rescue remedy If the cake is browning too quickly, cover it with a double thickness of greaseproof paper.

Sunken middle The mixture was probably under-baked (see above). The oven temperature might have been incorrect or the cake might have been baked in a smaller tin than specified, which would cause the mixture to be too thick to bake in the specified time. Too much baking powder also causes a cake to collapse, leaving a sunken middle, and a close texture.

Rescue remedy Once the cake is baked and cooled there is little to be done to remedy this problem, except cut a circle out of the middle and decorate and serve the cake as a ring cake.

Crusty top Possibly too much sugar or golden syrup in the mixture; reduce the amount the next time you make the cake.

Oily texture Was the correct margarine used? Fat separates out from spreads and low- or reduced-fat margarine, making the cake's texture unpleasantly oily. Over-beating the mixture, particularly when making all-in-one cakes, can also make the fat separate.

Fruit sank The oven might not have been pre-heated to the correct temperature. If it is too low, the mixture does not set quickly enough to support the fruit while the mixture bakes. Over-beating the mixture or curdling can result in the fruit sinking. If the mixture looks like it is beginning to curdle, stir in a little of the measured flour.

Dry texture Especially on edges or the crust, this often indicates that the cake was over-baked. Perhaps the oven was not pre-heated to the correct temperature or the adjustment for timing and temperature for a fan-assisted or fan oven was not made? Incorrectly sized eggs might have been used.

Rescue remedy In creamed cakes, the mixture should fall easily away from the spoon when ready to spread in the prepared tin. If it doesn't, this could lead to a dry cake, so beat in 1 to 2 tablespoons of milk.

Brown sugar Either white sugar that has been coloured with caramel, or molasses or raw cane sugar. Can be substituted for caster sugar in cakes and biscuits but will alter the texture and will not make successful meringues

Caster sugar Always use caster sugar for sponge cakes. It has smaller granules than granulated so it dissolves quicker and gives cakes, meringues, biscuits, pastry and puddings better volume.

Granulated sugar Used as table sugar; it can be used in cakes made by the melted method but, generally, caster sugar is better for baking.

Icing sugar Used for icings. It turns lumpy during storage and must be sieved. It has a small amount of corn flour blended in to prevent it from caking.

Jam sugar Contains natural apple pectin which helps give jams a good set.

Preserving sugar A large-crystal sugar designed for jam-making; the crystals dissolve quickly and are supposed to reduce scum formation.

Raw cane sugar moist sugars in varying shades of brown from light muscovado, through muscovado to molasses and also large-crystal demerara. These add flavour and richness to fruit cakes, gingerbread, brownies, flapjacks and biscuits but they also make them heavier and more moist.

Sugar crystals Useful for decorating the top of baked goods such as Bath buns.

Vanilla sugar Caster sugar to which powdered extract or essence of natural vanilla has been added. Sold in small sachets for flavouring sweet dishes. Make your own by leaving a vanilla pod in a jar of caster sugar.

Whisked cake did not rise properly The eggs and sugar were probably not whisked until the mixture left a definite trail when the whisk was lifted. Another possibility is that too much air was knocked out when the flour was folded in.

Other cakes did not rise properly Check that the baking powder or self-raising flour were not past their use-by date. Perhaps the raising agent was left out by mistake. Was the mixture creamed until very light and fluffy? Was the flour folded in correctly? Alternatively, the oven may not have been pre-heated to the correct temperature.

Cake cracked and not baked through Was the oven too hot when the mixture was put in, so that the top baked too quickly and the mixture underneath had to force its way up as it rose?

icing and decorating cakes

The fashion is now for plainer cakes without too much sweet icing; often cakes are topped with a cream cheese frosting, sweetened mascarpone cheese or with a rich chocolate cream.

Almond paste and marzipan This is made with equal quantities of ground almonds, caster sugar and icing sugar bound to form a stiff rollable paste with beaten egg white. Very good quality almond paste can now be bought readily in supermarkets and is easier to use than home-made. Shop-bought marzipan is either a bright yellow colour due to added colouring or white, which is free from colouring. To cover a cake with almond paste, first brush it with warmed, sieved apricot jam, then roll out the paste on a surface dusted with icing sugar to the appropriate size, drape over the cake and smooth the top and sides. You will need 450 g (1 lb) to 550 g (1¼ lb) to cover an 18 cm (7 in) round cake.

Butter icing A simple, quick icing ideal for birthday cakes. Beat equal quantities of softened butter with icing sugar until smooth. Add cocoa powder or orange or lemon zest, or vanilla essence to flavour as desired.

Frostings Popular in American baking, frosting often refers to whipped cake coverings. Sugar, water, egg whites and syrups are whisked over heat to make frostings similar to Italian meringue, or hot sugar syrup is added to whisked egg whites. Boiled fudge frosting is made by boiling chocolate, milk, butter and golden syrup, which is then cooled and whisked until thick.

Glacé icing Most often used to drizzle over tea breads and loaf-shaped cakes or to top small cakes in paper cake cases. Mix about 1 teaspoon of water to each 25 g (1 oz) of icing sugar. It can be coloured or flavoured with essences. Lemon or orange juice can be substituted for water.

Royal icing Used to coat Christmas and wedding cakes that have been covered first with almond paste (see below) and for piping a firm decoration. It will dry hard. Sift 450 g (1 lb) of icing sugar. Whisk 2 egg whites until frothy and gradually beat in the icing sugar with a teaspoon of lemon juice until the mixture forms soft peaks. It is important to beat for at least 8–10 minutes to get a smooth, shiny consistency. Always keep covered when not using. You will need 900 g (2 lb) to cover the top and sides of an 18 cm (7 in) round cake.

Sugar paste This fondant-type icing can now be bought ready to roll out. It can be coloured using concentrated paste colourings and moulded into decorations. To cover a cake, first brush it with warmed sieved apricot jam, then roll out the icing to the desired size, drape over and smooth out with the palm of your hand. You will need 450 g (1 lb) to 550 g (1¼ lb) to cover an 18 cm (7 in) round cake. Sugar paste can be used instead of royal icing.

luxury chocolate cake coverings

Chocolate ganache A rich chocolate cream with a silky texture that can be poured over profiteroles, used as a sauce for ice-cream, or chilled and used to fill or cover cakes. Bring 200 ml (7 fl oz) of double cream to the boil. Add 250 g (9 oz) of plain chocolate, broken into pieces, and stir until melted and smooth. Use to pour over dessert or chill the mixture for 3–4 hours or until it is thick enough to spread and fill a cake. This will make enough chocolate ganache to cover or fill a 20 cm (8 in) round cake.

Chocolate glaze To cover a cake with a smooth, shiny icing (e.g. sachertorte) is quite tricky. Dissolve 100 g (4 oz) of caster sugar with 150 ml (5 fl oz) of water, then boil to the soft-ball stage which is 115°C (240°F) on a sugar thermometer. Melt 150 g (5 oz) of plain chocolate with 3 tablespoons of water until smooth. Using an electric hand-held whisk, pour the sugar syrup in a thin stream on to the melted chocolate. Pour immediately over the cake and spread it over with a palette knife. This will make enough glaze to cover an 18 cm (7 in) round cake.

golden christmas cake

makes a 20 cm (8 in) round cake | preparation time: 40 minutes | cooking time: 2¼ to 2½ hours

Packed full of apricots, cherries and sultanas, this moist crumbly cake also contains hidden chunks of almond paste but, if you don't like almond paste, leave it out. The cake can be decorated with extra almond paste and icing or topped with fruit and nuts. It will cut into 14 slices.

100 g (4 oz) ready-to-eat dried apricots
100 g (4 oz) natural-coloured glacé cherries
100 g (4 oz) walnuts
100 g (4 oz) almond paste
2 large unwaxed oranges
175 g (6 oz) butter, at room temperature
175 g (6 oz) golden caster sugar
3 eggs, lightly beaten and at room temperature
225 g (8 oz) sultanas
225 g (8 oz) plain wholemeal flour
1 teaspoon baking powder
2 teaspoons ground cinnamon
2 tablespoons demerara sugar, for the topping

Pre-heat the oven to 160°C/325°F/Gas 3/fan oven 140°C. Grease a 20 cm (8 in), round, deep cake tin and line the base and sides with a double layer of greaseproof paper. Quarter the apricots, halve the cherries and chop the walnuts and then set them aside. Roll the almond paste into marble-size balls; then set aside. Grate the zest from the oranges, squeeze about 150 ml (5 fl oz) of the juice and set aside.

Put the butter and sugar into a bowl and cream together until light and fluffy. Gradually beat in the eggs, adding a little of the flour if the mixture begins to curdle.

Add the almond paste balls, the apricots, cherries, walnuts, sultanas, orange zest and juice. Sift the flour, baking powder and cinnamon into the bowl, adding any bran remaining in the sieve. Stir together until everything is well blended.

Spread the mixture in the prepared tin and level the top. Place the tin on a baking sheet and bake in the centre of the oven for 1 hour.

Reduce the heat to 150°C/300°F/Gas 2/fan oven 130°C and bake for a further 45 minutes.

Sprinkle the top with the demerara sugar. Continue baking for 30–45 minutes, until firm to the touch and starting to shrink away from the sides of the tin; a skewer inserted into the centre should come out clean.

Allow the cake to cool for 10 minutes in the tin and then turn it out on to a wire rack; peel off the lining paper and leave to cool completely.

storing and freezing

Store for up to 2 weeks in a cake tin.
Freeze for up to 1 month in a plastic bag or an airtight container.
Thaw for 8 hours at room temperature.

ultimate tea bread

preparation time: 15 minutes | cooking time: 60–70 minutes | makes two loaf cakes

Although you can't taste it, the success of the cake lies in soaking the fruit in cold tea overnight, until plump and juicy. You could also try soaking it in fruit juice for a different flavour. Delicious sliced and thickly buttered. These loaf cakes cut into 10 slices each.

Put the sultanas, currants and sugar in a large bowl and pour over the tea. Stir well and set aside overnight for the fruit to plump up.

When you are ready to bake, set the oven to 180°C/350°F/Gas 4/ fan oven 160°C. Grease two 500 g (1 lb) loaf tins and line the base and sides of each tin with greaseproof paper.

Add the egg to the bowl with the fruit and beat it in. Sift the flour, mixed spice and nutmeg over and beat in until the mixture is smooth and well blended.

Spoon the mixture into the prepared tins and level the tops. Bake in the centre of the oven for 60–70 minutes, until each is firm to the touch and a skewer inserted in the centre of each comes out clean.

Remove the tins from the oven and brush the top of each cake with a knob of butter or use a butter wrapper, to give a lovely shine. Leave the cakes to cool in the tins on a wire rack and then turn out and peel off the lining paper. Serve sliced and spread with butter.

225 g (8 oz) sultanas
225 g (8 oz) currants
225 g (8 oz) caster sugar
350 ml (12 fl oz) cold tea
1 egg
450 g (1 lb) self-raising flour
1 teaspoon ground mixed spice
1 teaspoon grated nutmeg
a knob of butter or butter
  wrapper, to finish

storing and freezing

Store for up to 3 weeks in a cake tin.
Freeze in a plastic bag or an airtight container for up to 1 month. Thaw overnight at room temperature.

big, rich, fudgy chocolate cake

makes a 20 cm (8 in) cake | preparation time: 35 minutes + chilling | cooking time: 30 minutes

The addition of soured milk makes a rich, moist cake. We have used four layers of chocolate icing but, if you like, halve the icing and fill with whipped cream or mascarpone instead. A little liqueur sprinkled over the cake before filling adds even more indulgence. It's up to you. The cake will cut into 10 generous slices and is the perfect grown-up birthday cake – just add the candles!

FOR THE ICING:
175 g (6 oz) plain chocolate
50 g (2 oz) unsalted butter
1 teaspoon vanilla extract
300 g (10 oz) icing sugar

FOR THE CAKE:
250 ml (8 fl oz) milk
3 teaspoons lemon juice
100 g (4 oz) butter, at room temperature,
225 g (8 oz) caster sugar
2 eggs, separated
225 g/8 oz plain flour
1 teaspoon bicarbonate of soda
50 g (2 oz) cocoa

To make the icing: melt the chocolate and butter in a bowl over a pan of simmering water. Gradually whisk in 100 ml (3½ fl oz) boiling water, until smooth. Leave to cool and then lightly and gradually whisk in the vanilla extract and icing sugar, to make a glossy icing. Cover and chill for 3–4 hours.

To make the cake: pre-heat the oven to 180°C/350°F/Gas 4/ fan oven 160°C. Grease and flour two 20 cm (8 in) sandwich tins. Add the lemon juice to the milk and allow to sour.

Cream the butter and half the caster sugar until light and fluffy. Then beat in the remaining sugar and the eggs. Sift together the flour, bicarbonate of soda and cocoa. Stir into the creamed mixture, with the soured milk, until smooth. Divide between cake tins and bake for 30–35 minutes, until risen and springy to the touch. Leave in the tin for 5–10 minutes and then turn out on to a wire rack and leave to cool.

Split each cake in two horizontally and use a little of the icing to sandwich the four layers. Spread the rest of the icing over the top and sides, swirling it with a knife. Decorate with chocolate truffles or whatever is appropriate for the occasion – birthday candles, chocolate Easter bunnies for Easter, and so on as desired.

storing and freezing

Store for up to 4 days in an airtight tin.
Freeze for up to 1 month in a plastic container. Defrost in the fridge overnight.

big, rich, fudgy chocolate cake

lemon drizzle cake

makes an 18 cm (7 in) cake | preparation time: 10 minutes | cooking time: 30 minutes

A delicious, moist, tangy cake. This cuts into 12 slices. Made using the all-in-one method, it is so easy and everyone enjoys it.

100 g (4 oz) soft margarine
100 g (4 oz) caster sugar
2 eggs, beaten
100 g (4 oz) self-raising flour, sifted
grated zest of 1 lemon

FOR THE GLAZE:
juice of 1 lemon
75 g (3 oz) caster sugar

Pre-heat the oven to 180°C/350°F/Gas 4/fan oven 160°C. Grease and line the base of an 18 cm (7 in) round cake tin.

Place all the cake ingredients in a bowl and beat until light and creamy. Spoon the mixture into the tin. Bake the cake for 30 minutes, until golden. Leave in the tin for a few minutes, then turn out on to a plate.

To make the glaze: stir the lemon juice into the caster sugar, spoon over the top of the cake and allow to soak in.

fairy cakes

Great for children's parties: make the mixture as for Lemon Drizzle Cake, omitting the lemon zest if you prefer. Divide between 12 individual paper cake cases and bake for 15–20 minutes until risen, golden and firm to the touch. Leave to cool, omit the lemon glaze, instead dust with icing sugar, top with melted chocolate or glacé icing or cut the tops off and fill with butter cream (page 203) and replace the cake tops.

muffins

American muffins have replaced fairy cakes and cup cakes in popularity, probably because they are easier to make. Instead of icing, the flavour comes from the ingredients themselves. They are best served warm but will keep well in an airtight container for 3 days.

Deep bun or muffin tins and paper cases are available in cookshops and department stores. But you can use ordinary bun tins, in which case the quantities given should make about 12 smaller muffins; cook for 18–20 minutes.

choc chip muffins

preparation time: 10 minutes | cooking time: 20–25 minutes | makes 6–8

Pre-heat the oven to 200°C/400°F/Gas 6/fan oven 180°C. Melt the plain chocolate in a heatproof bowl over a pan of hot (not boiling) water or in the microwave. Sift the flour, baking powder and salt into a bowl.

Mix the melted chocolate, sugar, milk, butter and egg in another bowl. Fold in the flour mixture with a metal spoon.

Stir in the chocolate chips and spoon the mixture into greased muffin tins (or line with paper cases, if you prefer). Bake for 20–25 minutes until well risen and firm to the touch. Leave in the tins for a few minutes, then transfer to a wire rack to cool. Serve warm or cold.

- 50 g (2 oz) plain chocolate, broken into pieces
- 150 g (5 oz) self-raising flour
- ½ teaspoon baking powder
- a pinch of salt
- 50 g (2 oz) dark muscovado sugar
- 120 ml (4 fl oz) milk
- 25 g (1 oz) butter, melted
- 1 egg, beaten
- 50 g (2 oz) white chocolate chips

muffin variations

Banana and walnut muffins Replace the chocolate with a large mashed banana and 1 teaspoon of ground cinnamon; then fold 50 g (2 oz) of chopped walnuts into the mixture instead of the chocolate chips.

Lemon and sultana muffins Omit the chocolate. Add the juice and grated zest of a large lemon and then fold in 50 g (2 oz) of sultanas with the flour, instead of the chocolate chips.

Berry muffins Omit the chocolate and the chocolate chips. Add half a teaspoon of vanilla extract and then fold in 100 g (4 oz) of raspberries or blueberries; sprinkle over a little demerara sugar before baking.

scones

preparation time: 12–15 minutes | cooking time: 8–12 minutes | makes about 8

Simple and foolproof, scones are a great treat to rustle up for unexpected guests for tea.

Pre-heat the oven to 200°C/400°F/Gas 6/fan oven 180°C. Sift the flour into a large mixing bowl and then rub in the butter or margarine with your fingertips until the mixture resembles fine breadcrumbs. Add the sugar and mix well.

Pour in enough milk to make a soft, spongy dough, mixing with a palette knife or fork. It is better for the dough to be slightly soft rather than too dry. Simply turn it out on to a floured surface.

Knead the dough briefly until it is just smooth. Do not over-handle or the scones will be tough. Lightly roll or pat out the dough to a 2 cm (¾ in) thickness (any thinner and the scones will not rise well) and cut into rounds with a 6 cm (2½ in) plain or fluted cutter. Gather up the trimmings, roll out and cut more rounds. You should get only about eight scones from this mixture.

Place on a baking sheet and brush the tops of the scones with beaten egg or milk for a glossy crust or sprinkle with a little flour for a soft one.

Bake the scones in the top of the oven for about 8–12 minutes, until golden brown and well risen. Leave to cool slightly on a wire rack and serve warm; split and spread with butter or cream and jam.

225 g (8 oz) self-raising flour

50 g (2 oz) butter or margarine

40 g (1½) oz caster sugar

120 ml (4 fl oz) milk

beaten egg or milk, to glaze

butter, whipped or clotted cream and strawberry or raspberry jam, to serve

scone variations

Wholemeal scones Replace half the flour with self-raising wholemeal flour. Add a little more milk, if necessary.

Fruit scones Sift 1 teaspoon of ground mixed spice with the flour. Stir 50 g (2 oz) of currants, sultanas or raisins (or a mixture) into the flour before adding the milk.

Cheese and bacon scones Omit the sugar and sift 1 teaspoon of mustard powder and a quarter teaspoon of salt and freshly ground black pepper with the dry ingredients. Stir 50 g (2 oz) of finely grated mature Cheddar, 4 rashers of chopped fried bacon and 2 tablespoons of chopped fresh mixed herbs into the mixture before adding the milk. After glazing, sprinkle a little Cheddar on top, if you like.

Mediterranean scones Omit the sugar. Drain 50 g (2 oz) of sun-dried tomatoes preserved in oil. Pat dry with kitchen paper. Chop into small pieces and stir into the flour mixture with 1 tablespoon of chopped fresh oregano (or 1 teaspoon of dried). Sprinkle with grated Parmesan before baking.

scones

fudge brownies

cuts into 16 squares | preparation time: 15 minutes | cooking time: 40–45 minutes

These moist, rich brownies are the ultimate indulgence – omit the icing if you want a little less guilt!

150 g (5 oz) unsalted butter
150 g (5 oz) plain chocolate
425 g (15 oz) caster sugar
a pinch of salt
2 teaspoons vanilla extract
3 large eggs
175 g (6 oz) plain flour
3 tablespoons cocoa powder
100 g (4 oz) pecan nuts, chopped

FOR THE ICING:
50 g (2 oz) plain chocolate
50 g (2 oz) butter
75 g (3 oz) icing sugar, sifted

Pre-heat the oven to 180°C/350°F/Gas 4/fan oven 160°C. Grease a 23 × 28 cm (9 × 11 in) rectangular cake tin and line with greaseproof paper.

Melt the butter and chocolate over a pan of simmering water or in the microwave. Cool slightly and then stir in the sugar, salt and vanilla. Add the eggs, one at a time. Stir well. Add the flour, cocoa and pecans and beat until smooth.

Spoon into the tin and bake for 35–40 minutes, until just set in the centre and a cocktail stick comes out almost clean. Remove from the tin and allow to cool.

Make the icing: melt the chocolate, 1 tablespoon of water and the butter in a bowl over simmering water or in the microwave. Remove from the heat and stir in the icing sugar. Spread over the brownies and cut into squares.

gluten-free christmas cake

preparation time: 30 minutes | cooking time: 2½ hours | serves 12

A moist, rich fruit cake with a light and crumbly texture. You could finish this cake by topping with sliced glacé fruits and brushing with a warm apricot jam glaze.

Pre-heat the oven to 150°C/300°F/Gas 2; fan oven 140°C from cold. Grease the base and sides of a deep 20 cm (8 in) cake tin and double-line with greaseproof paper.

Put all of the fruit mixture ingredients in a large bowl and stir until well mixed. Put the cake mixture ingredients in a separate bowl and beat with a wooden spoon until smooth.

Add the cake mixture to the fruit mixture and mix until evenly blended. Transfer to the prepared tin and smooth the top with a palette knife. Bake in the centre of the oven for 1 hour, then lower the heat to 140°C/275°F/Gas 1/fan oven 120°C and bake for a further 1½ hours, until a skewer inserted into the centre comes out completely clean. Leave to cool in the tin.

menu: afternoon tea

sandwiches

scones (page 211), strawberry jam (page 238)

lemon drizzle cake (page 208)

ultimate tea bread (page 205)

FOR THE FRUIT MIXTURE:

750 g (1½ lb) mixed dried fruit

125 g (4½ oz) glacé cherries, sliced

50 g (1¾ oz) flaked almonds

grated zest and juice of 1 lemon

1 tablespoon black treacle

FOR THE CAKE MIXTURE:

200 g (7 oz) unsalted butter, softened

200 g (7 oz) dark muscovado sugar

75 g (3 oz) ground almonds

75 g (3 oz) potato flour

75 g (3 oz) brown rice flour

75 g (3 oz) maize flour

1 teaspoon ground cinnamon

1 teaspoon ground mixed spice

4 medium eggs

egg- and dairy-free chocolate muffins

makes 8 | preparation time: 15 minutes | cooking time: 20 minutes

Irresistibly good, you would never believe that these cakes contain no dairy ingredients or eggs.

FOR THE MUFFINS:
2 tablespoons vegetable oil
½ teaspoon vanilla extract
2 teaspoons white wine vinegar
75 g (3 oz) plain flour
15 g (½ oz) cocoa powder, sifted
1 teaspoon bicarbonate of soda
a large pinch of salt
125 g (4½ oz) caster sugar

FOR THE ICING:
1 teaspoon cocoa
4 tablespoons icing sugar

Pre-heat the oven to 190°C/375°F/Gas 5/fan oven 170°C. Place eight large paper muffin cases in a muffin tray.

In a large bowl, whisk together the vegetable oil, 150 ml (5 fl oz) of water, the vanilla extract and vinegar. Sift the flour, cocoa and bicarbonate of soda into a large bowl and stir in the salt and caster sugar. Gradually stir in the vinegar mixture until well combined, taking care not to over-mix.

Divide the mixture between the muffin cases. Bake for 15–20 minutes until firm and springy to the touch. Allow to cool in the tin.

To make the icing, sift the cocoa and icing sugar together and add a drop of boiling water, just enough to bind it into a thick icing. Spread over the top of the cakes and allow to set.

egg- and dairy-free chocolate muffins

desserts

a meal can seem incomplete without a dessert. For everyday meals, fresh fruit and yoghurt are perfect. However, for special occasions and at weekends when there is more time, a dessert is a treat. Cold desserts have the advantage that you can make them in advance and, in most cases, keep them in the fridge until they are needed. Hot desserts have a homely appeal. Favourites such as apple or rhubarb crumble, apple pie and, more recently, sticky toffee pudding are perennially on the menu in cafés, restaurants and works canteens in Britain.

chocolate

Chocolate is an essential ingredient in many desserts, cakes, biscuits and confectionery. Virtually every restaurant menu has at least one chocolate dessert because many people feel it is not a special occasion without having chocolate! When making chocolate desserts at home, use the best-quality plain chocolate that you can find, unless the recipe stipulates milk or white chocolate.

Chocolate covering or chocolate flavour coating This is melted and used to cover cakes. It can contain a small percentage of chocolate or no chocolate. It is made of vegetable fats, chocolate (if used), chocolate and other flavourings, colourings and additives. It is an inferior product and does not produce a good chocolate flavour.

Cocoa powder Usually unsweetened and can include an anti-caking additive.

Drinking chocolate A mixture of sugar and cocoa, usually about one-third cocoa. Drinking chocolate can contain other ingredients, such as dried milk powder and flavourings.

Milk chocolate This usually contains about 20% cocoa solids.

Plain chocolate The cocoa content, expressed as cocoa solids on the ingredients list, or sometimes simply as 70% on the front of the bar of chocolate, determines the quality of the chocolate. Generally, the higher the percentage the richer or more intense the chocolate flavour and the better quality the chocolate. Plain chocolate contains 30–70% cocoa solids. Top-quality chocolate is considered to be around 70%; anything higher would not be necessary for most recipes and 50–60% would be adequate.

chocolate tips

- Cocoa powder can be substituted for chocolate in recipes. For each 150 g (5 oz) of plain chocolate, use 5 tablespoons each of sifted cocoa powder and caster sugar plus 50 g (2 oz) of vegetable fat or shortening.
- Store chocolate below 18°C/64°F to prevent a harmless white bloom appearing.
- To melt in the microwave, break chocolate into a small microwave-safe bowl. Cover the bowl. Heat on high for 2 minutes. Remove from the microwave and stir the chocolate until melted.

- To melt chocolate over hot water, break it up and put it in a bowl over a saucepan of simmering water until it has melted. The bowl must not touch the water. Keep the temperature below 44°C/111°F, to prevent the chocolate from stiffening. Remove and stir the chocolate until it has melted.

Rescue remedy If the chocolate stiffens during melting, add pure white vegetable fat (not butter, margarine or oil) by the teaspoonful. Stir until the chocolate becomes smooth.

White chocolate Not really chocolate but a mixture of fat, milk and sugar with added flavourings and cocoa butter to give it a mild chocolate taste. Doesn't contain any cocoa solids.

custard

The British love of nursery food, in particular steaming hot puddings, gives us an insatiable lust for lashings of custard. This trait is so well recognized that in France, pouring custard, when made with fresh eggs and flavoured with natural vanilla, is referred to as *crème anglaise* (English cream).

Before the invention of dry custard powder, custard was made exclusively from raw eggs. There are two types of egg custard: baked (set custards) and steamed (pouring custard). It is important to cook custards at the correct temperature because too much heat, particularly direct heat, curdles the egg mixture. To avoid direct heat, a fresh egg custard sauce is made in a double boiler (a smaller saucepan that sits inside a larger pan of simmering water). Pouring custard can be made in a saucepan directly over the heat but great care has to be taken not to let it get too hot – egg whites set at 62°C/144°F and yolks set at 65°C/149°F, well below boiling. The most foolproof way to make set custard is to bake it in a *bain-marie*.

Baked custard: 2 whole eggs plus 2 egg yolks will set 600 ml (1 pint) of milk.

Pouring custard: Use 4–5 egg yolks to 600 ml (1 pint) of milk.

Adding a teaspoon of cornflour to the milk before putting it in with the eggs, sugar and flavourings to cook ensures the custard will thicken and helps to prevent curdling.

flavoured custards

Baked custard is traditionally flavoured with lemon zest in the custard and a dusting of grated nutmeg on top.

Pouring custard is flavoured with vanilla. A split vanilla pod is added to the milk when it is heated and if you scrape the seeds from the pod into the custard towards the end of cooking it gives an attractive speckled appearance and strengthens the flavour.

Chocolate custard Add 50–75 g (2–3 oz) of chopped semi-sweet chocolate to the milk after it has been infused with the vanilla pod.

Coffee custard Add 2–3 teaspoons of dry instant coffee to the milk after it has been infused.

Liqueur custard Include 2 tablespoons of rum, whisky or brandy in the finished custard.

Orange custard Use orange zest instead of vanilla when cooking or infusing the milk. Add 2 teaspoons of orange-flower water or orange liqueur to the custard.

what went wrong?

Rescue remedy If the custard curdles, try sieving it or blending in a liquidizer. If this fails, start again. See cornflour tip above before you start.

Burnt custard If you catch a whiff of burning or scorching take the pan off the heat immediately without any further stirring. Pour off the majority of the custard, leaving any burnt or brown part in the pan – discard it. Re-heat the remaining custard in a clean pan and, if it is free from burnt aroma, it can be used – if not, start again.

Lumpy custard Swap the wooden spoon for a balloon whisk and whisk like crazy over a low heat. If that does not work either sieve the custard or blend in a liquidizer.

chocolate espresso cups

preparation time: 15 minutes + chilling | serves 4–6

This dessert is so rich you only need to serve it in tiny portions. Little espresso coffee cups or tiny ramekins are ideal.

Break the chocolate into small pieces, then place the chocolate and coffee in a bowl over a pan of simmering water. Leave to melt, stirring occasionally, or melt gently in the microwave. Remove from the heat.

Add the butter, egg yolks, icing sugar, salt and orange zest and then return to the heat until the butter has melted. Leave to cool slightly.

Beat the egg whites until they hold soft peaks. Carefully fold half of them into the chocolate mixture; then slowly fold in the remainder until the mixture is smooth. Pour the mixture into 8–10 espresso cups or individual ramekins and chill for at least 4 hours.

Lightly whip the cream and spoon over the mousse just before serving. Dust with cocoa or chocolate powder.

note This recipe contains raw eggs. Do not serve to babies, the very young, old people or pregnant women.

wine suggestion A noble-rotted dessert wine such as Sauternes or Coteaux du Layon from the Loire won't come to any harm. Some like the traditional sweet reds of southern France (Banyuls and Maury) with chocolate.

**225 g (8 oz) plain chocolate
(70% cocoa solids)**
1–2 tablespoons espresso coffee
175 g (6 oz) butter, cut into pieces
3 eggs, separated
100 g (4 oz) icing sugar
a pinch of salt
grated zest of 1 orange
300 ml (10 fl oz) whipping cream
**cocoa powder of chocolate
powder, for dusting**

meringues

makes about 16 | preparation time: 15 minutes | cooking time: 1 hour

Crisp, airy meringue, made simply from egg white and sugar, makes a versatile base for various desserts and gâteaux. Sandwich mini meringues with fruit and cream or create a stunning Pavlova. Try brown sugar instead of white to give a richer, more caramelized meringue.

2 egg whites
100 g (4 oz) caster sugar
300 ml (10 fl oz) double cream

Preheat the oven to 140°C/275°F/Gas 1; fan oven 120°C from cold. Line two baking sheets with non-stick baking parchment. Place the egg whites in a thoroughly clean, grease-free bowl and whisk until they stand in stiff peaks.

Sprinkle over a little of the sugar and continue whisking until thoroughly blended. Continue adding and whisking until two-thirds of the sugar has been added.

Using a tablespoon, gently fold in the remaining caster sugar. The mixture should be glossy and should stand in stiff peaks.

Fit a large piping bag with a plain or star nozzle, about 1 cm (½ in) in diameter. Spoon the meringue mixture into the bag, using a metal spoon. Pipe rounds, about 5 cm (2 in) in diameter on to the prepared baking sheets or use a large tablespoon to spoon out the mixture in neat ovals.

Bake for about 1 hour, until crisp. Cool. Whip the cream until it forms soft peaks. Sandwich the meringues with cream and serve within 1 hour.

cooked meringue

makes 8 nests | preparation time: 15–20 minutes | cooking time: 1 hour

This method of whisking the egg whites and sugar over a pan of simmering water produces a much more stable meringue, ideal for piping into nests and shapes. It will produce dry, powdery meringues.

4 egg whites
200 g (7 oz) caster sugar

Preheat the oven to 120°C/250°F/Gas ½; fan oven 100°C from cold. Place the egg whites and sugar together in a bowl over a pan of gently simmering water. Whisk with an electric hand whisk for 10–15 minutes, until the mixture forms firm peaks and begins to feel sugary around the edge of the bowl. Remove from the heat and continue whisking until the mixture is shiny and cool. Pipe into nests or shape and bake on trays lined with baking parchment for about 1 hour, until crisp and dry.

pavlova with lemon-scented cream and summer fruit

preparation time: 15–20 minutes │ **cooking time: 1–1¼ hours** │ **serves 8**

The secret of Pavlova is to have a soft marshmallowy centre, which is why vinegar and cornflour are added. Fill with whipped cream or a combination of cream and yoghurt or mascarpone and whipped cream, as in this recipe. Flavour with passion-fruit seeds or a fruit liqueur and any combination of soft or exotic fruits – whatever takes your fancy.

Preheat the oven to 140°C/275°F/Gas 1; fan oven 120°C from cold. Line a baking tray with non-stick baking parchment and, in the centre, draw around a dinner plate with a pencil. Place the egg whites in a clean, grease-free bowl and whisk until stiff. Gradually whisk in the sugar a couple of tablespoons at a time, with the cornflour and vinegar, and whisk until smooth and glossy.

Spread the mixture over the marked circle. Swirl to form a slight dip in the centre and peaks around the edge. Bake for 1¼ hours, until crisp.

Whisk the whipping cream until it just holds its shape. Beat the mascarpone and limoncello or liqueur until smooth and then fold them into the cream. Spoon into the centre of the Pavlova and top with fruit.

note Make and serve on the same day; if you want to make the meringue ahead, bake it and then turn off the oven and leave the meringue to dry out for another hour, so that it will be crisper. Place on a baking tray, wrap in a tent of foil and keep for 1–2 days.

4 egg whites
225 g (8 oz) caster sugar
1 teaspoon white wine vinegar
2 teaspoons cornflour
150 g (5 oz) whipping cream
250 g (9 oz) tub of mascarpone
**2–3 tablespoons limoncello or
   other lemon-flavoured liqueur**
**450 g (1 lb) summer fruits, such as
   peaches, strawberries
   and raspberries**

---

menu: summer buffet party

salad niçoise omitting tuna, if preferred (page 50)

classic caesar salad (page 52)

potato salad (page 53)

oven-poached whole salmon (page 143)

broccoli and filo flan (page 166)

pavlova with lemon-scented cream and summer fruit (page 221)

mango, raspberry and passion-fruit trifle (page 224)

fruity mascarpone 'semi-freddo' ice-cream

serves 6 | preparation time: 10 minutes + 2 hours freezing

Nothing could be simpler than this semi-frozen ice-cream. It's rich and creamy without being over-sweet. It's also great made with blueberries, raspberries or a mixture of soft fruit. You could even try rhubarb or apple, sweetened to taste.

450 g (1 lb) strawberries, hulled
175 g (6 oz) icing sugar
juice of 1 lemon
2 × 250 g tubs of mascarpone

Mash the strawberries well with a fork. Stir the icing sugar and lemon juice into the mascarpone until smooth. Mix in the mashed strawberries, leaving the mixture slightly rippled. Transfer to a rigid container and freeze for 2–3 hours, until semi-frozen. Serve in scoops.

The ice-cream will keep for up to 2 months in a freezer.

serving from frozen If the semi-freddo has been frozen for a few weeks, transfer to the fridge for 2–3 hours before serving, to get that 'semi-frozen' taste and texture.

crème brûlée

preparation time: 20 minutes | cooking time: 1¼ hours | serves 6

You will need to make this the night before or at least in the morning, in order for the custard to set. Finish off the caramel 2 hours before serving and allow to cool.

Split the vanilla pod lengthways and scrape out the seeds. Place, with the cream, in a pan and heat gently for 10 minutes. If you are using vanilla extract, add it to the cream and just bring it up to the boil, without actually boiling it.

In a bowl, whisk the egg yolks with 40 g (1½ oz) of the sugar and the cornflour, until pale and foamy.

Pour the cream into the egg mixture, stirring constantly. Return to the pan and cook very gently, stirring until the custard has thickened. This takes 10–15 minutes. Do not allow to boil. Pour into six small ramekins, allow to cool and then chill in the fridge for at least 4 hours or, preferably, overnight, until set.

Pre-heat the grill to high – this is vital to caramelize the sugar quickly. Sprinkle the set cream evenly with the remaining sugar and grill until it has melted and is golden and caramelized. Leave for about 2 hours before serving.

wine suggestion The noblest noble-rotted wine you can stretch to is what crème brûlée deserves, Sauternes for preference. Alternatively, there are fine examples of this style in Australia, Austria and California. Semillon is the grape to look for on the label.

1 vanilla pod or ½ teaspoon vanilla extract

600 ml (1 pint) double cream

6 medium egg yolks

125 g (4½ oz) caster sugar

1 tablespoon cornflour

panna cotta with summer fruits

serves 6 | preparation time: 15 minutes + overnight chilling

This heavenly set cream is incredibly easy to make. Don't be put off by the leaf gelatine; it is very simple to use and the result just melts in your mouth.

FOR THE PANNA COTTA:
2 sheets of leaf gelatine
3 tablespoons milk
600 ml (1 pint) single cream
50 g (2 oz) caster sugar
1 vanilla pod, split lengthways

FOR DECORATION:
225 g (8 oz) mixed red fruits, such as strawberries, raspberries and redcurrants
wild strawberries

In a bowl, soak the gelatine in the milk for about 5 minutes, until soft.

Meanwhile, heat the cream, sugar and vanilla pod in a pan over a low heat, stirring to dissolve the sugar, until almost boiling. Remove from the heat. Take out the vanilla pod, scrape some of the seeds into the cream and then discard the pod.

Whisk the gelatine mixture into the hot cream. Leave to cool slightly and then pour into six 120 ml (4 fl oz) dariole moulds or teacups. Chill in the fridge overnight.

Allow the panna cotta to stand at room temperature for 30 minutes before serving; then turn out on to large plates. If they do not slip out easily, quickly dip the bases of the moulds in hot water, to loosen. Decorate with mixed fruits.

mango, raspberry and passion-fruit trifle

serves 6 | preparation time: 30 minutes + chilling

Irresistibly fruity, creamy and alcoholic, and quick to make, too.

Cut the cake into slices. Put half in the base of a large glass bowl. Sprinkle with half the Madeira or sherry. Cut the mango into cubes. Place in the bowl with the raspberries.

Halve two of the passion-fruit and scrape the seeds into the bowl. Scatter over the remaining cake and sprinkle with the remaining Madeira or sherry. Pour over the custard and smooth the surface.

In a large bowl, beat the mascarpone and yoghurt together until smooth. Fold in the sugar and lemon zest. Add the seeds from the other passion-fruit and very lightly swirl into the cream. Spoon the passion-fruit cream over the custard. Chill for 2–6 hours before serving. Decorate with mint sprigs.

wine suggestion Cut the richness of this tropical trifle with well-chilled Italian Asti. Not only does its frothy texture work well with whipped cream, but the ripe, grapy flavours in it are good with fresh fruit.

raisin and vanilla cheesecake

serves 6–8 | preparation time: 20 minutes | cooking time: 50–60 minutes

This is the ultimate rich, creamy, baked cheesecake, flavoured with lemon and juicy raisins.

FOR THE BASE:
175 g (6 oz) plain flour
100 g (4 oz) butter
75 g (3 oz) caster sugar

FOR THE FILLING:
50 g (2 oz) unsalted butter
75 g (3 oz) caster sugar
450 g (1 lb) curd cheese
3 eggs
grated zest of 1 lemon
25 g (1 oz) cornflour
150 g (5 oz) thick Greek yoghurt
75 g (3 oz) seedless raisins
icing sugar for sprinkling

Pre-heat the oven to 160°C/325°F/Gas 3; fan oven 140°C from cold. Lightly grease and base-line a 20 cm (8 in) loose-bottomed cake tin.

To make the base: sift the flour into a bowl, cut the butter into small pieces and rub into the flour using your fingertips. When the mixture resembles fine breadcrumbs, stir in the sugar and then sprinkle the mixture evenly over the base of the cake tin. Press down lightly with the back of a spoon. Bake for 20 minutes.

Meanwhile, make the filling: beat the butter and sugar until light and fluffy. Add the curd cheese and beat well. Beat in the eggs, one at a time, and then stir in the lemon zest, cornflour, yoghurt and raisins. Set the tin on a baking sheet and pour in the mixture. Bake for 50–60 minutes, until firm around the edges. Leave to cool in the oven.

When it is cold, chill it until ready to serve; sprinkle with icing sugar, and cut into wedges.

freezing and serving Freeze for up to 1 month. Thaw for 4–6 hours at room temperature.

rice pudding

preparation time: 2–3 minutes | cooking time: 1½–2 hours | serves 6

There cannot be a quicker, simpler or more satisfying hot pudding. So why don't we make it more often? Try this classic variation or enrich it with cream or fruit.

Scatter the rice and sugar in a 600 ml (1 pint) ovenproof dish. Pour over the milk. Add a knob of butter and sprinkle with nutmeg, if you like. Set the oven to 150°C/300°F/Gas 2; fan oven 130°C from cold and bake for 1½–2 hours, until the rice is plump and most of the milk has been absorbed.

50 g (2 oz) short-grain pudding rice

2 tablespoons sugar

600 ml (1 pint) milk

a knob of butter

a little grated nutmeg (optional)

rice pudding variations

Creamy rice pudding Substitute single, or double, cream for 150 ml (5 fl oz) of the milk before cooking. Or, if you like, swirl clotted cream through the pudding once cooked.

Fruity rice pudding Add 50 g (2 oz) of sultanas, raisins or chopped apricots and the grated zest of a lemon or an orange before cooking. If you like, add a few flaked almonds too.

whisky bread and butter pudding

serves 6 | preparation time: 10 minutes | cooking time: 45 minutes

Use crusty bread rather than sliced bread, or even brioche or French bread, to give a crisp, buttery top to this favourite pudding. Omit the whisky and pecans for a more traditional dish.

50 g (2 oz) butter
8 slices of crusty white bread
2 tablespoons whisky
75 g (3 oz) seedless raisins
50 g (2 oz) pecan halves
4 eggs
75 g (3 oz) light muscovado sugar
300 ml (10 fl oz) full-fat milk
284 ml carton of single cream
1 teaspoon vanilla extract
½ teaspoon ground cinnamon
¼ teaspoon grated nutmeg

Pre-heat the oven to 180°C/350°F/Gas 4; fan oven 160°C from cold. Butter a 1-litre (2¼ -pint) ovenproof dish. Butter each bread slice on one side and cut into triangles. Arrange, butter-side up, in the dish. Drizzle over the whisky.

Scatter over the raisins and pecan halves. Beat the eggs in a bowl and then mix in the sugar. Stir in the milk, cream and vanilla; pour over the bread. Sprinkle with the spices.

Bake for 40–45 minutes, until just set, golden and crisp.

menu: winter supper party

smoked salmon and avocado pots (page 64)

venison and chestnut casserole (page 135)

whisky bread and butter pudding (page 228)

whisky bread and butter pudding

classic fruit crumble

serves 4–6 | preparation time: 15–20 minutes | cooking time: 40–50 minutes

A classic combination of blackberry and apple with a crumble topping. The blackberries can be replaced with plums or rhubarb, or just use apple if you prefer. The basic crumble mixture can top any fruit filling (see the variations at the end of this recipe). Demerara sugar gives the crumble its famous crunchiness. You can add 75 g (3 oz) toasted, chopped hazelnuts or walnuts, or add 50 g (2 oz) of porridge oats for a chewy, crunchy topping.

FOR THE FRUIT:
450 g (1 lb) cooking apples, peeled, cored and sliced
225 g (8 oz) blackberries
100 g (4 oz) caster sugar

FOR THE CRUMBLE:
175 g (6 oz) plain flour
100 g (4 oz) butter, chilled and cut into pieces
75 g (3 oz) demerara sugar
cream, custard, vanilla ice-cream or natural yoghurt, to serve

Pre-heat the oven to 180°C/350°F/Gas 4; fan oven 160°C from cold. In a 2.25-litre (4-pint) ovenproof dish, gently mix together the apples, blackberries and caster sugar. Spoon over 3 tablespoons of water and then level out the fruit.

Make the crumble: in a blender or food processor, briefly blend the flour and butter until the mixture is crumbly. Alternatively, in a bowl, rub the butter into the flour until crumbly. Stir the sugar and then spread evenly over the fruit. Bake for 40–50 minutes, until the crumble is golden brown and the fruit is cooked. Serve warm.

wine suggestion A fortified sweet wine, such as Moscatel de Valencia or one of the sweeter styles of madeira (Bual or Malmsey), will make a good support for this substantial English pudding.

crumble variations

Rhubarb crumble Use 750 g (1½ lb) of rhubarb, cut into sticks, and the juice of 2 oranges instead of the water, if you like.

Gooseberry crumble Use 750 g (1½ lb) of gooseberries, topped and tailed; delicious with oat crumble.

sticky toffee pudding with caramel sauce

preparation time: 15–20 minutes | cooking time: steam for 2 hours | serves 8

This moist, gooey, steamed pud is a favourite with everyone. It doesn't take long to make and is quick to cook if you microwave it.

Beat the butter and sugar until light and fluffy. Beat in the eggs, a little at a time. Stir in the vanilla and then fold in the flour, dates and milk, to form a soft, dropping consistency.

Turn the mixture into a buttered 1.5-litre (2½-pint) pudding basin and smooth the top. Cut a circle of greaseproof paper and a circle of foil about 5 cm (2 in) larger than the top of the bowl. Pleat both together in the centre. Place over the bowl and secure tightly with string. Place in a large saucepan. Pour in enough boiling water to come two-thirds of the way up the side of the bowl. Cover the pan with a tight-fitting lid. Simmer gently for 2 hours until risen and firm, checking every now and then to ensure the pan does not boil dry. Top up with boiling water if necessary.

Make the sauce: place the ingredients in a small pan and bring to the boil, stirring. Simmer for 5 minutes until thickened; serve with the pudding.

For microwave ovens, cover only with greaseproof, not foil. Cook on high for 4½ minutes, then leave to stand for 5 minutes and continue cooking for a further 5 minutes.

wine suggestion Only the sweetest and strongest can live with the lusciousness of this popular pudding. Try Australian Liqueur Muscat or maybe the sweetest (*dolce*) style of Sicilian Marsala.

100 g (4 oz) butter, at room temperature
100 g (4 oz) light muscovado sugar
2 eggs, lightly beaten
½ teaspoon vanilla extract
200 g (7 oz) self-raising flour
175 g (6 oz) chopped dates
4 tablespoons milk

FOR THE CARAMEL SAUCE:
150 g (5 oz) light muscovado sugar
150 ml (5 fl oz) double cream
100 g (4 oz) butter
½ teaspoon vanilla extract

christmas pudding

makes two puddings | preparation time: 20 minutes | cooking time: 3 hours

A rich, moist, classic pudding. Serve with custard, cream or Boozy Butter. Each pudding will serve eight people.

100 g (4 oz) plain flour

2 teaspoons ground mixed spice

½ teaspoon ground ginger

½ teaspoon freshly grated nutmeg

175 g (6 oz) vegetable suet

100 g (4 oz) dark muscovado sugar

100 g (4 oz) fresh breadcrumbs

100 g (4 oz) nibbed almonds

100 g (4 oz) dried apricots, chopped

100 g (4 oz) uncoloured glacé cherries, chopped

50 g (2 oz) candied peel, chopped

grated zest of 1 lemon

grated zest of 1 orange

225 g (8 oz) cooking apple, grated

225 g (8 oz) currants

275 g (10 oz) stoned raisins

350 g (12 oz) sultanas

3 eggs, beaten

250 ml (8 fl oz) brown ale

2 tablespoons brandy or rum

Sift the flour and spices together into a large bowl; then stir in the suet, sugar and breadcrumbs.

Add the almonds, apricots, cherries, candied peel, lemon and orange zest, apple and dried fruit; mix well. Add the eggs, ale and brandy or rum; mix well again.

Line the base of two greased 1.2-litre (2-pint) pudding basins with a round of greaseproof paper. Pack the mixture into the basins and smooth the tops.

Cover each pudding with two rounds of greaseproof paper and a round of foil, pleated across the middle and tied around with string. Set each pudding in a large pan and pour in enough boiling water to come halfway up the basins. Bring to the boil, reduce the heat and cover with a lid. Steam for 3 hours, topping up with boiling water occasionally. Check at intervals to ensure the pans never boil dry.

Remove the basins from the pans and leave to cool. Remove the paper and foil and tie down with fresh greaseproof paper. (The pudding will keep for up to 12 months in a cool, dry place.)

To serve: steam as before for 3 hours or cut into slices and microwave each slice for 30 seconds–1 minute. Take care not to overcook because Christmas pudding is so rich and can easily catch fire in the microwave.

wine suggestion Although a rich, noble-rotted dessert wine can work with the Christmas pud, practically nothing complements it more perfectly than vigorously chilled Asti or Moscato d'Asti.

gluten-free christmas pudding

preparation time: 25 minutes | **cooking time: 3 hours + reheating** | **serves 4**

This gluten-free recipe is so tasty, non-coeliacs will love it too. Store as you would a normal pud, in dry, cool conditions (see page 232).

Grease a 600 ml (1 pint) pudding basin and line the base with greaseproof paper. Break the bread into pieces and whizz to fine crumbs in a food processor; set aside. Sift together the rice flour, spices and baking powder. Add the melted butter, apple, raisins, sultanas, breadcrumbs, sugar and almonds. Mix thoroughly.

Heat the treacle until just warm. Remove from the heat and stir in the egg, lemon zest and brandy, if using. Mix into the flour and fruit and then spoon the mixture into the prepared basin. Cover with a double round of greaseproof paper and a round of foil pleated in the middle and tied around with string. Put into a large pan and pour in boiling water to come half way up the basin. Bring to the boil, reduce the heat and cover with a lid. Steam for 3 hours topping up with water occasionally, until the pudding is risen and firm to the touch. Cool completely and then top with clean greaseproof paper, wrap in foil and keep in a cool, dry place. To re-heat, steam for 2 hours or cut into slices and microwave each slice for 30 seconds–1 minute each. Take care not to overcook because Christmas pudding is so rich and can easily catch fire in the microwave.

75 g (3 oz) fresh gluten-free bread

25 g (1 oz) rice flour

a good pinch of ground cinnamon

1 teaspoon ground mixed spice

¼ teaspoon gluten-free baking powder

50 g (2 oz) butter, melted

100 g (4 oz) cooking apple, peeled and grated

100 g (4 oz) raisins

100 g (4 oz) sultanas

50 g (2 oz) light muscovado sugar

50 g (2 oz) ground almonds

1 tablespoon black treacle

1 egg, beaten

finely grated zest of ½ lemon

1 tablespoon brandy (optional)

boozy butter

preparation time: 10 minutes | **serves 8**

Add your favourite alcoholic tipple to this butter – brandy, Grand Marnier or Cointreau are favourites – then let it melt over hot Christmas pudding for a real treat.

Beat the butter until pale and soft. Gradually beat in the sugar, adding a little of your chosen alcohol each time. Beat in the remaining alcohol. Transfer to a bowl. Cover and chill for up to 2 weeks.

100 g (4 oz) unsalted butter, softened

100 g (4 oz) caster sugar

50 g (2 oz) icing sugar

3 tablespoons brandy, Cointreau or Grand Marnier

preserves

home-made jams and marmalades are a real treat and they make marvellous gifts for family and friends. Making a preserve such as marmalade or strawberry jam is a seasonal activity, which is rare in these days when ingredients are available all year.

Jam, marmalade, chutney and other preserves are a cooked mixture of fruit and sugar. The sugar concentration in them is so high that spoilage organisms cannot grow and in this way the fruit is 'preserved'.

equipment

Pans Any large, heavy-based saucepan can be used to make jam, so long as it is big enough for the contents to come only halfway up the pan. The extra capacity is needed to accommodate a 'fast rolling boil', during which the contents bubble to the top of the pan. A preserving pan is best because the sloping sides allow the jam to boil and fall back down the sides of the pan, reducing the danger of the mixture boiling over. Stainless steel is the best material because it is inert and, unlike aluminium, will not leach into the jam.

Jars Sterilized jam jars are needed for bottling the jam (see page 239). Preserves are best bottled into warmed jars to prevent the jars from cracking.

Thermometer Allows you to know when 106°C/240°F (setting point) has been reached. At this stage you can begin testing to see if the jam is ready to set.

Waxed discs Seal the top of the jam as soon as it has been bottled. Cellophane covers can also be applied when the jam is still hot. Discs and cellophane covers are sold in cook shops, some stationers and chemists, or by mail order.

Long-handled spoon for stirring.

Slotted spoon for skimming off scum and fruit stones.

Funnel with a wide neck, can be used for filling jars, but a jug will do just as well.

choosing fruit for preserves

A mixture of ripe and under-ripe fruit is best. The fruit should be sound, not blemished or going rotten.

The pectin content of fruit determines how well a preserve sets. Some fruits contain more pectin than others. Using a combination of fruit with high and low pectin levels is one way of getting round this problem. Another is to add lemon and lemon juice to aid setting – lemon also brings out the flavour of the fruit (2 tablespoons to just under 2 kg/4½ lb) of fruit). Preserving sugar with added pectin is another alternative. Sachets of pectin are also available for preserve-making; follow the instructions on the pack.

Rescue remedy If the jam or marmalade has not set once it has been bottled, return it to the preserving pan with a sachet of pectin (or the amount suggested

pectin content of fruit and vegetables used for preserving

Good Apples (cooking and crab); cranberries; currants (red and black); damsons; gooseberries; lemons; limes; medlars; Seville oranges (special bitter marmalade oranges, available January and February only); some plums; quinces.

Medium Apples (dessert); apricots; bilberries and blueberries; blackberries; greengages; loganberries; mulberries; some plums; raspberries.
Poor Bananas; carrots; cherries; elderberries; figs; grapes; marrows; melons; nectarines; peaches; pineapples; rhubarb; strawberries.

on the pack) and re-boil. Clean and prepare the jars again and re-bottle. A couple of pounds of jam will be lost through evaporation, but at least the preserve will set.

using fruit

Always go through the fruit carefully, discarding any mouldy or damaged fruit. Wash it and shake or pat dry then put it into the preserving pan with water and simmer as directed. Cooking time varies according the hardness of the fruit. Simmering releases the pectin and acid; it also cooks off some of the liquid to help with the set. The sugar should be added only when the fruit is sufficiently soft. This is particularly important for marmalade – the peel must be thoroughly cooked and soft before adding the sugar because it does not have enough time to cook further during the subsequent boiling with sugar.

sugar

The amount used depends on the pectin strength of the fruit. In general, use an equal weight of sugar to fruit: 450 g (1 lb) sugar to each 450 g (1 lb) of fruit. Too little sugar results in poor setting and jam that goes mouldy. Too much sugar produces dark, sticky jam; this spoils the flavour of the fruit and can also lead to sugar crystallizing out as the jam is stored. Granulated or preserving sugar is the best choice for a clear and bright jam – brown sugar produces a dark jam and influences the flavour, but it can be very successful in Dundee-style marmalade.

You can reduce the sugar in jam by about 20–25%. These reduced-sugar jams will be runnier and will not keep as well. Store them in the fridge and use within six weeks to two months.

bottling

Once setting point has been reached, remove the pan from the heat and allow it to stand for 10 minutes, so that the fruit or peel which is mainly at the top has time to sink back through the jam. This produces a more even distribution of fruit or peel when the preserve is bottled. Fill the jars and put the waxed disks and cellophane tops on, securing with an elastic band (supplied in the pack of discs and tops). Wetting the cellophane with a tiny amount of water on the outer surface helps it stretch and seal in the jam. Allow the jar to become completely cold. Wipe any sticky drips off the outside of the jars and label them. Store in a cool, dry place.

Strawberry jam is susceptible to the fruit rising. Instead of using warmed jars use cold ones, which discourage floating fruit!

jellies

Jellies are strained jams. After the fruit has been cooked in the water it is strained by being put into a jelly bag that is suspended over a large bowl to catch the juice. The pulp remains in the jelly bag. Often, jelly bags are sold on frames that stand over a bowl. If you do not have one, a large piece of muslin or a boiled tea-towel or piece of cotton sheet could be used. Tie the fruit pulp into the cloth and suspend the bag overnight. Never squeeze a jelly bag. Although this might extract more liquid, it will make the finished jelly cloudy.

The strained juice is boiled with sugar to make jelly. Usually, 450 g (1 lb) of sugar is added to each 600 ml (1 pint) of juice, but this amount of sugar can be reduced by 50–75 g (2–3 oz) for high pectin fruit. Bring to the boil and test the jelly for setting in the same way as you would for jam.

three-fruit marmalade

preparation time: 45 minutes | cooking time: 1¾ hours | makes about 3.6–4 kg (8–9 lb)

A tangy marmalade that can be made at any time of the year. If you prefer Seville orange marmalade, use 1.5 kg (3 lb) of Seville oranges.

Wash and sterilize nine jam jars (see page 239).

Scrub the grapefruit, lemons and oranges. Cut grapefruit in half and place in a large pan, or a preserving pan, with oranges, lemons and 3 litres (5¼ pints) of water. Gently simmer for about 1½ hours, until the skins are tender and easily pierced with a sharp knife.

Using a slotted spoon, remove the fruit from the pan. When cool, cut the fruit in half. Remove the pips, place them in a piece of muslin and tie with string. Attach this to the pan handle, so the pips float in the marmalade as it cooks. Warm the sugar in a bowl in a low oven for 10 minutes.

Meanwhile, cut the fruit into strips, as long, thin or as chunky as you like. Return to the pan. Add the sugar and stir until it dissolves. Bring to the boil and boil rapidly for about 10 minutes or until setting point is reached. Remove from the heat and test as described below. If it hasn't set, return to the heat, cook for a little longer and re-test.

Remove from the heat and leave to settle for 20 minutes. Remove the pip bag, skim off any scum, and then spoon the marmalade into warm, sterilized jars. Cover with a disc of waxed paper, waxed-side down. Dampen the outside of a cellophane jam cover and then secure tightly with elastic bands.

500 g (1 lb 2 oz) grapefruit
500 g (1 lb 2 oz) lemons
500 g (1 lb 2 oz) oranges
3 kg (7 lb) granulated sugar

how to test for setting point

There are two ways to check for setting point but you must remove the pan from the heat first, to prevent the jam or marmalade from overcooking.

If you have a sugar thermometer, place it in a jug of hot water so that it will register more quickly. Stir the jam and put in the thermometer. When it reads 106°C/240°F, the jam has reached setting point.

If you don't have a thermometer or you're making small quantities of jam or marmalade, the flake test is a useful technique. Chill a plate in the fridge. Place a little jam or marmalade on the plate and then chill it in the fridge for a few minutes. Gently push the jam with your finger or the back of a metal spoon; if the surface wrinkles and is not very runny, it has come to setting point. If it isn't ready, return the pan to the heat and repeat the test a few minutes later.

strawberry jam

makes about 3 kg (7 lb) | preparation time: 15 minutes | cooking time: 20–25 minutes

Take advantage of plentiful supplies of summer fruit and make your own jam. You can adapt the strawberry jam recipe for other soft fruits.

Strawberries should be unblemished If they're unripe, they won't soften enough, while over-ripe fruit will contain less pectin, colour and flavour. Select small strawberries, as they retain their shape better. Wash them only if they're muddy. Always use jam sugar with strawberries.

1.75 kg (4 lb) jam sugar
1.75 kg (4 lb) hulled strawberries
juice of 3 lemons

Pre-heat the oven to 110°C/225°F/Gas ¼/fan oven 90°C. Wash and sterilize the jars (see page 239). Warm the sugar on a plate in the oven.

Place the strawberries and lemon juice in a preserving pan or large, heavy-based pan. Cook over a low heat for 5–8 minutes, until the juices run and the strawberries are soft.

Using a wooden spoon, stir in the warmed sugar and heat until it dissolves. Bring to the boil and then boil quickly for about 10–15 minutes, until the jam reaches setting point (see page 237). Once the jam is at setting point, leave it off the heat to cool slightly, skimming off any scum from the surface and edges with a metal spoon. When the jam begins to cool, stir gently to distribute the fruit and then ladle or pour it into warmed sterilized jars to within 5 mm (¼ in) of the top.

To seal the jam jars, cover with a disc of waxed paper, waxed-side down, directly over the jam to cover the surface completely. Dampen the outside of a cellophane jam cover and then secure tightly over the jar with an elastic band. This cover will shrink and form a tighter seal as the jar cools.

Store in a cool, dry and dark place for up to 12 months.

what went wrong?

The preserve has set too firmly Too much sugar was added or the jam boiled too long after the sugar was added.

The preserve has gone mouldy The jars were not sterilized properly or the jam not covered straight away, leaving it vulnerable to mould spores in the air. Or the jars may have been damp or the jam was stored in a damp place. Throw it away.

The preserve did not set properly It was either underboiled (keep jam at a full rolling boil for the correct length of time and watch constantly) or there was not enough pectin in the fruit or acid (lemon juice) used. Add liquid pectin or use jam sugar next time. Try boiling it again and re-test for setting point, or freeze and use as an ice-cream sauce.

pear, apple and date chutney

preparation time: 30–40 minutes | cooking time: 4–4½ hours | makes 2.25–2.7 kg (5–6 lb)

This is a great way to use up a glut of apples and pears. Prepare the ingredients the day before making, as the need soaking overnight.

Wash and sterilize 6–8 jam jars (see below). Put the pears, apples, onions, dates, apricots, sultanas, ginger, garlic, lemon zest and juice and salt in a large mixing bowl.

Place the sugar, chilli flakes and vinegar in a pan over a low heat, stirring until the sugar dissolves. Turn up the heat and boil for 5 minutes. Pour over the ingredients in the mixing bowl, cover with a clean cloth and leave in a cool place for 12 hours, or overnight.

Transfer the mixture to a large preserving pan, heat gently and then bring to the boil. Lower the heat and simmer very gently for 4–4½ hours, until all the liquid has evaporated to leave a good, rich chutney. Stir occasionally, to prevent the chutney from sticking to the bottom of the pan as it thickens.

Transfer to hot, sterilized jars. Cover with a disc of waxed paper, waxed-side down to cover the surface completely. Dampen the outside of a cellophane jam cover and then secure tightly over the jam jar with an elastic band. This cover will shrink and form a tighter seal as the jam cools. Store in a cool, dry place for up to 12 months.

2 kg (4 lb) pears, peeled, cored and roughly chopped

1 kg (2 lb) cooking apples, peeled, cored and roughly chopped

450 g (1 lb) onions, chopped

225 g (8 oz) dried dates, chopped

100 g (4 oz) dried apricots, chopped

100 g (4 oz) sultanas

50 g (2 oz) fresh root ginger, grated

6 garlic cloves, crushed

finely grated zest and juice of 2 lemons

25 g (1 oz) salt

350 g (12 oz) light muscovado sugar

2 teaspoons dried chilli flakes, crushed

1.2 litres (2 pints) cider vinegar

tips for successful preserves

To sterilize jam jars, wash, rinse and drain. Place in a warm oven, 110°C/Gas ¼/225°F; fan oven 90°C from cold, for 15–20 minutes to sterilize them. Keep them warm until ready to fill.

You can use screw-topped lids instead of cellophane covers, but they should be plastic or plastic-lined. Metal lids will corrode. Add plastic lids while still hot, but do not tighten until the preserve is completely cold.

Add warmed sugar to the fruit as it dissolves more quickly and prevents crystals from forming in the jam.

Jam sugar contains natural apple pectin, which will help the jam give a good set.

You can also use preserving sugar – this is sugar granulated in a way to make it quicker to dissolve.

wine

the days when developing an interest in wine meant having a cellar to keep it in are far behind us. Anybody intending to 'lay down' some fine vintages now is more likely to have to make do with a space under the bed or in the cupboard under the stairs. Anywhere will do as long as it's dark, not too warm or prone to extreme variations in temperature, and just a little awkward to get at. This last feature will prevent you from rifling through your maturing stock too early on those days when you forgot to stop off at the wine merchant's. These guidelines, though, are really only intended to apply to the sort of wine that needs many years' cellaring or keeping. Most people will only keep bottles bought in bulk for a few months at most and, with this length of time, there is no earthly reason for you to go to the effort of squirrelling it away. Wine is a much more resilient product than people tend to give it credit for, and old textbooks that advised you to check on the level of humidity in the atmosphere of the storage space were presuming you would be keeping bottles for many years.

Many premium wines are aged by their producers before release on to the market. These include Rioja and similar styles of wine from Spain, Reserve wines from eastern Europe, and categories of port such as Late-Bottled Vintage or Vintage Character. Wines such as these are deliberately intended to be ready to drink as soon as you buy the bottle. By contrast, many wines – perhaps the bulk of what is sold in retail outlets with high turnovers, the off-licence chains and supermarkets – are not intended for ageing at all, but are meant to be enjoyed young and fresh, while the first flush of youthful fruit flavour is still on them, and while their crisp acidity lends them a lively, refreshing texture.

The wines that do need ageing are the solidly built reds of French regions like Bordeaux, Burgundy and the Rhône, Italians from Piedmont and Tuscany, and vintage port. The point of allowing these to mature is that, as the hard tannins in them soften up with time, the fruit flavours grow steadily more complex and fascinating. Some dry white wines, such as the grander categories of Chablis, other white burgundies, and vintage champagnes, need time to lose the brittle acidity of youth, while great sweet wines such as Sauternes can take several years for their sweetness and acidity to arrive at a harmonious balance.

serving wine

The correct temperatures for serving different types of wine are worth observing in order to get the best out of your bottle, but they don't have to be absolutely thermometer-precise. All white wines and rosés should be served chilled, quite vigorously for sparkling wines, pinks and the lighter styles of dry white (in the region of 7–9°C/45–48°F), a little less so for the richer whites such as oaky Chardonnay (9–12°C/48–54°F). Sweet wines can take the coldest temperatures of all (5–6°C/41–43°F), on account of their syrupy concentration of flavour.

Some lighter reds, such as Beaujolais and young wines made from Pinot Noir, benefit from being served slightly chilled (but no lower than about 11–13°C/52–55°F). Most reds are fine at room temperature, assuming you don't keep the central heating at tropical levels. There has been something of a fashion in the last few years in certain circles to serve all red wines at what is known as 'cellar temperature' (about 14–15°C/57–59°F). This is an acquired taste and, if you don't care for it, don't do it. What you should scrupulously avoid is the old-fashioned business of warming the wine artificially. That can easily spoil its aromas and flavours. If it seems too cold when you taste it, warm the first glass by cupping it in the palms of your hands while the remainder of the bottle warms up a little.

opening sparkling wines
Great care should always be taken when opening wines that have been bottled under pressure. The best technique is to remove the cork by pushing gently upwards against it, whilst turning the bottle. When you can feel it beginning to give, control its release little by little by placing your thumb over the top. If the bottle

has been badly shaken up, there is a chance it can erupt violently when you come to open it. Always point the bottle away from other people's faces (and your own) and, if the wine does begin spurting out, either pour it into the first glass quickly or put a finger in the neck of the bottle, allowing a little room for air to escape nonetheless. As a rule, the colder the wine is, the less likelihood there will be of explosions.

decanting

If an older wine has thrown a sediment, i.e. created a deposit in the bottle, it will need to be decanted. Leave the bottle standing upright for a day or so before opening, to allow the sediment to fall to the bottom. After opening it carefully, it is simply a matter of pouring it slowly but steadily into a decanter or jug, looking into the flow of wine itself against some convenient light source. As soon as you see the first hint of grainy sediment come through, stop pouring. Anything remaining in the bottle can then be filtered. A clean muslin cloth is the best vehicle for this. Unscented tissue will work nearly as well, but is messier. Avoid perfumed tissue or coffee filter-papers, which will spoil or even strip the wine's natural flavours.

how to spot faulty wine

cork taint

A significant minority of bottles suffers from a condition in which the wine is said to be 'corked'. This is nothing to do with fragments of the cork crumbling off and falling into the wine, which doesn't affect the flavour. A corked bottle is one where the wine has reacted with the chemicals used to treat the cork, or has simply picked up off-flavours from an old and dried-up cork, and gone bad. The longer the suspect cork is in contact with the wine, the worse the problem will be. At its most rank, corked wine has a dirty, musty smell, like an old dishcloth or sometimes like the blue mould that forms on stale bread. It completely masks the fruit aromas of the wine. Whatever you have heard, it isn't that hard to spot, and should always be the occasion

for taking the wine back to the retailer or refusing to accept it in the restaurant. The chances are it will be one bad bottle, so you can be reasonably confident that another bottle of the same wine will be healthy. If it isn't, don't chance another. The winemaker has obviously been sold a duff batch of cork.

If the wine is only just on the turn, the problem might not show itself on the nose but will become apparent when the wine is tasted. Sometimes, light cork taint only develops gradually while the first glass is being drunk. It makes no difference. The advice is the same: send it back.

oxidation

An oxidized wine has received too much air contact, either during the production or through an imperfect cork during long cellaring. It will taste dead, stale and flat, not mouldy like corked wine, just lifeless. It is particularly noticeable in white wines, where it not only gives the wine a cidery, even metallic flavour, but deepens the colour to something like Lucozade. This, too, is an out-of-condition wine, and should not be accepted.

tartrate

Sometimes wine that has been stored in chilly conditions develops a tartrate deposit. These are crystals of precipitated tartaric acid, as you will discover if you taste one. They are obviously more visible in white wine than in red, and often collect on the underside of the cork. Tartrate crystals don't affect the drinking quality of the wine, but it can be necessary to waste a little if you find a clump of them in the bottom of your glass.

sulphide

Occasionally, the sulphur dioxide (SO_2) that wine is treated with as an antioxidant undergoes a spontaneous chemical process to form hydrogen sulphide (H_2S), the characteristic odour of which is rotten egg. (Think of stinkbombs.) If it is only a trace, it can well blow off with air contact in the glass but, if it is overpowering and persistent, send the wine back.

reading a wine label

Domdechant Werner Hochheimer
Domdechaney Riesling
Trockenbeerenauslese 1994

Confused? You needn't be. The Gothic script at the top is simply the name of the wine estate, and proudly tells us that this has been a family company since 1780. Below that, a deGothicized version appears. Under the vintage – 1994, with its German -er suffix – is the identification of precisely where this wine was grown. The first name is the nearest town or village, in this case Hochheim, while the second name is the vineyard itself. Riesling is the grape variety, and Trockenbeerenauslese indicates the level of sweetness in the wine. This one is the very sweetest. Below that, Gutsabfüllung announces that it has been bottled at the estate, and Rheingau is the region. At the very bottom, Qualitätswein mit Prädikat is the German version of appellation contrôlée – the highest quality designation.

Muga Rioja Reserva 1995

The registration letter after Muga tells us that that is the name of the producer, or Bodegas Muga (the Muga Cellars) as it is shown further down. Rioja is the appellation, as is indicated by the classification printed beneath it, Spain's highest – Denominación de Origen Calificada. It is a 1995 Reserva, as the top of the label tells us, that is it has been given the second-longest maturation period of any Rioja, the longest being Gran Reserva. The company shield beneath the DOCa shows us that this company has been around since 1932, and below that, Embottellado en la propriedad is the equivalent of that German Gutsabfüllung, or the French mis en bouteille à la propriété – in other words, bottled at the estate, as opposed to some outside bottling plant. The sub-region, Rioja Alta, appears at the very bottom of the label.

wine glasses

The question of which glasses to use for wine has, in recent history, approached the level of rocket science in its complexity. Led by one particular widely respected Austrian glass company, there has been a trend towards insisting that every individual wine, and each of the leading grape varieties, should have its own respective design. You might not wish to buy dozens of different sets, however, and there is no reason to do so. Three or four types will cope with the demands of all the world's wines.

red and white wine glasses

A salient point to remember is that a wineglass can never be too big. It can, on the other hand, be too small. Those tiny round goblets beloved of pubs and wine-bars are practically useless because they don't allow much space for swirling the wine and enjoying its aromas. A tulip-shaped glass is the best design, one that tapers towards the rim and channels the wine's aromatic character to your nostrils. A deep bowl allows for vigorous swirling: remember, you don't have to fill it more than a third full. If you buy two sizes, use the larger ones for red wine. Choose glasses with long

stems (it isn't sensible to hold a white wine glass by the bowl because the heat of your hand will neutralize the chilling), and the thinnest rims you can find. Always go for plain rather than coloured glass, which obscures the precise shade of the wine. Cut crystal may look pretty, but it doesn't give as clear a view of the wine as an undecorated glass does.

sparkling wine glasses

The tall, narrow flute is the universally recommended glass for fizz these days. Its design minimizes the surface-area of the wine, meaning that fewer bubbles are breaking on it and slowing down the rate at which the wine loses its effervescence. It isn't clear who ever left their champagne sitting around in the old saucer glasses long enough for it to go flat, but it is a design thought fit only for cocktails now. Avoid flutes with short stems, and any that flare out towards the rim.

fortified wine glasses

Glasses for port, sherry and madeira should be slightly smaller than those used for table wines, on account of their higher alcohol levels, but don't use those little thimble glasses. You want to appreciate the aromatics in these wines just as much as with unfortified wines. Avoid liqueur glasses and those tiny, narrow creations known as schooners. These are wines, after all, not spirits or liqueurs, and deserve to be treated as such.

food and wine matching

The old rule of thumb about serving the right wine with the right dish used to advise: white wines with fish and white meat dishes, red wines with red meats and game. Modern gastronomic theory has made that seem laughably simplistic now, and yet the basic premises have never been disproved. It is just that sometimes a red wine works equally well with white meat and, occasionally, even with fish. (White wines with red meats, though, are hardly ever a good idea.) These guidelines are not meant to be learned by rote.

They are only intended to point you in some directions you might not have considered. When all is said and done, your own experimentation will continue to turn up unexpectedly successful combinations. The food-and-wine tasting has never yet been held that didn't uncover at least one major surprise. A recent discovery of my own was a delicate rosé champagne that beautifully complemented a bowl of earthy, home-made leek and potato soup!

apéritifs

An appetite-arousing mouthful of something dry, light and possibly fizzy is the best start to a meal. Bone-dry pale *fino* sherry is superb at performing this function, and is especially good if accompanied by tapas. Champagne (or New World sparkling wine) not only awakens the tastebuds but gets everybody in the right mood, too. Choose a fresh, vivacious non-vintage: the lighter style of young *blanc de blancs* works well. Failing either of those options, a light-bodied but flavoursome dry white is a sound choice. The more aromatic grape varieties, such as Riesling or Sauvignon Blanc, are the better bets. Avoid sweet wines as apéritifs. Sweetness has a satiating effect on the tastebuds, exactly the opposite of what you are trying to achieve.

first courses

Asparagus with hollandaise Sauvignon Blanc, especially from New Zealand.

Avocado with prawns Chablis or other unoaked or lightly oaked Chardonnay.

Chicken- or pork-liver pâté Gewürztraminer or Pinot Gris from Alsace.

Gravad lax Alsace wines or full-bodied, oaky Chardonnay or Sémillon from Australia.

Salads Any light, unoaked white with crisp acidity (Sauvignon, Riesling, Chenin, Italian dry whites), but vinaigrette with a straight wine vinegar in it will argue with the wine. Balsamic is friendlier. A dash of lemon juice shouldn't cause major problems.

Smoked salmon As for gravad lax, but it can take even higher oak and alcohol.

soups

Light-textured, liquidized soups are better taken on their own, although a glass of *fino* or dry *amontillado* sherry, or even champagne, makes an acceptable match. With a chunkier soup such as minestrone, a midweight Italian red is an appropriate choice. Consommé needs a tot of medium-sweet *amontillado* sherry, while a suitably fruity New World rosé works well with rich crustacean bisque.

pasta

Dishes with herb-scented tomato sauces need gutsy Italian reds such as Montepulciano d'Abruzzo, Barbera or Chianti Rufina. With a cream sauce, a richly constituted white is better. Carbonara is happiest with a big, smoky, oaked Chardonnay. For pasta dishes containing shellfish, a lighter, astringent white such as Italian Verdicchio or Arneis is the best route.

fish and shellfish

Crab With the white meat served in a salad, a light Spanish, Italian or Portuguese white is good. For dressed crab, something richer is called for – Chardonnay, perhaps, with a touch of oak.

Lobster As a salad, a light dry to medium white, such as classic German Riesling or a dry or *demi-sec* Vouvray. Lobster Thermidor needs a big, opulent Chardonnay – the best white burgundy you can afford.

Monkfish This sturdiest of white fish needs a big white such as old-fashioned oaky white Rioja or an aged Australian Semillon. If stewed with bacon in red wine, drink the same wine with it.

Oysters Bone-dry whites: non-vintage champagne, Chablis or Muscadet.

Red mullet Waxy southern European white (e.g. Vernaccia di San Gimignano, Portuguese Roupeiro), or a light-textured red such as Beaujolais, or Loire red like Chinon.

Salmon Depending on the sauce, it demands a fairly muscular specimen if white is preferred. With hollandaise, the most buttery Chardonnay is required (Burgundy, California, Australia or Chile). It also gets along very well with a lightly chilled young Pinot Noir red from Burgundy's Côte de Beaune or from New Zealand.

Scallops Delicately flavoured whites like Alsace Pinot Blanc or Soave Classico are best.

Tuna Big reds – Australian Shiraz, Chilean or California Merlot, Côte de Nuits burgundy or Moulin-à-Vent – hold no terror for it.

Other light-textured white fish (sole, John Dory, trout, skate, etc) Ring the changes from the world's array of light to medium-bodied whites.

Other firm-textured white fish (sea bass, cod, turbot, hake, etc) More densely textured whites such as Bordeaux blanc, Australian Semillon, *premier* or *grand cru* Chablis, Pinot Gris, and so forth.

poultry, meat, game and offal

Beef A grilled steak can take any fairly meaty-textured red with moderate tannin. Roast beef needs something a little lighter (Bordeaux, California, Washington or Chilean Merlot, Châteauneuf-du-Pape). If there is a hot accompaniment like horseradish or mustard, you will need an appositely spicy wine – Crozes-Hermitage, Zinfandel or a Spanish Garnacha-based red.

Calf's and lamb's liver Softer reds based on Merlot (Pomerol or St-Emilion), Pinot Noir (California or Oregon) or Cabernet Franc (Loire) are the most sympathetic matches.

Chicken Poached chicken needs a savoury, firm-bodied white such as midweight Chardonnay, Pinot Blanc or Gris, Sémillon, etc. With roasted, a medium-bodied red is better. Think Burgundy, southern Rhône, St-Emilion, or Merlots from the New World.

Duck Roast duck needs a spicy red such as California Zinfandel, Australian Shiraz-Cabernet or a top northern Rhône Syrah like Côte-Rôtie or Hermitage.

Game birds The darker-fleshed varieties, such as partridge or grouse, need the pungency of old Pinot Noir from wherever. With pheasant, a scented white wine such as Australian Riesling, California Viognier or Alsace Pinot Gris can be good.

Goose Much as for duck, but a bit more tannin can help. California Cabernet, Barolo or Barbaresco from Piedmont or a fine Haut-Médoc claret will provide the necessary weight.

Ham Roast ham works exceptionally well with aged semi-sweet German Rieslings, Chenin Blanc from the Loire or a Viognier from the northern Rhône or Languedoc. Or Provence rosé.

Lamb Cabernet or Cabernet-Merlot blends from almost anywhere make an impeccable match, or for the classic Iberian experience, go for a Crianza or Reserva Rioja or Portuguese red from the Douro or Alentejo.

Pork Very flexible, but is probably a bit better with a soft, supple red such as a Merlot or southern Rhône blend than with next-best oaky whites.

Rabbit Relatively bland, lightly oaked whites are best, unless there is a pungently flavoured sauce or stuffing, in which case a midweight red will shine. Try Brunello di Montalcino from Tuscany or a Côte de Nuits burgundy.

Sweetbreads Best with an assertively flavoured white, such as Alsace or New Zealand Gewürztraminer, southern French Viognier or an oaked Chardonnay from Chile.

Turkey As for chicken, but with a bit more sinew to reflect the texture of the bird. Whites such as Hermitage or Châteauneuf-du-Pape blanc or Rioja Blanco, reds of the order of Shiraz from Australia or Zinfandel from California.

Venison Best with robust, chewy reds. Go for strapping New World Cabernets or try Nebbiolo reds from Italy.

oriental cuisines

As a very rough guideline, most Thai and Chinese dishes are better with white wines than with reds. The chilli-heat in Thai cooking means that there is no point in serving wines of great subtlety, and so well-chilled neutral whites, such as Muscadet, Soave or Rueda, will fit the bill quite adequately. However, a certain amount of upfront fruity or floral aromatic quality makes a more diverting marriage. Wines made from Gewürztraminer, Pinot Gris, Sauvignon Blanc or Riesling are the ones to opt for: think Alsace, New Zealand and Australia.

With Indian food, a wider canvas comes into play. Red wines with a fair amount of acidity and moderate tannic weight can negotiate the hotter dishes very well. A lamb dish absolutely demands them, but even the richer dishes such as dhansak or dopiaza can take a red when made with chicken. Otherwise, the pungent, aromatic whites referred to above will all prove worthwhile investments.

cheeses

No one wine can hope to satisfy all the cheeses on a cheeseboard but, if you are serving one mature specimen in fine condition, it is unthinkable not to drink a wine with it. Goats' cheese needs a high-acid unoaked white from either Sauvignon (Loire or New Zealand) or Chenin (Loire or South Africa). Ripe, soft cheeses, such as Camembert, Brie and so forth, are fine with either a rich white or a light, soft red (Pinot Noir is good). Hard English cheeses like Cheddar, Gloucester, Leicester, etc. can take a sturdier red, such as Cabernet or Merlot or good port, but are also very successful with a richly oaked Chardonnay (try Australia). With blue cheeses, a sweet wine can be a heavenly match (Sauternes or sweet Alsace wines with Roquefort being the classic juxtaposition), because the high sugar-levels balance any saltiness in the cheese.

desserts

Nowadays, it is considered a little *infra dig* to drink sweet wines with desserts, and yet some combinations are pleasurable enough to be worth hanging on to. The richest egg- or cream-based desserts, such as crème brûlée, mousses, bavarois, charlottes and so on, are well served by noble-rotted sweet wines (i.e. those that have had their sugars concentrated by allowing the grapes to rot on the vine) from Sauternes, the Loire, Germany, Austria or elsewhere. A lighter style of late-harvested wine is the best option for a frangipane-based fruit tart or hot fruit-based soufflé: go for Riesling, Muscat or Gewürztraminer. Chocolate desserts can be good with the fortified styles of Muscat, such as Beaumes-de-Venise. With Christmas pudding, the most refreshing match is Italian Asti or Moscato d'Asti. A glass of malmsey madeira or Australian Liqueur Muscat is excellent with a piece of traditional English fruitcake. The only desserts really to avoid serving wine with are ice-creams, parfaits and sorbets, where the coldness tends to desensitise the palate's responsiveness to other flavours.

grape varieties

There are thousands of varieties of the wine grape *Vitis vinifera* growing throughout the world's viticultural regions, but only a handful of what are known as the international varieties now make the bulk of the wine we consume. Most of these are French in origin. One or two others are sufficiently important within one country to be worthy of note on their own.

chardonnay

Style Well on its way to becoming the most widely planted white wine grape in the world, Chardonnay has become everybody's favourite variety. It is something of a chameleon, and can produce wines in a range of styles from light and sharp and relatively neutral in flavour to big, blowsy, oak-powered creations that can stand up to the richest food. At the lighter end, it can have little more than a faint tinge of lemon or green apple, but no other obvious fruit, while the oak-barrel versions derive most of their classic tasting notes of butter, cream and soft spices like nutmeg or cinnamon from the wood treatment they are given.

Regions It is the the sole white grape of Burgundy, including Chablis, and is grown in every other wine-producing country on earth.

riesling

Style Riesling is easily as versatile a grape as Chardonnay is, with the added attraction of the fact that it makes superlative sweet wines. It doesn't have much of an affinity with oak, but it hardly needs it, since this is one of the most aromatic white grapes of the lot. It typically has a strong scent of lime, which can be mixed with luscious soft fruits like peach or apricot in the sweeter versions. When it has been allowed to develop noble rot for making the very sweetest wines it can be smothered in honey or marmalade, and it also often displays a strangely pungent but appealing aroma of petrol when it has been given some bottle-age. A wine made from Riesling nearly always has highly defined acidity, which adds refreshing tang to a dry version, and balances out the intense sweetness of the rot-affected wines. German Rieslings are among the lowest in alcohol of any fine wines, and yet the best lack nothing in terms of flavour concentration, which, together with that high acid, means that they age superbly.

Regions The Rhine and Mosel valleys in Germany are its favourite stamping-grounds, but fine Riesling is made in Alsace, Australia and New Zealand, and, increasingly, California.

sauvignon blanc

Style Another aromatic grape, but one that tends to make simpler wines than Riesling, Sauvignon is the epitome of the fresh-and-fruity, drink-it-young style of dry white wine. It generally shows green fruit and vegetable flavours in abundance, from apples and pears through to green peppers, asparagus or fresh herbs like basil, although the southern-hemisphere wines can have an even broader repertoire of fruits, including mango, passion-fruit and peach. Peculiarly for a white wine, there is often a hauntingly precise scent of blackcurrant in it, perhaps the leaves of the bush rather than the berries themselves. Something even more piercing still often comes through, particularly in the French versions, that is famously (or notoriously, depending on which way you look at it) referred to as cat's pee. If you have a cat, you won't have difficulty spotting it. Sauvignon is nothing without a tongue-tingling zap of acidity and, although some producers do experiment with oak-ageing it, it tends to be happier without. Sauvignon makes a good blending partner with Sémillon, as in the wines of Bordeaux.

Regions The Loire valley, where its best wines are Sancerre and Pouilly-Fumé, Bordeaux, Hungary and parts of Spain such as Rueda are its most successful European areas, but New Zealand is thought by many to make the best Sauvignon in the world. Good in Chile too, and, occasionally, South Africa.

sémillon

Style Sémillon has two quite distinct personalities. On the one hand, it can make very rich, fleshy, full-bodied dry wines that can not only stay the distance in the cellar, but often develop a strange hint of toastiness as they age, as if they have been matured in wood even where they haven't. On the other hand, its great susceptibility to noble rot makes it, like Riesling, outstanding at producing classic, lusciously concentrated, long-lived sweet wines, often with a dash of Sauvignon added just to sharpen the overall balance on the palate. This is the style made world-famous by the wines of Sauternes. Dry Sémillon has long been a speciality of the Hunter Valley of New South Wales, Australia, and its fat-textured and yet oddly austere style there is now imitated by certain enterprising growers in Bordeaux. It is also used widely in Australia as a blending partner for Chardonnay, which tends to result in a palatable but rather indifferent wine.

Regions Bordeaux and the Hunter Valley are its pre-eminent homelands, but decent varietal Sémillon has also emerged from California.

chenin blanc

Style Chenin is a much misunderstood grape variety that is very much an acquired taste to wine beginners. It always has very high, some would say searingly high, levels of acidity, on account of the fact that it ripens only very slowly in the vineyard. Like Riesling and Sémillon, it is very hospitable to noble rot in the right conditions, and can make some disarmingly beautiful (and relatively keenly priced) dessert wines. In the Loire, it is also widely used to make *demi-sec* wines with just a touch of residual sweetness, which might not be a hugely fashionable style but is, nonetheless, an attractive one that has its gastronomic place. The aromatic range of Chenin is often what puts people off.

It can have a trace of exotic fruit, but more often it exhibits a baffling aroma of damp wool ('wet dog' is how some less charitable commentators describe it). This is particularly noticeable in the driest versions from the Loire. Good Chenin – even the lighter, drier versions – ages well in the bottle, and can demand it if that youthful acid is just too aggressive.

Regions The central Loire, especially Vouvray and Savennières. Elsewhere, it is of lesser importance. It is the most widely grown white grape in South Africa, but rarely rises to the heights in quality terms.

gewürztraminer

Style No fine-wine grape has a more singularly exotic range of scents and flavours than Gewürztraminer. This, more than any other, is a real love-it-or-hate-it variety. In its heartland of Alsace it produces a rich, high-alcohol, deeply coloured wine that nearly always has a noticeable hint of residual sugar in it. But it is the aromas that shock and amaze: a mixture of sweet-smelling flowers with something soapy underneath, allied to tropical fruits such as mango and banana and strong spices like cinnamon, ginger and cloves. Without wishing to compromise its dignity, it's fair to say it sometimes smells more like something you would add to the bathwater than pour out at the dinner-table. With the proviso that a little tends to go a long way, it can be a memorable wine, and is adept at producing great rotted sweet wines too. Typically low acidity, though, means they might not have quite the staying-power in the cellar as the best sweet Rieslings or Sémillons.

Regions At its very best in Alsace, but it has also turned in some convincing performances in Australia, New Zealand, California and Chile.

other important white grapes

Melon de Bourgogne Important only as the grape of Muscadet in the western Loire, dead-neutral, bone-dry, high-acid wine made for drinking young.

The Muscat family Grapy or raisiny, frequently orangey in flavour, the Muscat grapes make decent sweet wines all over the world, including Muscat de Beaumes-de-Venise, Asti, Moscatel de Valencia and the Liqueur Muscats of Australia.

Pinot Blanc More neutral in flavour than Pinot Gris, but good at solid, vaguely appley wines in Alsace.

Pinot Gris Muskily aromatic grape, making fleshy dry whites in Alsace and Oregon, and lighter styles in northern Italy (as Pinot Grigio).

Viognier Once confined to tiny enclaves in the northern Rhône, now grown more widely in the Languedoc, California and Australia, it has a characteristic apricot scent, sometimes backed up with a touch of ginger spice.

cabernet sauvignon

Style The world's most famous red grape variety is a surprisingly tricky customer. It needs plenty of sun to bring out its character, and nearly always benefits from the influence of wood-ageing (and one or two other grapes in the blend) to round it out. Dark purple fruits such as damsons, black plums and – classically – blackcurrants are its characteristic tasting notes, but there is also a woody austerity in the most complex wines. Seen at its most distinguished in the classed-growth wines of Bordeaux, Cabernet is sometimes described as having the aroma of cigar-boxes or cigar-wrappers, and the scent of freshly sawn cedarwood can also be detectable. The hotter the climate it is grown in, the darker the colour and the higher the alcohol will be, and the greatest Cabernets can evolve for many years in the bottle.

Regions Originally Bordeaux (particularly the area known as the Haut-Médoc), but Cabernet is grown nearly all over the world now. It is made in a magisterial, densely textured style in California and Washington State, softer and more voluptuously in Australia and Chile. For years, Bulgaria has made bargain-priced Cabernet of genuine class.

merlot

Style Merlot has traditionally been seen as the foremost and best blending partner of Cabernet Sauvignon, because that was the recipe followed by the Bordeaux châteaux of the Médoc. Here, it performed the obliging function of cushioning some of the hardness and austerity of the Cabernet. However, modern wine thinking has increasingly allowed Merlot to take centre stage, and rightly so because, vinified on its own, it can be a real charmer. Its fruit tends to the softer plums-and-blackberries end of the spectrum, and there is sometimes a chocolatey hint in there too. Generally less tannic than Cabernet, Merlot wines are more approachable in their youth, although the best can easily match Cabernet for longevity. There was a fashion in California for a while of trying to make Merlot wines with the same degree of iron-bound toughness as Cabernet, but that style has thankfully now been all but eclipsed by the kinder, gentler approach.

Regions It forms the greater part of the blend in the wines of the Pomerol and St-Emilion districts of Bordeaux, as well as appearing solo in varietal wines of the Languedoc. Chile has some fantastic varietal Merlot now, as does California and the north west of the USA. South Africa is also doing great things with it. It is widely grown in the north east of Italy to make featherlight, everyday quaffing wines.

pinot noir

Style The great red grape of Burgundy is at its best when made as a midweight, lightly oaked, aromatic red with a subtle undertone of meatiness. This is the benchmark style of burgundy itself, but depends very heavily in that region on the overall quality of the vintage from year to year. In its youth, it can display attractive scents of red summer fruits such as raspberries or cherries, backed up by that beefy substructure that helps it to age. The other element that assists its maturation is high acidity, a factor that tends to make it quite painful to drink if you catch it too young. Only rarely is it noticeably high in tannin although, despite its relatively light body, it is nearly always fairly alcoholic. Great Pinot Noir ages sublimely, and takes on feral, gamy scents as it does so – a quality that makes it a traditional choice to partner well-hung game birds. This is one of the most site-sensitive grapes in the fine wine collection, being notoriously unforgiving if it is grown in too hot or too cool a climate. The margin for error in making classic Pinot is perilously thin.

Regions Burgundy is the homeland of Pinot Noir, but very fine Pinot is now being made in California and Oregon, and also cool-climate New Zealand. Australia has been generally less successful with it but is improving all the time, while the cooler regions of South Africa could yet produce some of the most appealing Pinot Noir from anywhere.

syrah/shiraz

Style In France, where it is native to the Rhône valley, they call it Syrah, but the rest of the world – under the influence of Australia, where it is the most widely planted red grape – calls it Shiraz. Either way, it is a top-quality variety of fascinating character. In the northern Rhône, it is used unblended in the reds, and is responsible for wines that have a strongly floral scent (think violets or roses) wrapped up in lush chocolatey texture, and with an intriguing spice note exactly like freshly ground black pepper. Although the wines can be very tannic and demand time to age, they also have a charming soft centre that can make them hard to resist at two or three years old. In Australia they are less peppery, but full of sinuous, creamy, brambly fruit and a scent often compared to warm, supple leather. Syrah is also a very compatible blending partner for a whole range of other southern French grape varieties, such as Grenache, Cinsault and Mourvèdre.

Regions The Rhône, Languedoc and Roussillon in southern France are the speciality regions for Syrah, but Australia, particularly the Barossa Valley, is a definite rival for quality. California and Chile are doing good things with the grape, although it is by no means yet a major influence in the Americas.

tempranillo

Style No other red grape indigenous to Spain is as important as Tempranillo. It is grown virtually all over the country, and is the backbone of the celebrated red wines of Rioja in Castile, as well as cropping up under various pseudonyms in such regions as Navarra, Ribera del Duero and Valdepeñas. Characteristically, it has a scent of light red fruit, and is best at producing a full-bodied but gently textured style of oak-aged wine. In the past, it was hardly ever noticeably tannic but modern producers – determined to beef it up a little to compete amongst the Cabernets and Merlots on the world stage – have emphasized the tannin. It has a glorious affinity with the unapologetically rich, vanilla-like flavours of new oak, and is traditionally and successfully aged in the spicier American oak by many producers. Like Cabernet, Tempranillo never feels quite at home on its own, and is best blended with grapes like Garnacha and Graciano.

Regions As well as its Spanish heartlands, Tempranillo also makes an appearance over the border in Portugal (where they call it Tinta Roriz) and in Argentina.

sangiovese

Style The widely grown Italian variety Sangiovese is perhaps most familiar internationally as the principal ingredient of Chianti. It is nearly always blended with other grapes (principally Canaiolo, but increasingly nowadays a healthy dose of Cabernet Sauvignon), but nonetheless has its own distinctive characteristics. At its best, it has an unmistakable aroma and flavour of bitter cherries mingled in with a strong herbal scent of oregano or rosemary. It also tends to be quite light in both texture – tannin and Sangiovese are not obvious bedfellows at all – and colour. Unfortunately, the reputation of Sangiovese as a classic grape has been hampered by the overproduction and poor winemaking that marked out too many producers, many of them giant combines, in central Italy. This was a shame because, as a handful of quality-conscious growers has demonstrated, Sangiovese can form the basis of a highly individual and long-lasting wine. Not for nothing has it been adopted by a few far-sighted Californian winemakers as representing an interesting stylistic alternative to the ubiquitous Cabernet and Merlot.

Regions Central and eastern Italy are its main hangouts, but those Californian pioneers, as well as some Argentinian growers who are beginning to take it seriously, should help to raise its international profile.

other important red grapes
Cabernet Franc Grassy, lightweight cousin of the more famous Cabernet, used unblended in red wines of the central Loire.

Gamay Strawberry-scented variety used almost exclusively for the light-bodied red wines of Beaujolais.

Grenache Southern French/Spanish variety much used in blending, but increasingly seen as a solo performer in the Languedoc and in Australia. Red fruits and ginger are its identifiers.

Pinotage A cross between southern French Cinsault and Pinot Noir, it is the USP grape of South African reds. Slightly sour but interesting style.

Zinfandel Of Italian origin, this is now a speciality of California. Sweet-fruited, toweringly structured reds of great longevity. Increasingly important in Chile too.

the world's classic wines

The following pages offer a guide to the most significant wines produced in each of the world's major viticultural regions. It is by no means an exhaustive listing, but does include the wines most commonly encountered on high-street retailers' shelves.

france

However much wine fashions have tilted towards the New World in recent years, the major French wine

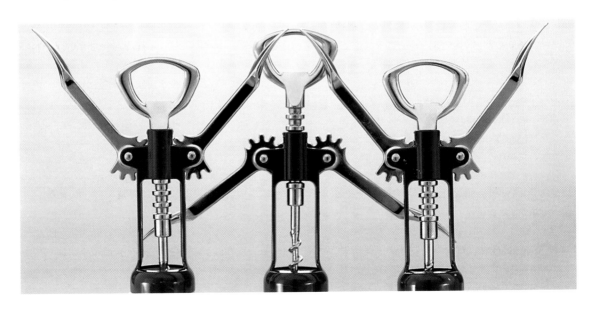

regions remain the benchmark for nearly all quality winemaking the world over. All oaked Chardonnays are descended in some sense from the white wines of Burgundy, all Cabernet Sauvignons and Merlots from the classified wines of Bordeaux. Tastes can change from year to year, and the country certainly has more than enough rivals now to cope with, but a world of wine without France is quite unthinkable.

bordeaux

The most productive region in France is home to red wines known as clarets (made from varying blends based on Cabernet Sauvignon, Merlot and Cabernet Franc) and dry white and sweet white wines (made chiefly from Sémillon and Sauvignon Blanc). Its most illustrious wines are grouped in a system called *cru classé* (classed growth), at the top of which are the red wine châteaux of Lafite-Rothschild, Mouton-Rothschild, Latour, Margaux and Haut-Brion and the great sweet wine producer of Sauternes, Château d'Yquem. Below the classed-growth wines are an intermediate category called *crus bourgeois*, with the remainder known as *petits châteaux*. Bordeaux Supérieur and basic Bordeaux bring up the rear. Below are listed the various principal sub-regions.

Barsac Village within Sauternes. The area is noted for its sweet wines of similar concentration, but slightly lighter body.

Entre-deux-Mers Large production area between the Garonne and Dordogne rivers (hence its name), making dry whites of mostly humdrum quality, although there are a few stars.

Graves South of the city of Bordeaux, the Graves makes fine, earthy reds and austere, minerally dry whites.

Haut-Médoc Left bank of the river Gironde, incorporating the major districts Pauillac, St-Julien, St-Estèphe and Margaux.

Margaux Haut-Médoc district. Powerful, intense, streamlined reds.

Médoc Northern end of the left-bank section of Bordeaux. Quality not quite as good as Haut-Médoc.

Pauillac Heart of the Haut-Médoc, producing Cabernet-based, rich but austere, long-lived classic claret.

Pessac-Léognan Northern sector of the Graves, making its best wines – sturdy, minerally reds and great, exotically fruity dry whites.

Pomerol Right-bank region using principally Merlot to make soft, plummy, but supremely ageworthy reds.

St-Emilion Right-bank district making grassy reds, not quite as refined as Pomerol but still capable of ageing.

St-Estèphe Earthy and full of classic cigar-box aromas. The toughest of the Haut-Médoc reds in their youth.

St-Julien Haut-Médoc zone making the most sinuous, soft-centred reds.

Sauternes In the south of the Bordeaux region, Sauternes makes oak-driven, decadently rich sweet wines that can last for decades.

burgundy

Whilst its wines are just as much sought-after as the best wines of Bordeaux, Burgundy produces only a fraction of that region's output and, whereas Bordeaux is always a blend of different grape varieties, Burgundy's reds are made solely from Pinot Noir and its whites from Chardonnay. There are many small growers scattered about the region, often making minuscule quantities of fine wine from tiny plots of land. These are some of the more important denominated wines or *appellations contrôlées* (ACs).

Beaune Mainly light, strawberryish reds.

Chablis Famous unoaked or lightly oaked whites, with enough lemony acid grip to make them worth ageing. *Premier cru* better than basic Chablis; *grand cru* best of all.

Chassagne-Montrachet Largely white wines of gentle, nutty richness.

Côte de Beaune-Villages Basic AC for soft, simple reds from the south of the Côte d'Or.

Côte de Nuits-Villages As above, from the north of the Côte d'Or.

Gevrey-Chambertin Sturdy, meaty reds of great longevity.

Hautes-Côtes-de-Beaune Good-value, fruit-filled wines above Côte de Beaune-Villages in quality.

Hautes-Côtes-de-Nuits As above, in relation to Côte de Nuits-Villages.

Mâcon-Villages Straightforward bottom-end reds and whites from the south of Burgundy.

Meursault Fat, intensely rich, oaky whites. The area produces great savoury depth of flavour as well as ageability.

Montagny Simple, even anonymous whites. *Premier cru*, uniquely, refers to the alcohol level rather than a particular vineyard.

Morey-St-Denis Almost exclusively reds of deep concentration and power.

Nuits-St-Georges Plummy, muscular reds with good keeping quality. A little foursquare white.

Pommard Beefy reds from the Côte de Beaune that need ageing longer than most of their immediate neighbours.

Pouilly-Fuissé Oaky whites from the Mâcon district, generally somewhat overpriced.

Puligny-Montrachet Elegant, hazelnutty, wood-matured whites and some simple red.

Rully Light but appealing whites and attractively fruity reds.

St-Véran Fairly neutral, light whites made in the far south of Burgundy.

beaujolais

To the south of Burgundy, Beaujolais makes light-textured, low-tannin reds (and a soupçon of dry white). Basic Beaujolais can be pretty dire, as can Nouveau, but Beaujolais-Villages is usually reliable. Better are the wines of ten *cru* villages: Brouilly, Chénas, Chiroubles, Côte de Brouilly, Fleurie, Juliénas, Morgon, Moulin-à-Vent, Régnié and St-Amour. Of these, Moulin-à-Vent is the heaviest and longest-lived, Morgon slightly less so, and Fleurie is full of violet-tinged charm. Brouilly is one of the lightest, a cherry-scented, easy-drinking wine.

rhône

This southern region makes exciting, aromatic reds, either wholly from Syrah or from a blend in which Syrah and Grenache play major roles. Whites have less character but, from good producers, can be rich and full. The region is traditionally divided into its northern and southern sectors.

Châteauneuf-du-Pape (S) Big reds with chewy, berry fruit flavours, and some fairly neutral, hefty whites.

Condrieu (N) Expensive but beautifully scented whites from the Viognier grape. Drink young.

Cornas (N) Spicy reds of great weight that need time to develop.

Côtes-du-Rhône (N/S) Blended reds and whites of mainly reliable, if rustic, quality. Huge production. Better quality if -Villages is added to the name.

Côte-Rôtie (N) Highly prized Syrah reds, peppery, floral, liquoricey.

Crozes-Hermitage(N) Peppery Syrah reds that represent fine value.

Gigondas (S) Full-bodied, fiery, fearsomely tannic blended reds.

Hermitage (N) The pinnacle of Syrah reds. Opulent berry fruits and plenty of ageing potential.

Muscat de Beaumes-de-Venise (S) Sweet fortified Muscat, full of orange scents and refreshing rather than cloying.

St-Joseph (N) Blackcurranty, peppery Syrah reds; nutty, solidly built whites.

Tavel (S) Rosé only. Weighty, serious, alcoholic style meant for ageing.

loire

This extensive region stretches along the course of France's longest river, from Brittany in the west to the centre of the country at the other end.

Muscadet Bone-dry, dead neutral whites meant to be drunk young and crisp. Best are labelled Muscadet de Sèvre-et-Maine *sur lie*, and have been kept on their yeast sediment for a short while before bottling.

Pouilly-Fumé Sauvignon whites with, traditionally, a wisp of smokiness floating over the sappy green fruit.

Sancerre Sauvignon whites full of gooseberry tang and a cutting-edge of youthful acidity.

Savennières Chenin whites that are hard and neutral in their youth, but should go creamy and nutty if you keep them.

Vouvray Chenin whites made in the full range of styles: dry, off-dry, mildly sweet, syrupy-sweet or fizzy. The Loire produces some great sweet wines from botrytised (noble-rotted) Chenin Blanc in appellations like Coteaux du Layon and Bonnezeaux, and light, raspberryish reds such as Bourgueil, St-Nicolas-de-Bourgueil, Chinon and Saumur-Champigny from unblended Cabernet Franc. Three other good-value ACs for Sauvignon whites are Ménétou-Salon, Quincy and Reuilly.

alsace

In the north-east of France, Alsace was, before the Pays d'Oc, the only region to label its wines by their grape varieties. These are exotically floral Gewürztraminer, musky Pinot Gris, appley Pinot Blanc, sharply citric Muscat, steely, lime-tinged Riesling, the faintly cabbagey Sylvaner, and some wafer-thin Pinot Noir, the only red. Many fine sweet wines are made, labelled either Vendange Tardive or – even richer – Séléction des Grains Nobles. Also excellent fizz, Crémant d'Alsace.

champagne

The greatest sparkling wine in the world, made by re-fermenting the wine in the bottle, is made in France's northernmost wine region. Styles include everyday Brut Non-Vintage (the flagship brand of each house), Vintage wines that need up to a decade's ageing to reveal their opulent, biscuity richness, and Rosé, mostly made by adding a little still red wine to the bottle. Blanc de Blancs champagne is made solely from Chardonnay and Blanc de Noirs champagne is made from the two red grape varieties of the region, Pinot Noir and Pinot Meunier.

southern france

The central southern region, Languedoc-Roussillon, is increasingly important as a source of varietally labelled wines made under the country-wine designation, Vin de Pays d'Oc. Traditional ACs here include Corbières, Minervois and Fitou for textured Grenache-based reds that have improved greatly in recent years. Côtes du Roussillon-Villages is a reliable AC for sturdy, spicy reds. In the south-west of France, Cahors makes fine, weighty, damsony reds, Gaillac some sharply appley whites, Madiran tough and tannic reds that need time, and Jurançon a range of attractively perfumed dry and sweet whites from a pair of grapes called Petit Manseng and Gros Manseng.

italy

The great diversity of Italy, which makes wine in every single one of its constituent regions, is much under-represented on the export markets. It has many local grape varieties contributing to some unique flavours, although it has to be said that most of the best wines are red. This list of the most noteworthy *denominazioni* (i.e. appellations) indicates the region each wine comes from.

Aglianico del Vulture (Basilicata) Coffee-scented, lush-textured reds scoring highly for individuality.

Asti (Piedmont) Sweet, foaming, grapy fizz unfairly underrated. Low alcohol, high reliability.

Barbaresco (Piedmont) Towering, tough-textured reds from the Nebbiolo grape. Potentially brilliant, but needing years to come round.

Barbera d'Alba/Barbera d'Asti (Piedmont) Mid-weight, cherry-fruited reds. Nicely priced.

Bardolino (Veneto) Wafer-thin reds (and pinks) of no great class.

Barolo (Piedmont) Companion wine to Barbaresco. Aromatic, muscular reds, if anything even tougher.

Brunello di Montalcino (Tuscany) Well built, complex reds at sky-high prices aged for three years in barrel. Rosso di Montalcino is released younger.

Chianti (Tuscany) Big-production, lightish reds based on Sangiovese grape. Quality extremely patchy. Best sub-regions are Chianti Rufina and Chianti Classico.

Dolcetto (Piedmont) Light-textured, blueberryish reds of great appeal made in seven districts, of which Alba is the best.

Franciacorta (Lombardy) Fine champagne-method sparklers, as well as reds and whites – labelled as Terre di Franciacorta – made from international varieties.

Frascati (Lazio) Neutral, but refreshing white in trattoria house-wine style.

Gavi (Piedmont) Solidly built, lemony whites mostly priced way above their quality.

Grave del Friuli (Veneto) Extensive region for international varietal wines in all styles, with reds from Cabernet and Merlot the best.

Lambrusco (Emilia-Romagna) Catch-all *denominazione* for cheap and cheerful, usually slightly fizzy wines in all three colours.

Marsala (Sicily) Great fortified wines with a haunting flavour of burnt caramel, much under-appreciated.

Montepulciano d'Abruzzo (Abruzzi) Good midweight plummy reds at competitive prices.

Moscato d'Asti (Piedmont) Less fizzy version of Asti, even lower alcohol. Can be excellent.

Oltrepò Pavese (Lombardy) All styles, but Barbera-based reds probably the best bets.

Orvieto (Umbria) Neutral, simple whites in dry, off-dry and sweet styles.

Prosecco (Veneto) Variable sparkling wines. Can be appealing in a tutti-frutti sort of way.

Salice Salentino (Puglia) Silky, plummy, gently spicy reds based on local Negroamaro grape. Worth seeking out.

Soave (Veneto) Famous, neutral, soft-textured white. Some have a touch of savoury class.

Teroldego Rotaliano (Trentino-Alto Adige) Light, juicy, blackcurranty, dependable reds.

Valpolicella (Veneto) Much improved cherry-scented reds from local grapes. Superiore better than the ordinary. Amarone and Recioto are speciality versions made from dried grapes, the former exceedingly bitter but unforgettable.

Vernaccia di San Gimignano (Tuscany) Almondy whites of reasonable quality for drinking young.

Vin Santo (Tuscany) Classically a sweet wine of luscious intensity from raisined grapes, although some is made in a bone-dry, sherry-like style. Deliberate oxidation makes it an acquired taste.

Vino Nobile di Montepulciano (Tuscany) Very fine, damsony reds made for the long haul.

spain

Once associated with a mere handful of famous wines, Spain now has many up-and-coming wine regions experimenting with a wide range of styles, from producers determined to compete in the modern world. That old way of doing things, which generally meant ageing wines in old oak barrels until most of their fruit and vitality had gone, are now happily in decline, and the result is a dynamic wine scene with plenty to offer. And prices, for the time being, look very attractive. The Spanish equivalent of AC is DO (*denominación de origen*), given largely to whole regions rather than individual villages, as in France.

Cava Produced mainly in Catalonia, these are traditional sparklers made by the champagne method from indigenous grapes, plus a little Chardonnay. Can be rather rough-and-ready but the best achieve nutty, biscuity class. Non-vintage, vintage and rosé.

Conca de Barberá North-eastern region making crisp whites and well built reds, as well as a fair amount of cava.

Costers del Segre Excellent north-eastern zone with fine international varietals, as well as plush-textured Tempranillo, making the running.

La Mancha Vast central region once responsible for indifferent bulk wine, but now starting to produce some good modern varietals led by white Airén and red Tempranillo (here known as Cencibel).

Málaga Endearing, dark brown, caramel-rich fortified wines, heading towards extinction through lack of commercial interest. Snap them up while you can.

Montilla-Morilés Inland southern region making fortified wines in the same range of styles as sherry. Quality distinctly less good, but prices are lower.

Moscatel de Valencia Speciality of Valencia in eastern Spain, this isn't actually wine as such but sweet grape juice that has been 'alcoholized' with grape spirit. Well chilled, it can be orangey and appealing.

Navarra Northern region on the up. This region produces some excellent whites from the local Viura grape and Chardonnay. Good Tempranillo/Garnacha-based reds.

Penedés Catalonia wine heartland, home to the internationally renowned house of Torres. A wide palette of international and Spanish grapes, as well as large amounts of cava.

Priorato Mightily structured, alcoholic, usually bitter-tasting northeastern reds that age for years.

Rias Baixas North-western DO in Galicia. Graceful, floral, even slightly spicy whites from local Albariño grape.

Ribera del Duero Outstanding region for spicy, ripe, oak-influenced reds led by Tempranillo (here called Tinto Fino) but also often including Cabernet and Merlot.

Rioja Spain's most famous table-wine region makes Tempranillo/Garnacha-based reds and Viura/Malvasia based whites. Wines labelled Crianza have been aged for a while in oak, Reserva a little longer and Gran Reserva for the longest of all. Old-style whites used to be among the woodiest white wines in the world, but changing tastes have fashioned a lighter, more lemon-fresh style.

Rueda Northern region specializing in white wines blended from local Verdejo grape with Sauvignon Blanc. Crisp, fresh and appetizing.

Sherry One of Europe's great fortified wines, made in a gamut of styles from astringently bone-dry (*fino*) to lusciously toffeeish and sweet. Tawny *amontillado* and deep brown *oloroso* versions are thought of as being medium-sweet and sweet, but both styles can be made bone-dry too. The best sherry is made by a complex method of blending, *solera*, indicated on the label.

Somontano Northeastern region making headway with fine international varietals and blends, particularly for fresh, fruity whites.

Toro Mainly powerful, oak-driven, spicy reds of great weight and pedigree.

Valdepeñas South of La Mancha. Mainly classy Tempranillo-based, oaky reds.

portugal

Among the winemaking countries of western Europe, Portugal is the one that has made the greatest leaps and bounds in recent years. As well as its classic fortified wines, the following regions are the current stars.

Alentejo Southeastern region with a range of excellent savoury, oak-matured reds and aromatic whites.

Bairrada Peppery, rustic reds and head-turning, spicy, oak-aged whites.

Douro The port country in the north now has some world-class reds from local and international grapes.

Ribatejo Southeastern region fast approaching Alentejo for quality. Same broad range of styles.

Terras do Sado Exciting western region with a cosmopolitan spectrum of grapes, including good creamy Chardonnay and some attractive, liquoricey red from local grape Castelão Frances.

Portugal's two historic claims to fame are its fortified wines, port and madeira. Port, from the northern Douro region, comes in a bewildering range of styles. Top is vintage-dated port, followed by late-bottled vintage, which has been aged by the shipper to save you the trouble. Tawny port is lighter and nuttier in flavour than red, while white port tends to be a little chunky and coarse. The best madeira comes in four versions. From lightest to richest, they are Sercial, Verdelho, Bual and Malmsey. All have an enlivening streak of acidity underpinning the smoky richness of the wine.

germany

Fine German wines are the most underrated in the world. Because of the country's long association with cheap, artificially sweetened wines like Liebfraumilch, very few consumers bother to investigate its better offerings. You are definitely missing out.

At the top of the quality system are wines labelled QmP (*Qualitätswein mit Prädikat*). These are subdivided into five categories – Kabinett, Spätlese, Auslese, Beerenauslese and Trockenbeerenauslese – in ascending order of their natural sugar levels. Wines in the first three categories are sometimes fermented out to a semi-dry (*Halbtrocken*) or even fully dry (*Trocken*) style. Nearly all of the best German wine is made from Riesling, but there is good wine from Grauburgunder (France's Pinot Gris), Weissburgunder (Pinot Blanc) and Silvaner. The cranberry-scented Dornfelder is responsible for some of Germany's rare red wines.

Pre-eminent wine regions are the Rheingau, west of Frankfurt, the Palatinate or Pfalz, a little to the south, and the Mosel valley, which includes the historic towns of Bernkastel and Trier.

central and eastern europe

The old winemaking nations of western Europe now have serious competition from elsewhere on the continent. Once the bedrock of bargain-basement wine, the countries of the old eastern bloc are aiming high these days, while Austria is poised on the brink of entering the first division for the quality and versatility of its wines. Winemaking expertise from the New World has transformed the Hungarian wine industry, and it

won't be too long before Greece is knocking on the door too. There has never been a better time for branching out and trying something new. Here are a few pointers to what to look for in each country.

austria
World-class winemaking across the board. Exotically perfumed whites from the Alsace and German grape varieties, including fine, full dry Riesling, plus an indigenous speciality, Grüne Veltliner, making floral, spicy creations of singular charm. Reds good too, not only from lighter varieties like Zweigelt and Blaufränkisch, but good old Cabernet and Merlot too. Superb noble-rotted sweet wines from a north-eastern region, Neusiedlersee. What more do you want?

bulgaria
Quality took a bit of a knock after the break-up of the old state winemaking industry, but Bulgaria is gradually coming back. Overwhelmingly, its best wines are reds, the Reserve Cabernets and Merlots, as well as local varietals like Gamza and Mavrud, all softly fruity, carefully matured and underpriced. Whites less great, although there is some nice, creamy Chardonnay about.

greece
There will be fine varietal wines from local grapes emerging from Greece in the next few years, such as cherry-fruited Agiorgitiko reds from the Peloponnese and crisply citric Assyrtiko whites from round Halkidiki.

hungary
International white varietals are the strong suit, with richly buttery, oaked Chardonnays, sappy, pungent Sauvignons and even the odd piercingly intense Gewürztraminer all showing well. Traditional oxidized sweet wine, Tokaji, has been revived in the last few years. Its sherry-like intensity takes some getting used to, but is a highly individual style worth preserving.

romania

Rich, earthy reds are what to look for – Cabernet, Merlot and especially rough-edged but recognizable Pinot Noir from the Dealul Mare region.

other european wine-producing countries

Switzerland has light, fairly neutral but brittle-textured whites – the most visible Swiss wine presence in our market. They have a certain Alpine purity about them, but are terribly overpriced. The English wine industry is growing all the time. The quality is still very patchy, although there are good floral, high-acid dry whites from grapes like Bacchus and Reichensteiner. Sparkling wines from the Home Counties are well worth trying, although the reds are not for the time being.

united states and canada

There is more broad-minded experimentation going on in the USA today than there is in any other non-European wine-producing country, most of it in California. After the Golden State, the next most important zone is the Pacific Northwest, which takes in Washington State, Oregon and Idaho. American wines are not especially cheap on the export markets but the quality is, by and large, unimpeachable, and has achieved overall a happy blend of Old and New World winemaking philosophies. Canada has been chiefly noted so far for Icewines, sweet wines made in the German tradition by allowing the grapes to freeze on the vines deep into the cold northern winter, but there will also be fine dry varietal wines from grapes like Chardonnay and Pinot Noir as their industry gears itself up for a vigorous export effort. Below are listed are the main varietal wines of North America.

Barbera The most widely planted of the Italian grapes in California makes a fuller, more intensely brambly wine than it tends to in Piedmont.

Cabernet Sauvignon Once made universally in a thunderously tannic, jet-black style, California Cabernet is still a big-hitting wine, but the textures are a little softer now, the wines approachable younger, and the glorious layers of blackcurrant and cedar that are Cabernet's best shot allowed full expression. Washington has some slightly gentler Cabernet, still packed with impeccable ripeness.

Chardonnay Arguably the best Chardonnay outside Burgundy is now being made in California, with the buttery richness and savoury spice of the best oak-aged creations constituting a truly individual new classic style. Best drunk fairly young (within a couple of years of the vintage), they are brilliant food wines. Good ones, too, from Washington State.

Merlot Varietal Merlot is very much the mood of the moment in America right now. Its soft, voluptuously plump textures and concentrated blackberry-and-plum fruit are indeed hard to resist, though some are made more tannic for cellaring. California and Washington are equally good at this variety.

Pinot Noir California Pinot from areas such as Carneros and the Napa Valley is fully capable of rivalling the best burgundies for its combination of meaty, savoury depth and raspberry fruit intensity. Oregon has established a reputation for great Pinot in the more obviously Burgundian style, since its climate is that bit cooler.

Riesling The best comes from Washington State, where there are some luscious, fully sweet versions.

Sparkling wines Made by the champagne method from Chardonnay and Pinot Noir, many of these are now excellent.

Syrah Small amounts of varietal violet-and-plums Syrah are made by a handful of producers. Others are concentrating on the classic Rhône blend with grapes like Cinsault, Mourvèdre and Grenache, with promising results.

Sauvignon Blanc Not hugely successful in the USA. Too many producers try to play down the grape's pungent cattiness, which is half the point for Sauvignon devotees. Some wines labelled Fumé Blanc in imitation of Pouilly-Fumé might or might not have been oaked.

Vidal One of the most popularly used grapes in Canadian Icewine.

Zinfandel California's very own red grape, making wines across the stylistic spectrum from light, gracefully raspberryish specimens to big, chunky, long-lived winter warmers, but always with an intriguing touch of sweet spice to them. Some pink wine (Blush), as well as a pure white version, are usually uncomfortably sugary in style.

south and central america

Led by Chile, the winemaking countries to the south of the USA are home to some forward-thinking and innovative wineries. European (and Californian) expertise has contributed significantly and, for the time being, the wines are selling at prices that make them look very tempting compared to those of their northern neighbours. In terms of price-quality ratio, Chile, in particular, is currently offering some of the best-value red and white wines in the world.

argentina
Slower out of the starting-blocks than Chile, Argentina is nonetheless coming up fast on the inside track. Chardonnays, Cabernets and Syrahs all look good, while Malbec (a minor grape in Bordeaux) is something of a speciality for earthy, peppery reds. Spain's Tempranillo is also quite at home here. Most of the best vineyards are concentrated in a region called Mendoza.

chile
Its best whites are memorably intense, butterscotch-rich, oaked Chardonnays, but some of the unoaked examples are full of luscious tropical fruit too. Best reds are the silky, often slightly gamy, purple-fruited Merlots, some of which rival the best of France's Pomérol. Sauvignon Blanc is crisp, grassy and gooseberryish from the good growers, and decent, floral Gewürztraminer crops up here and there. Cabernet Sauvignon reds can be redolent of the purest essence of blackcurrant, more so than anywhere else in the world, Pinot Noir has been improbably good from a handful of producers, while Syrah and even Zinfandel are beginning to show their paces. Best regions are Maipo, Curico, Rapel (especially for Merlot) and the cooler Casablanca.

mexico
A little Mexican red finds its way to the UK. Cabernet Sauvignon and Petite Sirah (not to be confused with Syrah) are hearty enough to stand up to your spiciest red meat dishes.

uruguay
One to watch. The international varietals will achieve recognition in the not-too-distant future, while a southern French red grape, Tannat, is used to make big wines full of chocolatey promise.

australia

The love affair of British wine drinkers with the wines of Australia has been one of the most sensational success stories of the last decade. No country outside Europe sells more wine here than does Australia, and it's not hard to see why. It led the way in the 1980s for wines that tasted nothing like their Old World counterparts, but were brimful of sunshine and ripeness, with labels that were easy to understand and at prices that substantially undercut what California was offering at the time. So popular is Australian wine now that keeping up with demand has been a bit of a problem for its growers of late, at least for red wines, but if present market trends continue as they are, we look set to carry on gratefully drinking whatever they can spare. Here is a guide to the main styles.

Cabernet Sauvignon Supple, velvety textures, astonishing levels of blackcurrant and blackberry fruit concentration, luxurious vanilla oak tones: this is Cabernet's best side, and Australia does it consummately well. It makes a fine blending partner for Shiraz as well as Merlot. Best regions: Barossa Valley, McLaren Vale, Coonawarra, Eden Valley.

Chardonnay The trailblazer for Oz wines, once made in a bright yellow, high-octane, blowsy style, rich as clotted cream, now lighter and more elegant, and with less oak by and large. Best regions: Barossa, Coonawarra and Western Australia.

Grenache Making a name for itself as a red varietal, these tend to be huge, alcoholic, tannin-rich wines. A little goes a long way.

Marsanne Fat-textured, banana-scented white wines from a northern Rhône variety.

Muscat Some lightly sweet, surprisingly delicate wines. Also massively rich, orange-chocolate, fortified wines called Liqueur Muscat, made in Victoria. Amazingly sweet and sticky but somehow not cloying.

Pinot Noir Has been a bit heavy and oak-smothered, but better ones are now emerging from Yarra Valley, Margaret River and Tasmania.

Riesling Very attractive lemon-and-lime dry whites from the cooler areas, notably Clare Valley.

Sauvignon Blanc Not generally outstanding, but a few have the right herbaceous charm.

Sémillon A genuine classic. Dry wines – some oaked, many not – with a strange mineral intensity, taking on toasty complexity as they age. Hunter Valley (New South Wales) is the pre-eminent region.

Shiraz The star among reds, either solo or in a duo with Cabernet. Strapping, brambly, creamy reds of great power and long life. Good from many regions, but classically brilliant from the Barossa, where it often takes on a bewitching minty topnote.

Sparkling wines Many world-class bubblies, some made by the champagne method. An individual Oz style is deep red sparklers from Cabernet or Shiraz, full of ripe plummy fruit and even tannin. Worth trying at your next barbecue.

new zealand

The most recently established of all the New World winemaking industries, and with an annual production dwarfed by that of Australia, New Zealand has nonetheless gained a firm foothold in our market with some exuberantly fruity varietal wines.

Cabernet Sauvignon Was once a bit thin and stalky, owing to the cool climate, but now putting on more flesh in the warmer climate of the North Island.

Chardonnay Probably fruitier here than anywhere else in the world when unoaked. The oaky wines have bags of lean, buttery class.

Gewürztraminer Can be almost as attractively floral/spicy as the Alsace versions.

Pinot Noir Coming on strong with high-acid, but ripely cherryish wines. Wairarapa is one of its best regions.

Riesling Good, steely, racy dry wines and concentrated sweet wines of true class.

Sauvignon Blanc Star of the show for fruit-drenched whites. Best without oak. Its heartland region is Marlborough (South Island) but Hawkes Bay (North Island) is good too.

Sparkling wines Lean and austere, but many full of unmistakable finesse.

south africa

South Africa's wine industry emerged blinking into the international spotlight after the end of the apartheid era. There is still a fair way to go before its wines will be taken fully to heart by wine-lovers, but the potential is undoubtedly there.

Cabernet Sauvignon Too much is disappointingly lean and even bitter but, blended in the Bordeaux style with other grapes, it can produce some richer, more elegant wines.

Chardonnay Some oak-matured wines have lemony, buttery charm, but many suffer from overly keen acidity.

Chenin Blanc Sometimes labelled Steen. Neutral, light, dry whites traditionally, but some growers are coaxing some pleasant, melony fruit out of it.

Merlot Could be as successful one day as it is in Chile. Ripe, musky, black-cherry flavours in the best.

Muscat The basis for some classic, strong, sweet fortified wines.

Pinot Noir One or two producers in the cooler areas are making waves with fine, raspberry-scented, complex Pinot.

Pinotage Speciality grape of the Cape. Best use barrel-ageing to soften its juicy, sour-cherry fruit.

Sauvignon Blanc Occasionally sharp and fruity, too often dull and neutral.

Sparkling wines Plenty of rich, yeasty, champagne-method fizz that will one day be rightfully recognised as world-class.

equipping a kitchen

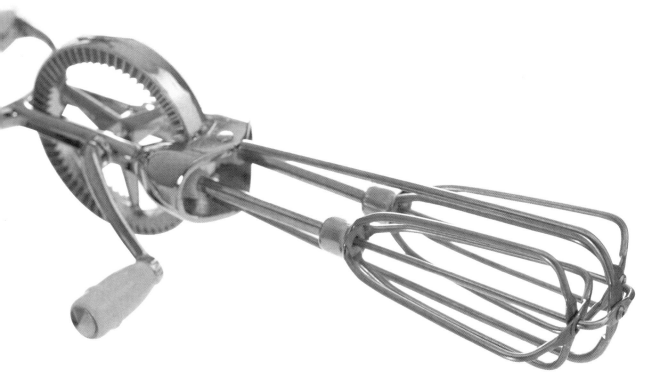

nvesting in the correct tool for the job will save time and make results more professional. Buy the best that you can afford – view the equipment as an investment and buy utensils that will last; the satisfaction of using good-quality equipment, the professional results it gives and the long life of the equipment will pay dividends. Basic equipment suffices for most jobs in the kitchen, so there is no need to invest in a vast professional *batterie de cuisine* (unless you really want to!).

absolutely essential equipment

Bread board
Can opener
Carving knife and fork
Casserole dish(es)
Chopping board
Colander
Fish slice/slotted spoon/ladle
Flexible spatula
Grater
Kettle
Knives:
   7.5 cm (3 in) vegetable knife
    (parer)
   13 cm (5 in) filleting knife
   18 cm (7 in) general-purpose
    cook's knife

bread knife
palette knife
Measuring jug
Mixing bowl(s)
Oven cloth/gloves
Pepper mill
Potato/fruit peeler
Pudding basins,
   in 3 graduated sizes
Roasting pan, with rack
Salad bowl/large glass bowl
Saucepans:
   21 cm (81/2 in) with lid
   15–18 cm (6–7 in) with lid
   12 cm (5 in)
   20 cm (8 in) frying pan

Sieve
Weighing scales
Wooden spoons

Miscellaneous:
   aluminium foil
   all-purpose, non-PVC
    cling film
   corkscrew
   food/freezer bags
   greaseproof or parchment
    paper
   ice-cube tray/bags
   measuring spoons
   plastic containers with lids for
    storing food

useful equipment – beyond the basics

American cup measures
Apple corer
Baking tins/cake tins
   (round, square, rectangular,
   loaf, sandwich, shallow, deep,
   loose-based, spring-form)
   baking sheets
   bun/muffin tray
   flan rings
   Swiss roll tin
Baking/confectionery equipment
   biscuit/scone/pastry cutters
   ceramic or metal baking
   'beans'
   flour dredger
   rolling pin
   pastry board
   patty tins
   icing bags and nozzles
   pastry brush(es)

Blow torch
Clam or oyster knife
Conical (chinois) strainer
Cooling trays
Citrus zester
Double saucepan
Egg slicer
Fish kettle
Freezer knife
Fruit/grapefruit knife
Funnel
Garlic press
Girdle (griddle)
Ice-cream scoop
Kitchen scissors
Lemon (citrus) squeezer
Mandolin grater
Meat cleaver
Melon baller (parisienne cutter)
Mezzaluna

Mouli–légumes
Omelette pan
Pan rests
Pasta machine
Pestle and mortar
Potato masher
Poultry shears
Preserving pan
Pressure cooker
Ramekin dishes
Skewers
Soufflé dish(es)
Steamer
Stock pot
Thermometers
   (meat, sugar, oven)
Tongs
Vegetable (scrubbing) brush
Whisk
Wok

electrical kitchen equipment worth thinking about

Food mixer Expensive but it is best for speeding up baking and bread-making. Most have attachments to do the jobs that a food processor does and, in addition, they also have meat-mincers, juicers, pasta-makers, coffee-grinders – even wheat mills. However, food mixers are large and heavy, so work-surface space is essential if the machine is not to be lifted in and out of the cupboard frequently.

Food processor Takes up less space and does the basic jobs of cutting, slicing, shredding, chipping and liquidizing (not very smooth purées). Not good at whisking and creaming cakes or kneading dough.

Hand-held blender Good for puréeing small quantities, making frothy sauces and milk shakes; can be used in saucepans, avoiding dirtying an extra bowl.

Hand-held whisk Makes short work of creamed cake-mixes, egg whites, cream, etc.

Ice-cream machine Electric machines make professional-standard ice-creams and sorbets and are simple to use. Ones with built-in refrigeration units are heavy but worth having if the storage space is available.

Liquidizer Often an attachment for a food processor. Gives a smoother result than a processor; also makes breadcrumbs.

microwave ovens

The microwave oven is useful for defrosting food quickly. It is also useful for re-heating, but food needs to be stirred and standing times need to be observed for the heat and cooking to be even. Microwave cooking has many health advantages. Vegetables and fruit cooked quickly in the minimum, or no, water retain their colour, texture and nutrients. Steamed puddings cook much more speedily. Creamy porridge and scrambled egg can be made in 2 minutes in a jug (and no scorched saucepan to wash). Fish cooks without added fat and without much smell. Butter, chocolate, sugar and syrups melt quickly without sticking to and dirtying saucepans.

Combination microwave ovens combine conventional heat with microwaves and are most effective at saving time. Crisp-skinned baked potatoes cook in 10–15 minutes and savoury and sweet dishes cook in much reduced time with conventional browned or baked finishes. Combination microwave ovens can be used in several ways: microwave only, convection only (standard oven), microwave and convection, grill only, microwave and grill, grill and convection.

Microwave ovens vary in their ability to re-heat food. This is reflected in the heating category label on microwave ovens and food packs. There are five categories: A to E. Ovens can have the same wattage (power output) but the speed at which they cook small portions of food or re-heat/cook microwave meals can vary – hence one 650-watt oven can be labelled category B and another category C. Ovens manufactured before 1992 will be labelled only with wattage, from 550 to 750. The higher the wattage, the faster the cooking time.

Follow the cooking or re-heating instructions on the food pack, which are given in both the new categories and wattage (columns one and two below).

Food labels do not include instructions for use in combination ovens, so re-heat using microwave-only (or you will have to use a system of trial and error). It is safer to use combination ovens specifically for recipes in manufacturer's handbooks.

Microwave Instructions	Column 1		Column 2
	B Heating Category **D**		Power rating 650W
Cook on full power Stir and re-cover Cook on full power	3 mins 3mins	2½ mins 2½ mins	3 mins 3 mins

how to season a cast iron wok or pan

Do this before using for the first time. Put the wok or pan on a high heat and brush it lightly with vegetable oil. Wipe it clean with kitchen paper. Repeat twice, rinse and dry thoroughly. After use, always wipe the wok or pan with paper. Never wash it. The wok or pan will rust if not oiled and used frequently. If this happens, scour off the rust, rinse and brush with oil.

labelling

food labelling in the UK is in a state of flux. As this book goes to press, comments from consumers are being sifted as part of the government's Food Labelling Initiative. The Initiative was announced by Baroness Hayman, stating, 'Clear, informative food labelling is essential to help consumers to exercise informed choices when selecting foods to buy and eat. Labels cannot carry all the information individual consumers might want to see but we believe they could be improved.'

Many consumer and lobbying groups would agree that labelling should be clearer and more informative and be purged of misleading descriptions and spurious health claims. More than half of all consumers in a survey conducted as part of the government's initiative wanted more information and believed it should be presented in a standard format.

While 68% look at labels before buying, more than half could not find the information they were looking for. Three-quarters of consumers found use of terms such as 'fresh', 'natural', 'pure' and 'traditional' misleading. These terms have been devalued by misuse. Though quality and price are still the main buying criteria, nearly half look at the ingredients list and method of production. It will be the job of the new Food Standards Agency to take the information gathered during the Food Labelling Initiative and develop it into advice on food-labelling policy.

food labelling requirements

For most foods, the labelling requirements are:

- name of product
- ingredients list, in descending order of weight
- best-before or use-by date
- storage instructions
- name and address of manufacturer, packer or EC seller
- instructions for use
- weight.

food names

Names of 'traditional' foods (cheese, pork pie) are often established by law but some can be customary or local names (Eccles cake, Bakewell tart). If the name isn't descriptive, there must be a subsidiary explanation ('multi-grain cereal with raisins, apple and almonds'). Processes such as smoking (bacon, mackerel) have to be declared on the label, as does drying (for example, dried apricots). Pictures on packs are not permitted to be misleading (artificially flavoured strawberry yoghurt cannot show a picture of strawberries on the pot).

ingredients list

Food sold unpackaged, such as delicatessen and bakery items, fruit and vegetables, does not need an ingredients list but tickets must show if food additives are present (such as 'contains preservative' notices on cured meats on delicatessen counters).

Food additives must be declared in the list of ingredients. The specific name of an additive, its E number (which indicates it has been approved for use by the EU) or its number (those without E prefixes that are allowed in the UK and not in other EC countries) must appear. The type of additive (preservative, artificial sweetener) must be given before its name or number.

'best-before' or 'use-by' date

Date coding shows how long a food will remain good or safe to eat if stored according to the storage instructions. Date codes refer to the product before the pack is opened. After opening, follow storage instructions and eat within 2 days.

Use-by dates are put on chilled foods (sandwiches, cook-chill meals), which should be stored in the fridge. These foods are highly perishable and, after the use-by date, the product will start to deteriorate and might not be safe to eat.

Best-before dates are put on products with a longer shelf life (biscuits, crisps), some of which might last up to three months. The date can be expressed as a day and month or a day, month and year.

'Best before end' is seen on products with a shelf life of more than three months (cans, jars of baby food). Some dates will be given as a month and year and, if the shelf-life is longer than 18 months, either a month and a year or a year only.

Unpackaged food does not need date coding and neither do wines.

nutritional information

This is notably absent from the list of legal requirements for labelling. Where nutrition information is given, it is given voluntarily – unless a claim such as 'low-fat' or 'high-fibre' is made, in which case nutritional labelling to support the claim has to be included.

Information is given per 100 g or 100 ml of product; some labels give details per serving or portion as well.

Two systems of nutrition labelling are accepted by the EU and, where nutrition information is given it must follow one or other system:

* Energy, protein, carbohydrate, fat: 87% of British manufacturers show this information, the highest rate in the EU;
* Energy, protein, carbohydrate, sugars, fat, saturates, fibre, sodium. Some manufacturers and retailers also give information about polyunsaturated and mono-unsaturated fat content.

NUTRITION INFORMATION TYPICAL VALUES AS SOLD		
	PER ½ POT	PER 100g
Energy	458kJ	183kJ
	110kcal	44kcal
Protein	1.3g	0.5g
Carbohydrate	14.8g	5.9g
of which sugars	8.8g	3.5g
Fat	5.0g	2.0g
of which saturates	2.5g	1.0g
Fibre	2.5g	1.0g
Sodium	1.3g	0.5g

QUID labelling will soon be introduced in the UK. QUID stands for 'quantitative ingredient declaration'. It shows the percentage of the main ingredient used in the food, for example, the percentage of meat in a sausage or apples in an apple pie.

Some symbols that appear on food labels are universally recognized, such as the frost symbol if the product can be frozen, attached to freezing instructions; bar codes can be read by checkout scanners; microwave symbols and cooking instruction symbols are other examples. In addition, some retailers devise their own symbols and logos, for example, to denote 'healthy eating', products that contain less fat or sugar than standard or to show whether products are 'suitable for vegetarians'.

what the label does not tell you

Despite the apparent mass of information that appears on some labels there is still a lot that the label does not tell you, for example: a soft drink might claim brazenly that it is free from artificial sweeteners (or another food additive) but a close reading of the ingredients reveals that it contains lots of other additives, such as preservatives and colourings. Fruit-juice 'drinks' aimed at children can be packaged to look like fruit juice and claim to provide a large percentage of children's daily vitamin and or mineral requirements, from added vitamins and minerals, but they do not say they are basically sugar or sweeteners, flavourings, colourings and water, and that it would be far more nutritious to have a glass of fresh juice. Meat pies, burgers and sausages might state how much meat they contain (lower than you might expect, in many instances), but the pack does not say that the 'meat' is reformed from a slurry blasted off the carcass, of bits of the animal that you would not give the cat.

So-called 'traditional recipe' foods, from ice-cream to biscuits and sausage rolls, often contain a myriad of far-from-traditional food additives and have only been made possible using all sorts of tricks of food technology.

Processing aids to make anything from wine to bread are not listed on the label, so you do not know if the wine you are drinking has been fined using unpalatable animal ingredients or the bread contains genetically modified yeasts. Fish 'fillets' can be made from minced fish and there can be several types of meat in a mince product or even in a named variety meat pie or sausage.

There is no way of telling from a food label what food additives or other chemicals were in the food fed to the animals it is made from. There is no indication of what drugs might be present as residues.

The list of examples could go on and on, but the point is that, despite a certain amount of food-labelling legislation, consumers are still in the dark about many aspects of food processing.

food-labelling lobbyists' 'wish list'

Food-labelling campaigners have called for far more informative labels that identify the following in our foods:

- Pesticides used in the production of the food
- Genetically-modified ingredients
- Irradiated ingredients
- Meat varieties
- Method of slaughter of animals
- Identification of potentially allergenic substances
- All additives and processing aids to be listed by name and number
- Levels of saturated fat, sugar and fibre to be listed on all foods
- A ban on incorrect and meaningless health claims
- Health claims only to be allowed if they can be supported by scientific research
- Inclusion of unwrapped foods, restaurant and takeaway foods and alcoholic drinks in labelling regulations

if you are not satisfied

Complaints about inadequate or misleading food labels should be made directly to the maker, packer or seller, whose name and address should be on the pack. Or complaints can be made to a local Trading Standards Department, which is responsible for enforcing food-labelling laws.

glossary and conversion tables

Acidulated water Water to which lemon juice or vinegar has been added. Fruit and vegetables that brown easily are put in the water during preparation to prevent discoloration.

Agar-agar A tasteless white powder made from seaweed, for use as a vegetarian substitute for gelatine.

Antipasti (singular, *antipasto*) Italian selection of hot or cold foods served as an appetizer.

Arrowroot An alternative to cornflour for thickening sauces and glazes. Arrowroot gives a clear gloss; cornflour produces an opaque finish.

Aspic jelly A savoury jelly used for setting and garnishing savoury dishes.

Au gratin A dish coated with sauce, sprinkled with breadcrumbs and/or cheese and browned under the grill or in the oven. A gratin dish is a low-sided, heatproof dish.

Bain-marie French term for a water bath, used for dishes like bread and butter pudding and créme brûlée; they stand in a shallow pan half-filled with hot water to protect them from direct heat in the oven.

Baking blind Pastry cases for flans and tarts are cooked or partially cooked without a filling, so the pastry sets (see *Easy Lemon Tart,* page 192).

Baking powder A raising agent consisting of an acid, usually cream of tartar, and an alkali, usually bicarbonate of soda, which react to produce carbon dioxide. The gas causes cakes and breads to rise during baking.

Barding Covering lean meat or the breast of poultry or game birds with rashers of bacon or strips of fat, to prevent the flesh from drying out during roasting.

Basting Spooning cooking juices or melted fat over meat, poultry, game or fish during roasting, to keep it moist. Marinating foods are basted with the marinade.

Beating A method of incorporating air into an ingredient or mixture by agitating it vigorously with a spoon, fork, whisk or electric mixer. Also used to soften ingredients.

Blanching Immersing food briefly in boiling water to whiten it, or to assist removal of the skin, for example, tomatoes. Vegetables to be frozen are blanched, to destroy spoilage enzymes and preserve colour, flavour and texture.

Boning Removing the bones from meat or poultry, so that it can be rolled or stuffed.

Braising A slow cooking method used for cuts of meat, poultry and game that are too tough to roast. A pan or casserole with a tight-fitting lid is used, to prevent evaporation. The meat is first browned, then cooked on a bed of chopped vegetables with just enough liquid to cover the vegetables. The dish can be cooked on the hob or in the oven.

Brining A method of preserving by immersing food in a salt and water solution.

Brochette Fish, meat or vegetables, cooked on a skewer or spit, also called kebab.

Butterfly To split a food, such as a large prawn, almost in half and open out flat, so that it resembles a butterfly because it has two mirrored halves; allows food to cook more quickly. When applied to a poussin, the term 'spatchcock' is used.

Caramel Substance obtained by heating sugar syrup very slowly until it turns a rich brown.

Caramelize Cooking sugar or sugar syrup to the caramel stage. Also used when grilling, or using a blowtorch on a sugar topping on a dessert such as a crème caramel. Also applied when reducing meat or other cooking juices to a sticky glaze.

Chining Joints such as loin or neck of lamb, veal or pork are chined to make them easier to carve into chops or cutlets after cooking. Chining severs the rib bones from the backbone, by sawing through the ribs close to the spine.

Clarifying The process of removing sediment or impurities from a food or liquid. After clarifying, butter and dripping can be used for frying at higher temperatures. Clarified butter is known as ghee in Indian cookery. Jellies such as consommé can be clarified with egg white, which gathers up all the impurities and forms a scum on the surface that can be discarded.

To clarify butter, heat until melted and all bubbling stops. Remove from the heat and allow to stand until the salt and sediment have sunk to the bottom, then gently pour off the fat, straining it through muslin, discarding the sediment. Chill the clarified butter and use as required.

Coulis A French term applied to a liquid purée of vegetables, fish, poultry or fruit.

Court-bouillon A light, seasoned stock (carrots, onion, celery, bay leaf, bouquet garni and white wine), in which meat, poultry, fish or vegetables are boiled or poached.

Creaming Beating together fat and sugar until the mixture is pale and fluffy and resembles whipped cream. Used in cakes and puddings which contain a high proportion of fat and require the incorporation of a lot of air.

Crimping Decorating the edges of a pie, tart or shortbread by pinching it to give a fluted effect.

Croûte A circle or rectangle of fried or toasted bread on which meat and other savoury foods are served. The term can also refer to a pastry crust, usually crescent-shaped, served with savoury dishes.

Croûton Small cubes of toasted or fried bread, served as a garnish for soups, salads, etc.

Curdle Creamed cake mixtures are said to have curdled when the mixture separates, usually because the egg has been beaten in too quickly. Some sauces and custards curdle when overheated and milk can be curdled by adding lemon juice.

Deglaze Pans are deglazed when stock, wine or other liquid is heated with the cooking juices left in the pan after roasting or sautéing meat. The liquid is stirred to dissolve the sediment, to produce a sauce or gravy.

Dice To cut food into small cubes or smaller pieces than if chopped.

Dredging Sprinkling food with flour, sugar or other powdered coating. Fish and meat are often dredged with flour before frying, and a pastry board is dredged with flour before pastry is rolled out.

Dropping consistency When raw cake or pudding mixture falls easily from a raised spoon within a few seconds. This is the correct texture for cake mixture prior to baking.

Dusting Sprinkling food or a preparation surface lightly with flour, cornflour or icing sugar.

En papillote A French term applied to food that is cooked in a parchment or greaseproof parcel.

Fillet The undercut of a loin of beef, veal, pork or game; boned breasts of birds; and boned sides of fish.

Flambé Flavouring a dish by pouring over alcohol, usually brandy or rum, and then igniting; the alcohol is burned off but the flavour and aroma remain. Christmas pudding and crêpes Suzette are often flambéd.

Folding in Method of combining a whisked mixture or dry ingredient such as flour or sugar with other ingredients, by cutting through the mixture, usually with a large metal spoon. The method allows ingredients to be mixed while retaining air. Used mainly for meringues, soufflés and certain cakes.

Frosting American-style icing for cakes. Also refers to coating fruits, flowers and the rims of glasses (also salt on a Margarita) with a fine layer of sugar that resembles frost.

Frying The various methods of cooking food in hot fat or oil. Shallow-frying uses a little fat in a shallow pan. Deep-frying totally immerses the food in oil. Dry-frying of fatty foods such as bacon and sausages can be done in a non-stick pan without extra fat. Stir-frying is a Chinese technique of continuously stirring and turning evenly sized pieces of food, to cook it in a small amount of very hot oil. A wok is designed for stir-frying.

Garnish A decoration, often edible, e.g. parsley or croûtons, added to a savoury dish.

Glaze Glossy coating to sweet and savoury dishes, to enhance their appearance and, sometimes, add flavour. Ingredients for glazes include sieved jam, syrups, milk and beaten egg.

Hanging Leaving meat or game suspended in a cool, airy, dry place, to allow time for naturally present enzymes to tenderize the flesh and develop (an often gamy) flavour.

Hulling Removing the calyx from soft fruits, e.g. strawberries.

Infusing Method of imparting flavour to a liquid. Aromatic vegetables (onions), herbs, spices (vanilla pod) or coffee beans are infused in milk, water or syrups.

Julienne Vegetables or citrus zest cut into very fine strips.

Knead To massage and pummel dough with the heel of the hand.

Knock back To knock the air out of a dough after its first rising. A second kneading and rising usually follow this.

Liaison A combination of ingredients such as flour, cornflour, arrowroot, rice or potato flour, or egg yolk, that thicken or bind.

Macerate To soften and flavour raw or dried foods by soaking in a liquid.

Mandolin A flat wooden or metal frame with an adjustable cutting blade for slicing vegetables thinly.

Marinate To tenderize and flavour meat, poultry or game by soaking in a mixture of oil, wine, vinegar or yoghurt and flavourings such as garlic, ginger, chillies. The mixture is called a marinade, and it can also be used to baste the food during cooking.

Mincing Chopping, cutting or grinding food into very small pieces, either by hand or using a mincer or food processor.

Parboiling A short, partial cooking before finishing by another method, e.g. parboiling potatoes before roasting them.

Paring Thinly peeling vegetables or fruit.

Piping Forcing cream, icing, mashed potato, cake mixtures or meringue through a nozzle fitted to a piping bag.

Poaching Cooking food gently in liquid at a simmer.

Proving When bread dough is left to rise after kneading.

Purée Fruit, vegetable, meat, fish or pulse such as lentils which has been pounded, sieved or liquidized to a smooth pulp.

Reduction The concentrated liquid that results from fast-boiling a stock or other liquid in an uncovered pan to evaporate much (usually half) of its water content.

Refresh To pour cold water over blanched and drained food, to stop the cooking process and, in the case of vegetables, set the colour.

Roux A mixture of equal amounts of fat and flour cooked together to form a thick paste. Liquid is stirred in over the heat to make a thickened sauce.

Rubbing in Method of incorporating fat into flour with the fingertips. It is used for pastry, cakes, buns, scones and biscuits. See explanation on page 200.

Sautéing Cooking food in a small quantity of fat in a sauté pan (a frying pan with straight sides and a wide base), which browns the food quickly.

Scalding Pouring boiling water over food to clean it, loosen hairs or remove skin. (Food should not be left in boiling water or it will begin to cook.) It is also the term used for heating milk to just below boiling point, to retard souring or to infuse it with another flavour.

Scoring To cut narrow parallel lines in the surface of food to improve its appearance or help it cook more quickly.

Searing Browning meat quickly in a little hot fat before grilling or roasting.

Sieving Pushing food through a sieve to make a purée.

Sifting Shaking dry ingredients through a sieve, to remove lumps and introduce air.

Simmering Keeping a liquid just below boiling point.

Skimming Removing froth, scum or fat from the surface of stock, gravy stews and jam. This is done using either a skimmer, a spoon or absorbent kitchen paper.

Souring Adding acid, often lemon juice, to cream or milk to give it a sour taste.

Steaming Cooking food in the steam of rapidly boiling water, or over a stew e.g. cous cous.

Steeping Covering food with hot or cold water and leaving it to stand, either to soften it or extract its flavour and/or colour.

Sweating Gently cooking food (usually vegetables) in a little, or no, melted fat in a covered pan, until the juices run or until vegetables become slightly softened. Non-stick pans are most suited to the job.

Tenderizing Beating raw meat with a spiked mallet or rolling pin, to break down the fibres and make it more tender for grilling or frying.

Trussing Tying or skewering into shape before cooking. Applied mainly to poultry and game.

Conversion tables

metric and imperial solid measures

Metric	Imperial	Metric	Imperial	Metric	Imperial
5 g	⅛ oz	275 g	10 oz		5¼ lb
10 g	¼ oz	300 g	11 oz	2.5 kg	5½ lb
15 g	½ oz	350 g	¾ lb (12 oz)		5¾ lb
20 g	¾ oz	375 g	13 oz	2.75 kg	6 lb
25 g	1 oz	400 g	14 oz	3 kg	7 lb
40 g	1½ oz	425 g	15 oz	3.5 kg	8 lb
50 g	2 oz	450 g	1 lb (16 oz)	4 kg	9 lb
65 g	2½ oz	550 g	1¼ lb	4.5 kg	10 lb
75 g	3 oz	750 g	1½ lb	5 kg	11 lb
90 g	3½ oz		1¾ lb	5.5 kg	12 lb
100 g	¼ lb (4 oz)	1 kg	2¼ lb	6 kg	13 lb
120 g	4½ oz	1.25 kg	2½ lb	6.5 kg	14 lb
135 g	4¾ oz		2¾ lb	6.75 kg	15 lb
150 g	5 oz	1.5 kg	3 lb	7.25 kg	16 lb
165 g	5½ oz		3¼ lb	7.5 kg	17 lb
175 g	6 oz		3½ lb	8 kg	18 lb
185 g	6½ oz	1.75 kg	4 lb	8.5 kg	19 lb
200 g	7 oz		4¼ lb	9 kg	20 lb
215 g	7½ oz	2 kg	4½ lb	9.5 kg	21 lb
225 g	½ lb (8 oz)		4¾ lb	10 kg	22 lb
250 g	9 oz	2.25 kg	5 lb		

metric and imperial liquid measures

Metric	Imperial	Metric	Imperial
1 × 1.25 ml spoon	¼ teaspoon	450 ml	15 fl oz (¾ pint)
(or pinch)	(or pinch)	475 ml	16 fl oz
1 × 2.5 ml spoon	½ teaspoon	500 ml	17 fl oz
1 × 5 ml spoon	1 teaspoon	550 ml	18 fl oz
1½ × 5 ml spoons	1½ teaspoons	575 ml	19 fl oz
2 × 5 ml spoons	2 teaspoons	600 ml	1 pint (20 fl oz)
1 × 15 ml spoon	1 tablespoon	750 ml	1¼ pints
1½ × 15 ml spoons	1½ tablespoons	900 ml	1½ pints
2 × 15 ml spoons	2 tablespoons	1 litre	1¾ pints
3 × 15 ml spoons	3 tablespoons	1.2 litres	2 pints
4 × 15 ml spoons	4 tablespoons	1.25 litres	2¼ pints
5 × 15 ml spoons	5 tablespoons	1.5 litres	2½ pints
6 × 15 ml spoons	6 tablespoons	1.6 litres	2¾ pints
7 × 15 ml spoons	7 tablespoons	1.75 litres	3 pints
15 ml	½ fl oz	2 litres	3½ pints
20 ml	¾ fl oz	2.25 litres	4 pints
25 ml	1 fl oz	2.5 litres	4½ pints
35 ml	1¼ fl oz	2.75 litres	5 pints
40 ml	1½fl oz	3.4 litres	6 pints
50 ml	2 fl oz	3.9 litres	7 pints
60 ml	2¼ fl oz	4.5 litres	8 pints
65 ml	2½ fl oz	5 litres	9 pints
85 ml	3 fl oz		
100 ml	3½ fl oz		
120 ml	4 fl oz		
135 ml	4½ fl oz		
150 ml	5 fl oz (¼ pint)		
175 ml	6 fl oz		
200 ml	7 fl oz (⅓ pint)		
250 ml	8 fl oz		
275 ml	9 fl oz		
300 ml	10 fl oz (½ pint)		
325 ml	11 fl oz		
350 ml	12 fl oz		
375 ml	13 fl oz		
400 ml	14 fl oz		

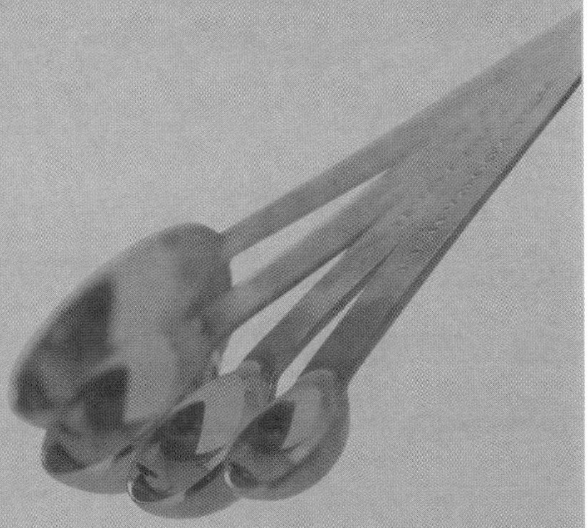

metric and imperial measurements

Metric	Imperial	Metric	Imperial	Metric	Imperial
3 mm	⅛ in	5 cm	2 in	20 cm	8 in
5 mm	¼ in	6 cm	2½ in	23 cm	9 in
1 cm	½ in	7.5 cm	3 in	25 cm	10 in
2 cm	¾ in	9 cm	3½ in	28 cm	11 in
2.5 cm	1 in	10 cm	4 in	30 cm	12 in
3 cm	1¼ in	13 cm	5 in	33 cm	13 in
4 cm	1½ in	15 cm	6 in		
4.5 cm	1¾ in	18 cm	7 in		

oven temperatures

Oven Description	°C	°F	fan oven °C	Gas
Very cool	110	225	90	¼
	120	250	100	½
Cool	140	275	120	1
	150	300	130	2
Moderate	160	325	140	3
	180	350	160	4
Moderately hot	190	375	170	5
	200	400	180	6
Hot	220	425	200	7
	230	450	210	8
Very hot	240	475	220	9

One American cup is equivalent to 225 ml (8 fl oz). To measure flour, always sift, except for wholewheat and bran. Fill the cup and level off the top, but never pack flour.

To measure white sugar: fill cup and level off as above. For brown sugar, pack cup so firmly that the sugar, when turned out, will hold the shape of the cup.

To measure butter, lard, margarine, etc. by the spoon: pack it solidly into the spoon, levelling off the surface.

By the cup: again, pack so solidly that it will hold the level of the cup when turned out. Always level off the surface.

converting from american measures

Butter, margarine etc

25 g (1 oz) = 2 level tablespoons = ¼ stick

100 g (4 oz) = 8 level tablespoons = ½ cup = 1 stick

Eggs (quantity depends on size)

4–6 eggs = 1 cup   1 egg white = 1½ tablespoons

8–10 egg whites = 1 cup   1 egg yolk = 1 tablespoon

12–14 egg yolks = 1 cup

american/metric/imperial liquid measure equivalents

USA	Metric	Imperial	USA	Metric	Imperial
⅛ cup	25 ml	1 fl oz	1¼ cups	300 ml	10 fl oz (½ UK pint)
¼ cup	50 ml	2 fl oz	1½ cups	350 ml	12 fl oz
⅓ cup	65 ml	2½ fl oz	1¾ cups	400 ml	14 fl oz
½ cup	100 ml	3½ fl oz	2 cups	475 ml	16 fl oz (1 USA pint)
⅔ cup	150 ml	5 fl oz	2½ cups	600 ml	20 fl oz (1 UK pint)
¾ cup	175 ml	6 fl oz	3 cups	750 ml	24 fl oz
1 cup	250 ml	8 fl oz (½ USA pint)	4 cups	900 ml	32 fl oz (1 quart)

index

Please note that page numbers in *italic* refer to the illustrations

Food photography by David Munns

This book is published to accompany the television series entitled *Food and Drink*
produced for BBC television by G.M.G. Endemol Entertainment plc
Executive Producer: Tim Hincks

Since it was first broadcast in 1982 the series has been produced by
Henry Murray, Peter Bazalgette, Tim Hincks, Alison Field, Elaine Bancroft and
Geraldine McClelland.

Published by BBC Worldwide Limited,
Woodlands, 80 Wood Lane,
London W12 0TT

ISBN 0 563 53708 6

Commissioning Editor: Vivien Bowler
Cover Art Director: Pene Parker
Book Art Director: Lisa Pettibone
Project Editor: Vicki Vrint
Copy Editor: Deborah Savage
Designer: Isobel Gillan
Recipe Writer: Mitzie Wilson
Home Economist: Linda Tubby
Recipe Stylist: Sue Rowlands
Other styling: Lisa Pettibone

Set in Helvetica Neue
Printed and bound in France by Imprimerie Pollina s.a. (85) - n° L80205
Colour separations by Imprimerie Pollina s.a.

For information about this and other BBC books, please visit our website on
www.bbcshop.com/bbc_shop